THE MIRROR

Book One:
Welcome to the Evil Sisterhood

by Michael M. McConaughey

Produced by:

FriesenPress
Suite 300 – 852 Fort Street
Victoria, BC, Canada V8W 1H8

www.friesenpress.com

Distributed to the trade by The Ingram Book Company

Table of Contents

I dedicate this book to the many children who have been cruelly deprived of a loving parent through the brutal form of child abuse known as parental alienation.

Especially my own, whom I will always love. Their father never abandoned them, despite constant adversity and persecution. Not once; he loves them too much. May they all one day see the truth.

I have changed the names of most of the people in this story, unless otherwise mentioned. Canada apparently has the worst protection for freedom of expression in the English-speaking world. Telling the truth about naughty or even wicked people can hurt their feelings, so in Canada they're allowed to sue you for libel if you do this.

The opinions expressed in this book are solely those of the author unless otherwise noted.

Introduction

*All truths are easy to understand once they are
discovered; the point is to discover them.*
—GALILEO

I am writing this book to expose certain truths. This may result in my
becoming the most hated man alive.

So be it.

The reason for this is simple. My children were deliberately subjected to
child abuse. Expert-confirmed, child protection-sponsored, court-ordered,
government-approved child abuse. Some experts in the field hold this form
of child abuse to be even more harmful to kids than sexual abuse. I was
even forced to fund it. This wasn't supposed to happen in a decent and just
country. Yet it did. In fact, it regularly does.

Read on, and you'll understand why.

The Children's Aid Society (CAS) of the County of Simcoe is a child
protection agency. It interfered in a divorce to help Canadian mother Elaine
Campione get exclusive care of her two young daughters. Campione later
murdered them while under CAS supervision. After the jury returned a
guilty verdict at her 2009 murder trial, the judge burst out with a disgraceful
tirade that made national headlines.

Read on, and you'll understand why.

Russ Williams was a Canadian Colonel who commanded Canada's largest air transport base. He was also a deranged murderer of women. His mother made him so.

Read on, and you'll understand why.

People used to refer to radical feminists as feminazis. They were correct in intuitively relating these deranged women to the evil Nazis.

Read on, and you'll understand why.

Linda Gibbons is a simple woman who looks like she should be someone's loving grandmother. She lives in Canada. Perhaps it is more accurate to say that she lives in Canadian prisons. She's spent over nine years in them. This is because she believes that abortion is the moral equivalent to the Holocaust. In which, if you recall, the Nazis murdered over six million Jews. Gibbons is closer to the truth than she realizes: the Holocaust and abortion are two sides of the same coin.

Read on, and you'll understand why.

American Rush Limbaugh once controversially stated that feminists wanted women to have abortions. I am not a follower of Mr. Limbaugh's. However, he was right. Yet he didn't go far enough. (I am probably the only person who has ever accused Mr. Limbaugh of this.) Feminists also want women to be victims of breast cancer, domestic violence, and rape.

Read on, and you'll understand why.

Nicole Doucet was a woman who tried to hire a hit man to kill her ex-husband. Twice. Her ex-husband was worth a million dollars to Doucet dead. Despite irrefutable and admissible video evidence, The Supreme Court of Canada let Doucet off free as a bird. It even chastised the Royal Canadian Mounted Police (RCMP), whose conduct in the case was exemplary and beyond reproach.

Read on, and you'll understand why.

Edward Gibbon was one of the great minds of the Enlightenment. His magisterial work *The Decline and Fall of the Roman Empire* remains a classic by any definition. Ominously, what Gibbon identified as the symptoms of and causes for the *Decline* are rampant today. Yet our social elite wallows in ignorance and self-delusion.

Read on, and you'll understand why.

"Why?" is a question I've asked all of my life. I can't help it. My mind continually seeks to find order in the chaos of human affairs. In asking why my kids were subjected to expert-confirmed child abuse, I had a series of insights that were simple, elegant, and very, very profound. It is these insights above all else that I wish to share with you.

The title of this book is a not-so-subtle clue as to these insights. It all has to do with mirrors, in a sense. Not real, physical mirrors. Ones more like the magic mirror in Disney's *Snow White*. The sort where the mirror has to tell the wicked queen what she wants to hear about herself. The sort where if it doesn't, she flies into a terrible and evil rage.

There are people like this in real life. In particular, feminists. They have cunningly turned our society into their own collective magic mirror. And no one ever recognized what they were really doing, nor why.

Until now.

For the record, I'm aware of the distinctions between 1st, 2nd, and 3rd wave feminism, and equity, radical, gender, gynocentric, and ideological feminism. Etc., etc., blah, blah, blah. These terms are all rubbish to the average person. They're all rubbish to me too. I use the term "feminist" in the sense that it is generally understood. If you're an emotionally healthy woman who refuses to dominate people via indirect power and control, I have news for you.

Call yourself what you will: you're not a feminist.

Due to the *Child and Family Services Act* of Ontario, Canada, I cannot reveal my true name. Nor those of anyone whose identity could lead to revealing the identities of my three children. Also, Freedom of Expression is apparently not well respected by Canada's judges. I thus had to change the names of most of the people involved in my scandalous and true story. Otherwise, they could sue me for telling the truth about them.

Sometimes the truth hurts. So does a malicious libel lawsuit when you live in Canada.

My experience has been, sadly, that the Rule of Law is a joke in Canadian courts. Here, it is the Rule of Lies. This is probably true in American, Australian, British, and New Zealand courts too, to varying degrees. Still, on principle, please know that I am exercising my constitutional freedoms of thought, belief, and expression in writing this book. And my right to liberty. Not that feminists, especially feminist judges, care about freedoms or rights or the Rule of Law. They have made Canada's *Charter of Rights and Freedoms* a collection of absolutely meaningless words on a piece of paper.

Ask any divorced father. Especially this one.

If it isn't already apparent, the nature of this work is such that it predicts it will seriously upset certain individuals. This work cannot help but be most controversial, for which I make no apology. If you live in quiet fear of upsetting feminist gorgons and hags, and those who appease them, brace yourself. This is going to get very ugly indeed. Those hideous feminist gorgons messed with absolutely the wrong kids.

Mine.

Some mistakes you live to regret. Let history record that the demise of feminism began with these words. No quarter: none asked, none given.

M.M.M.

Narcissus' Sister

1
Genesis

Now, the snake was the most subtle of all
the wild animals that Yahweh God had made.
— NEW JERUSALEM BIBLE, GENESIS 3:1

I was born in 1965, in a small town hospital in Nova Scotia, Canada. If horoscopes interest you, I am a wood snake in the Chinese tradition. I seem to resemble the descriptions of such people that I've read on various websites. If you Google this, you'll get a good basic description of my nature.*
I've never believed much in astrology and horoscopes. But since learning of the wood snake thing, I'm no longer certain.

I like a harmonious home environment. I like to think about things. I am easy to get along with, and I avoid fights and conflicts. They're generally not worth the effort. However, with snakes in general, and this one in particular, once pushed past a certain point, they strike back.

Or write books.

Dad's father—Grandpa—was a Navigator in the Royal Canadian Air Force (RCAF) who flew overseas during World War II. Dad was a

---

* e.g., http://www.futurescopes.com/chinese-astrology-zodiac-signs/
snake/8461/wood-snake-chinese-astrology (11 February 2013)

Radio Officer in the RCAF, and later cross-trained to Navigator. I am an RCAF Navigator with 30 years of service as of this writing. Mom was an Administration Officer in the RCAF when she met my father, so I'm second generation RCAF on my mother's side as well.

Ours was a moderate Catholic family. I have two younger sisters whom I'll call Elizabeth and Ann. I loved them back then, and I still do. Same for my parents. We went to church on Sundays. We said grace before eating supper. We tried to be good people. There was a lot of love in our house, although there was the odd swat on the backside when we really deserved it. I was taught to tell the truth, to be generous with charity, and to be nice to people.

And to change my underwear, so that if I got into a car accident, I wouldn't embarrass Mom. It's hard to argue with that sort of upbringing.

We moved around a fair bit due to Dad's being in the RCAF. When I left for civilian university under a military ROTP sponsorship (I believe in the United States it's called ROTC), it was something like my tenth move. I was often bullied in some of those places, as I was always the new kid. I really don't like bullies.

The best thing about school as a kid was football, the North American kind. Not organized, just boys going out to a field or playground and having a great time. No pads and full tackling. I was good at it. Dad had taught me how to be a great little receiver, as he had been quite an athlete in his day. It started in Grade 3, and continued until I went to high school.

Geometry was far and away my favorite subject. It was fun. It was challenging. It made so, so much sense to the way my mind works. Everything fit together perfectly. You *knew* it was right because you could *prove* it. In my day, they started teaching geometry in Grade 9.

I was an avid reader as a kid, too. It started around the same grade as did the football. Boys' mysteries (*Brains Benton, The Three Investigators*) led to the best of science fiction and epic fantasy. These ultimately yielded to classics and novels. *Catch-22* remains my favourite. I can so relate to it.

I was also an avid chess player in high school. I loved thinking a few moves ahead and trying to discern the strategy and tactics of my opponent. Geometry, books, and chess made much more sense than did girls.

This probably explains why I didn't have many dates.

Although you might not know it by my Grade 12 marks, I did very well on my provincial school aptitude tests. I recall being in the mid- to upper-90's in terms of percentiles for most if not all subject areas. I later learned that I had very strong verbal, non-verbal, and mathematical language reasoning abilities. I wasn't necessarily anything particularly special in this regard, though. Looking back, so did most of the guys I flew with in the RCAF—they were a really sharp bunch. Regardless, it's nothing I can take credit for. I just got a lucky roll of the genetic dice when it was my turn at the craps table of life. Besides, if you want to see someone who gets vexed trying to assemble Ikea furniture, look no further.

I was accepted out of high school to the University of Waterloo for math. I didn't go, as I was too naïve to know that Waterloo was probably one of the five best universities in the world for math. It was an incredible opportunity that I wasted.

Or perhaps not. You decide.

My father never learned about personal finance and budgeting until he was around 35. He had an honours degree in physics. During my time in high school, he was a Base Administration Officer (even though he was a navigator) before his tour as a Squadron Commanding Officer. As the Base Admin O, he was responsible for the financial aspects of the base's administration. Dad felt a university education in commerce would be more valuable to me in life than an education in science or math.

He didn't pressure me, but being a good wood snake (which I didn't know at the time), I strove for domestic harmony. I ended up with a compromise degree program from an east coast university. It was a combination computer science and business administration degree. You could get either a degree in science or commerce, depending upon the elective courses you took.

I stacked most of my science courses into the first two years, during which I was on the Dean's List due to good marks. However, when I got to years three and four, I had mostly commerce courses, and I couldn't stand them. My marks plummeted, and I was put on academic probation.

I spent my summers doing military training, initially with the Canadian Army. Canada is a little different from other nations, in that its Navy, Army, and Air Force are all one legal military service. It's like if the United States forced its Navy, Army, and Air Force to join its Marine Corps. (It's only taken us 40+ years to sort that out.) I did the basic parachutist course and the infantry section commander's course in the summer after my second year of university.

For the section commander's course, our platoon commander was a guy who was commissioned from the ranks. He was a graduate of the US Army Ranger course. On which candidates are allegedly so starved that they actively hunt rattlesnakes for food. He ran during our physical training (PT) sessions with a four-foot log that was nearly a foot thick. I had trouble even lifting it.

We had two sergeant section commanders. Mine was also a Pathfinder. If you think paratroopers are tough (they are), Pathfinders are guys who find that being a regular paratrooper is too easy. Pathfinders are the guys who free-fall parachute with 120 pounds of gear behind enemy lines for a few days or weeks to scout things out. Then they take out the enemy sentries and mark the drop zone for the regular paratroopers. Or sometimes they do challenging things instead. They have slogans on the walls of their training facilities like: "Pain is only a sign that you're still alive."

The other section commander was waiting for his free-fall parachuting course. He had to take this before taking the Pathfinder course, which is reputed to be one of the toughest courses in all of NATO. This guy could run a mile in 4 minutes 15 seconds. I couldn't run that fast falling off the side of a mountain.

At the end of the training day we would have our platoon run. My Pathfinder section commander wore army boots and not running shoes. He didn't want his feet getting soft and out of shape. As we were lined up, dreading what was about to begin, the platoon commander and the two sergeants would stand in front of us and smoke cigarettes. Then they'd absolutely run us into the ground.

On what was, for them, a sissy run. They were probably ashamed to do it without first having had a smoke.

We eventually graduated to running while hefting filled sandbags or doing 50 yard sprints with guys on our shoulders in the fireman's carry. Needless to say, I was psychologically toughened by my exposure to such hard men, and it was to serve me well. They weren't the sort of chaps you'd necessarily take with you to have tea with the Queen. However, you couldn't ask for better guys to watch your back in a dark alley.

At the risk of being somewhat cryptic, if you're reading this and happen to be a Mason, you might find this interesting. I once had a fine gentleman who worked at my university casually mention that he was a Mason, and that it had been a very beneficial experience. I didn't pursue the topic, and it was dropped. Perhaps the Great Geometer had a different plan for me. I may have needed to remain a rough, unworked stone in order to write this book.

Before my third year of university, I had a serious motorcycle accident that kept me out of military training for the summer. It was after midnight on the main highway in New Brunswick, half an hour from the nearest city. It was in the middle of nowhere.

I remember being blinded by a truck's high beams, but perhaps I fell asleep. Based on the injury, the doctor who put my right leg back together figured that:

a) When my motorcycle hit the guardrail in a turn, I was catapulted off.

b) I landed head first and cartwheeled into the guardrail. I hit my right knee against the guardrail on the knee's outer side.

The force of the impact blew my right knee in towards my left knee. The femur bone in the thigh was cleanly snapped in two around eight inches above the knee. One of the two ligaments deep inside the knee snapped apart. The ligaments on the inner side of the right knee were torn from the lower bone.

And I had a scratch on my left elbow.

As I lay on my back in a bit of a state of shock, I realized that my right leg was broken. If pain is really just a sign that you're still alive, I was truly alive that night. The military had taught me first aid. One applies traction to a broken bone as the proper protocol, or at least we did back then. However, you were supposed to be doing it to someone else. Regardless, I tried to sit up and put traction on my leg by pulling my lower leg away .

That was a bad idea. I do not recommend that you try this if you ever break a femur. I quickly learned that this causes the muscles on either side of the break to contract. This, in turn, sort of worsened the funny angle that my femur was at. This, in turn again, made me much more alive. It's a bit weird when you look at your leg and it bends *before* the knee instead of at the knee.

Luckily, I had a closed fracture, which meant that the broken bones weren't poking through the skin. After pondering my predicament for a moment, I hit upon a novel solution. If I couldn't put traction on the leg by pulling from the bottom, I could do it from the other end. This required stepping on my lower broken right leg with my good left leg, and then pulling my upper body away from the break.

That's just what I did, and it worked.

Later, a trucker stopped, placed a blanket on me (it was cold out), and drove off to phone for help. While I was waiting, another trucker stopped. By his accent, this second trucker was clearly from the deep south of the US. I've said "God Bless America" with sincerity ever since.

I asked this trucker—I never knew his name—if he knew first aid. He responded that he didn't. He took directions well, though. I said, "See the foot that's lying on its side? I want you to pull on it as firmly as you can. When you've got my leg fully straightened out, slowly rotate the foot while still pulling on it until it's straight up and down like the other foot." (My lower right leg was rotated 90 degrees from the upper part.)

That's exactly what he did, and it worked. Thank you Canadian Army training. The ambulance came, off I went, and the rest was history. I never saw either trucker again, but if they ever read this book, thanks guys.

I'm not the type to do pushups on broken glass every morning to make myself tough. However, thanks to some exceptional training courtesy of the Canadian Army, I can dig deep when the going gets unpleasant. The motorcycle accident wouldn't be the last time that I needed this ability.

Most importantly, as a matter of public record I can confirm that I indeed had clean underwear on when I was carted into hospital. No doubt the nurses were really impressed. Hopefully the men who read this book will learn from my experience.

Moms just don't make this stuff up.

Early in my career, an older officer who knew my father told me that Dad would have become a general if he hadn't gotten out of the military early. Notwithstanding Dad's obvious leadership talents, his professional accomplishments pale when compared to mine. Ironically though, while Dad's star was generally a rising one, mine peaked rather early as an officer cadet in college.

My glorious personal Vimy Ridge, my very own career D-Day, happened one evening when a fellow officer cadet and I were deep into the single malt whisky. For me, it was medicinal; it's the only reason I ever touch the stuff. I have learned that it is the nature of young strategic thinkers and single malt whisky that the world's problems tend to get solved in a single evening.

And so they were.

The next morning I awoke to something we in the profession of arms refer to as "the fog of war." It happens after we declare war on our excess brain cells. All three of them. As I slowly tried to roll out of bed, I noticed some hieroglyphics on the marble base of my bedside lamp. Some drunken buffoon had written them the night before with a big, black marker.

I wracked my brain—what was left of it—for a Rosetta Stone to decrypt what had been written. Slowly, it all started coming back to me. My buddy and I used to go to the formal Navy mess dinners, and we had gotten to know the Commander of the Royal Canadian Navy. He was a superb gent by the name of Vice-Admiral Jim Wood (his real name). So, having solved the world's problems, we had phoned dear old Jim late in the night and made an appointment to speak with him.

Surely the Commander of the Royal Canadian Navy would appreciate our thoughtfulness in this.

What was written on my lamp's base were the appointment details. My buddy and I dutifully showed up at the appointed time expecting to face a firing squad. A lesser man would have done just that, but not Admiral Wood. He kindly had us in and gave us a tour of the old house he was refinishing. He then sat us down with a drink and did indeed have a chat with us. What a prince of a man. He was just that sort of guy: talented enough to lead a Navy, and real enough to have a drink and a chat with a couple of—ahem—not-quite-perfect future officers.

Of course, there is the other career 'incident' that must be considered. At one of those mess dinners, I had to give the toast of the day. Along with a humorous story, of course. A politically-incorrect humorous story, as it turned out. This story remains one of the most deeply classified secrets of the Royal Canadian Navy in the modern era. Suffice it to say that I had Navy captains bent over double trying not to laugh out loud. The captains let loose once they saw the admirals at the head table busting a gut with laughter.

Maybe Admiral Wood had a soft spot for me.

Mail from the university was sent to my parents' address, which by this time was in Ottawa, Canada's capital city. Like all good moms, mine read my mail without asking. Just to keep informed, of course. Towards the end of my fourth year, she was horrified to read a letter basically saying: "Dear Mr. McConaughey, You were told last year that if your marks didn't improve, you would not be allowed back. You're not allowed back."

About a week later, Mom was thrilled to read another letter from the university, which read: "Dear Mr. McConaughey, as you have already graduated, please disregard our last letter."

Being a resourceful young military officer, I had read through the university calendar and requirements for graduation. I found a loophole just big enough for me to squeeze through. I ended up managing to "pack" a three year basic science degree into four years.

Bully for me.

I was actually carrying on with a family tradition of academic distinction. When my father graduated with his honours degree in physics, his father was there. Sort of. In the Dean of Science's office. Since it was a Catholic university, the Dean was also a Jesuit priest. The sort of guys who got roasted alive in some spots for spreading Christianity. Grandpa's (in)famous words said it all: "Tell me, Father—will there be criminal charges?"

It seems that Dad as a college senior had imbibed a bit with the guys. (Given my history, I must say that I was shocked AND appalled to learn of such behaviour from my father.) After which, Dad and the guys thought it would be a good idea to don women's stockings as bank robber masks. And then slip into the convent to scare the nuns. Jolly good and harmless fun, or so it seemed at the time. Until the school threatened to not have graduation until the culprits confessed. So Dad took one for the team. While the rest of the grads were getting their degrees in the big ceremony, Dad was playing pinball at Bud's Burger Joint.

Dad's degree was bestowed upon him in the Dean's office. After it was decided that there would be no criminal charges. "Hail Mary, full of grace..."

Shortly after graduating, I met a military nurse, and we began seeing one another. She, too, was from an intact Catholic family, so it seemed to me that there were positives in the relationship. There would be no disagreements about religion, and we would think similarly about family and children. She would understand the rigours of being a military spouse, with the postings and moves and all of that.

It was a good lesson that trying to apply logic to women is illogical. Sort of.

We were together for about five months before I had to leave for a year of Navigator training. We thus had to decide whether or not we were going to further pursue the relationship. After I was established at Navigation School, we decided to get married. We did so around eight months later.

It was a fateful decision. She was a Chinese tiger. Although I didn't know it at the time, tigers and snakes are a terrible mix. There was also something much worse than a Chinese horoscope mismatch, but it would take me 20 years to discover it.

By then it was too late.

2
Life

The unexamined life is not worth living.

—SOCRATES

I met most of Mary's family for the first time at the wedding. It went reasonably well. However, for my sin of not contributing enough to the planning, I had to pick our china pattern. I was then nicely chided for picking the most expensive one, and was over-ruled.

Like I cared about china patterns.

Mary was the third child of four. First was Rebecca, a medical specialist and sub-specialist. She had a medical specialist husband named Ken, who was so smart that he never bothered to study during medical school. They had a daughter Melanie and a son Darren.

Next came Mary's brother, Gordon. He was late-30's, single, and living in his parents' basement apartment. A nice guy with serious brains. He'd read virtually every classic ever written, and had graduated as the top graduate student at his university for his master's degree. He then went to law school to become a lawyer. He was reputedly later courted to become a judge, but wasn't interested. Gordon was socially reserved, although very pleasant to talk to.

Mary had gone to a teaching hospital for three years to become a registered nurse, and afterward joined the Canadian Forces (military). Her other work experience was working at Revenue Canada (the Canadian Internal Revenue Service) for a summer as an income tax assessor. She was good with bookkeeping and finances.

Her younger sibling was Darlene, who was working towards a master's degree in something or other. All in all, Mary and her siblings were a pretty intelligent and accomplished bunch. Her parents seemed nice enough, but came from humbler backgrounds.

When I graduated from Nav School and went to fly on the east coast, Mary voluntarily released from the military. If you follow these things, I eventually became a Tactical Coordinator on the Lockheed P-3 Orion maritime patrol aircraft. Only for some reason, Canada can't call an Orion what everyone else in the world calls it, so it was a CP-140 Aurora. Basically, I was a tactician who hunted submarines. Hunting generally invisible things like nuclear attack submarines isn't an easy task. The people I flew with were quite intelligent and professionally competent. They were also a hell of a lot of fun to be with.

There is one event from my Nav School period that even now remains fresh in my mind. It probably happened around the summer or fall of 1989. Mary and I had had a civil marriage before the church wedding; this was between the two. We were sharing a hotel room with Mary's younger sister to save money. At one point in the conversation, Mary gave me a slap on the back of the head. It wasn't a full-fledged whack, nor was it a "love tap." It was quite condescending and demeaning. It was a Three Stooges "you idiot" sort of slap.

I looked at her in disbelief, and judging by her sister's reaction, I wasn't alone in this. Yet Mary carried on as if she was the life of the party. Hah, hah, hah—aren't I funny? What I really couldn't believe was that about five minutes later, *Mary did it again.* She seemed incredulous when I expressed my unhappiness with her actions. It was as if, "Well, la-di-dah! Isn't someone sensitive?" She was utterly clueless as to how insulting and condescending her actions had been, and how much I did not like being hit.

It's a snake thing.

Mary didn't particularly like being in the military, and so she was happy to get out. She had claimed that her military nursing superiors were not nice individuals towards her. She implied that she had been a victim of mild injustice. She once showed me one of her annual performance reports. I didn't have the heart to tell her that it used a technique informally known as "damning with faint praise." Dad had taught me about it. If this was indeed the case, then Mary was not particularly well thought of as an officer by her superiors.

I was happy for Mary to stay at home and not work as a civilian nurse if she didn't want to, which thrilled her. She became pregnant about two months after the church wedding.

Our first child, daughter Hillary, was born in 1990. I was there when she entered into this world. So, too, for her two brothers.

My parents lived an hour and a half away, and they often visited after Hillary was born. She was their first grandchild. On one of these visits my mother made a comment as to how Hillary looked just like me. What mother wouldn't say that? Hillary also had my blood type.

Shortly after that visit, Mary had a crying fit about Mom's comment and the fact that Hillary had my blood type and not Mary's. I thought it was just postpartum hormones – a crying fit about our daughter having my blood type? My mind tucked the incident away regardless. It has this disconcerting habit of searching for patterns that no one else notices. Even if I don't want it to. It just does. It's like it says, "Hmmm... that's odd. I'll remember that."

I was an active father. I carried Hillary around in a Snugli baby carrier whenever I was home. I did my share of the dirty diapers, burping, and feeding when Mary later weaned Hillary. I read books to her, took her for walks in the stroller, played with her, bathed her, and all of that good father stuff.

I soon noticed a habit of Mary's of trying to make me feel guilty. I thought this strange, as I contributed to the child care and housework. I did have this slight impediment commonly known as a *job*. This did interfere with my ability to do housework now and then. When I spoke to her about this, Mary basically laughed it off with a glib comment. I wouldn't feel guilty if I had nothing to feel guilty about. All a joke, ha, ha, ha. Mary occasionally mentioned that her father's favourite saying was "half in jest, whole in earnest."

My mind tucked that away too.

As a colleague of mine was to later say about wives' habit of trying to make their husbands feel guilty: "They make you feel guilty for trying to make them feel guilty about making you feel guilty." I bet he never thought he'd see that in print. I hope for his sake that his wife doesn't.

Mary's parents came to stay with us for a week or two shortly after Hillary's birth. This was the second time that I had met them. I noted that her dad seemed to treat her mother with a degree of contempt. It was a little bit as if he couldn't stand her. I quietly resolved to never grow old and bitter towards Mary.

Thank God.

After some weeks of parenthood, Mary and I were both exhausted due to broken sleep caused by Hillary's nursing schedule. She hadn't yet slept through. As Mary and I lay in bed one night with Hillary starting to howl, Mary said in a slightly ugly tone, "It's your turn to get Hillary." It was almost a command. The last thing that I remember thinking before I fell fast asleep was, "You're the one with the breasts."

We awoke the next morning to sunshine and singing birds. And no crying baby. We both raced to her crib, afraid that she had died of Sudden Infant Death Syndrome during the night. She hadn't—she was fast asleep. From that point on, Hillary slept through the night, ten hours or more every time. She slept so much that at times Mary would have to wake her for breakfast.

The sleep thing gets important shortly. I learned from Hillary that at some point you have to let babies cry themselves to sleep. This is how they actually learn to fall asleep. When I mentioned this to my mother, she related a similar experience with my youngest sister. At some point, after you've ensured they're fine, you have to let babies cry a little to tire themselves and learn how to fall asleep.

Hillary was around a year old when Mary ambushed me one morning. As I was about to leave for work, Mary suddenly said she didn't feel well and didn't think she could look after Hillary. Most employers don't like it when their employees show up late to work. My employer has its own laws, its own police force, its own courts, and its own jail. Showing up significantly late for work for no good reason has its own name. It's called being Absent Without Leave, or AWOL. It's something that you don't want to be.

Since Mary was a nurse, I assumed that it was something serious. Yet when I asked, she was evasive and couldn't provide me with any definite answer. But she was a nurse—surely it must be serious. In desperation, I phoned my mother and had her drive an hour and a half to look after Mary and Hillary. This ended up happening more than once.

I was to later learn from my mother that Mary would sit on the couch and sort of lord it over Mom. Mom would do some type of house cleaning, and Mary would give direction. "Vacuum behind the headboard, would you?" This repeated itself a few times before my mother refused to come, and I finally had to tell Mary to deal with it. Then it stopped. Mary had not been ill at all. Mom didn't tell me the truth for years, out of fear that I wouldn't have believed her. She was probably right.

Mary had been faking being ill.

Our second child, Hugh, was born almost four years after Hillary. Mary's pattern of strange behaviours took a dramatic turn for the worse. She absolutely could not bear to hear Hugh cry—she always had to pick him up, no matter what time of day or night. I can understand doing this with a newborn. I'm not a heartless military stereotype; exceedingly few of us really are. There are genuine reasons for an infant to be in distress, like a dirty diaper, illness, or hunger. This was nothing like that.

Hugh ended up not sleeping through the night until he was 20 months old. That number is etched in my memory. I have never been so tired in all my life. Every time he cried, Mary *had* to run and pick him up. It wasn't that she was just tired and had her judgment impaired by fatigue. Mary was beside herself with grief when Hugh cried. She *had* to pick him up and console him.

It wasn't for his sake; it was for hers.

It was as if she was a feral animal. She was completely beyond reason, and our home life was hell because of it. I tried to tell her that she was actually causing Hugh to not sleep by constantly picking him up to soothe him. *Mary was actually causing the distress in Hugh that she was so concerned about.* She was rewarding him for crying by picking him up, and thereby training him to not fall asleep on his own. Mary was training Hugh from birth to need her. My mind tucked this one away too; it was a very important clue.

At one point, when Hugh had been incessantly howling during the day, Mary and I had a substantial argument. When wood snakes have it out with their spouses, it must be serious. I could not get it through to her that **she was causing the problem**. She responded as if I was a heartless ogre and that *her* baby needed her. When I say she was beyond reason, I'm not being dramatic in the slightest. It was literally like I was dealing with an animal and not with a rational adult. It was disturbing to see Mary like this. It was sick.

I've since read internet articles that suggest there is debate as to whether sleep deprivation is simply cruel treatment or whether it actually constitutes a form of torture. What Mary was doing to Hugh and the family wasn't trivial. She was tearing us apart. She was being cruel to an infant, if not outright subjecting him to torture.

The situation came to a head the day that Mary gave me a vicious slap across the face. After everything that she had subjected Hugh to; after my being exhausted from months of sleep deprivation; and with my really, really not enjoying being hit in the face, my self-discipline wavered for a moment.

I hit her back.

It appears as if I am no threat to win the title of heavyweight champion of the world. There was no swollen black eye, no hiding marks with makeup or sunglasses. There was no trip to the emergency room. There was no corny cover story like a door swung and hit her in the face when she was bent over. It was trivial in terms of physical impact. One respectable woman whom I later told about the incident merely said, "Meh. Shit happens."

However, it wasn't trivial to Mary. She spent the next three days being ugly and accusing me of having hit her. She conveniently seemed to ignore that she had hit me first and provoked the response. As with Hugh's inability to sleep, Mary seemed incapable of recognizing that *she had provoked the entire incident.* I spent those same three days glaring at her with cold rage. I hardly spoke to her. Had it not been for the kids, I would have divorced her on the spot and been rid of her. For me to feel this way was incredible—I was one seriously unhappy snake.

After three days, during which I hadn't backed down—her efforts to "guilt me" having proved futile—, she finally broke down crying. She claimed that she was afraid she was going to lose me. I bought it, naive fool that I was. Yet there were the kids and the Catholicism. No getting divorced. We reconciled.

Six months after Hugh finally slept through the night, our third child Leo was born. The pattern repeated itself, and he didn't sleep through until he was 16 months old. No wonder Hugh later ended up being afflicted with night terrors.

So, by the summer of 1996, we had a six-year-old daughter, Hillary, a two-year-old son, Hugh, and a newborn son, Leo. I don't want to give the impression that life was a total hell, because it wasn't. There were good times too. Hillary was a cute, vivacious, and ever-so-slightly mischievous girl. Hugh was the most wonderful, contented toddler that you could hope for. And Leo would soon develop into an adventurous Irish-type of lad. Yet Mary's unfathomable behaviour was always there lurking as a potential threat.

It was somewhere around this time that Mary surprised me with news that our family doctor had scheduled a barium swallow for Hillary. Mary said that this was because Hillary was having stomach problems. I was surprised—this was the first that I had ever heard of it. The swallow came back negative—no fault found. The stomach issue just seemed to fade away.

It would later return with a vengeance.

As an engaged father, I did many things with the kids. I was the bedtime story parent and the bedtime snack parent. I was the parent who bought Hooked-On-Phonics, to give Hillary a head start in school. The Miquon Math program, too. I've always understood the importance of the kids' educations. When away on aircraft deployments, I typically bought Christmas presents for the kids. Then when Christmas came, most of the shopping was already done. I was also the homework parent.

I coached Leo's age four soccer team one summer, took the kids to swimming and skating lessons, and helped out with Hugh's young hockey team. The family photos show that I was pitching in to help at nearly every birthday. I was the dad who wrestled the Hugh and Leo tag team duo, and who gave the kids horse-back rides (I was the horse) and piggy-back rides. I was the dad who taught them to ride bikes and climb trees.

I was there, as are many, many dads. Fathers love their children as much as mothers do, although we tend to express our love a little differently.

For some reason, Mary always seemed to act as if she needed to protect the children from me. I could never understand why. She could be angry with the kids one moment, and then angry at me the next for my being 'mean' to them. She was to some extent unpredictable. If one of the kids upset her, she would be in a black mood.

Personally, I rarely have bad moods. God knows I've had reason to in the past few years, given some of the vile women I've had to deal with. Those rare times when I am grumpy, I try to temporarily isolate myself from family so as not to upset anyone. Not Mary. If she was upset, she was miserable with everyone, including the kids. She wanted you to know. She wanted you to feel bad for someone having upset her. She wanted you to feel sorry for her.

To spare the kids from having their mother be miserable to them, I had to teach them not to upset her. "Your Mom is like fine china," I would explain. Or "Your Mom is like a delicate flower. Don't upset her." Little did I know that my efforts to protect the children from Mary's moods – in effect, teaching them to placate her – would come back to haunt us. It was an insidious family dynamic.

Mary's irrational behaviour continued. As my mind could not yet find the pattern, it kept noting things of interest. The clues kept piling up, but I didn't have the key.

I used to love playing with the kids, and they loved it too. For example, Hillary used to love it when I played "tickle spiders" with her when I put her to bed. I'd say something like, "Oh, no! The tickle spiders are coming!" and I'd wiggle my fingers—the spider legs—as my hands were the spiders descending on a thread to get her as she lay in bed with a huge grin on her face. She'd squeal with delight as I began tickling her.

At some point she'd be nearly out of breath with laughter and would shout, "Stop please, Daddy!" I'd pretend that I'd misheard her. "Stop peas?" I'd reply, and then begin tickling her again. "Stop please, Daddy!" she'd gasp again. "Stop trees?" I'd ask, again pretending to mishear before I began tickling her anew. "Stop please, Daddy!" she would again gasp. "Stop fleas?" asked I, her hard-of-hearing father.

"Stop PLEASE, Daddy!" she would scream after being nearly tickled to death. So I'd stop and let her catch her breath. After which, she would mischievously tell me, "I said stop PEAS, Daddy!" and so she'd get me to start the tickle spiders all over again.

An incident involving Hillary stands out in my mind. Darlene and her husband (a wonderful guy) had adopted a baby from a different country. One day Mary came to tell me that they were going to Disney World for a long weekend and had volunteered to take Hillary with them. Wasn't that so fantastic of them?

Actually, I thought it was kind of dumb, but I wisely kept my mouth shut. Who takes an infant to Disney World? How can you go on the rides with an infant? It sounded like a big disappointment in the making for Hillary.

Sure enough, it was. Just as I suspected, Darlene felt it wasn't fair that she had to look after their infant while her husband and Hillary went on rides. Gee, didn't see that one coming. I think Hillary only got on one or two rides before they went back to the hotel, where they spent most of the weekend.

Hillary didn't even get to swim in the hotel pool, as it was a zoo because of the long weekend. It was more of a torture session for the poor kid. Almost like bringing her into a chocolate factory and telling Hillary she couldn't have any. It was almost cruel.

Hillary brought me back a Mickey Mouse baseball cap. In one of my bigger goofs as a parent—my kids never came with an instruction manual—, I didn't wear it. Truth be told, I was too insecure to be walking around town in a Mickey Mouse cap when I had my military flying crew baseball cap. I probably hurt Hillary's feelings, although I certainly wasn't trying to.

Sorry Sweetheart, if you're out there somewhere. Daddy tried his best, but at times he wasn't perfect. Few if any parents are. If it's any consolation, I still have my old crew ball caps, but I don't wear them. They really mean nothing to me. I do wear my Mickey Mouse cap now, and it really does mean something to me. A big something.

Better late than never.

Somewhere around this time, I began encouraging Mary to start her own small business doing personal income tax preparation. She had always managed our own finances, as she was very good at it. She had her background as an income tax assessor. I thought it would be good for her, as it was something she could do while at home with the kids. It would give her something that she could be successful at and feel good about doing.

Her reply was always "Oh, I can't do that." At every step she always found reasons to seek encouragement and support. I could see why she wasn't well thought of as an officer while in the military. I helped her every step of the way, often doing the set up work for her. I got her the income tax software for the computer. I wrote her initial advertising pamphlets, and got the post office to distribute them. I recognized that she was far more insecure than she seemed. What I did not recognize was that she was manipulating me to feed her ego. It wasn't the last time this would happen.

Mary's family didn't really express love, whereas mine did. I always ended a phone call to my mother or one of my sisters with "I love you." I didn't with my Dad, because we didn't need to say it. I remember the first time Mary ever said that to her mother at the end of a phone call. How she beamed with pride and joy. I was happy for her. Yet my mind tucked away the beaming thing. Clues, clues, clues.

Mary had an unpleasant habit of undermining me in front of the children. On occasion she would tell the kids not to listen to me. She did this in a half-in-jest sort of way, reminiscent of her father's favourite saying. She'd say that she (and not I) was the one who took care of them. I had to grit my teeth when she would say this. Mary just wasn't capable of dealing with any personal criticism.

Talk about a Judas wife, undermining me with my own kids.

She would even say this in front of our good friends Morris and Leslie. They had three kids, each within six months age of our three kids. We got along famously. I later learned that one evening, after leaving our house, Morris turned to Leslie and said to her, "If you ever treat me like Mary treats Michael, I'll divorce you." He wasn't joking. I had to tolerate some degree of emotional abuse for the sake of the kids. I knew that I couldn't speak to Mary about it, as this would set her off and she would be miserable with the kids.

In a way, our family's dynamic had a dimension of emotional terrorism to it. Mary was the emotional terrorist, and the kids were her hostages. "Placate me, or I'll be miserable to you and especially the kids" was her demand.

Mary not only acted to undermine my relationships with the children. She also acted to undermine my relationships with the women in my family. She'd often say things like, "Don't get me wrong, I think your sister Elizabeth is great, but ..." and add something negative. Or "I love your Mom, but ..." and something negative again. But, but, but. Everyone has imperfections. Yet Mary always seemed to focus on them (which were trivial, really) exclusively. I'd counter with all their positives and virtues, which were substantial, for a balanced perspective.

Later in the marriage I tried to speak to Mary about this. What I got was "I guess I'm just a negative sort of person." As if I was being mean to her and it wasn't her fault that she was this way. I subsequently learned from my mother and sisters that Mary did the same thing if only two of them were with her. Mary would make slightly negative remarks about the one who wasn't there. As Mom and my sisters have good relationships, they recognized this and ignored Mary.

Mary's father had passed away within a couple of years of Hillary's birth. After his funeral, all Mary's mother could muster was, with a big sigh, "Well, he was a good provider." Her innuendo was that if you can't say anything nice about someone, say nothing at all. I then made a second quiet resolution. There was no way in hell I was going to work all my life and die leaving everything I'd earned to Mary, just so she could sigh and say the same bloody thing. Mary did her parents' income tax for them. She knew that her father had left her mother with a mortgage-free home, over $120,000 in the bank, and a positive cash flow from pensions.

There was something weird with this.

Another pattern I noted after Mary's younger sister Darlene got married was that she and her sisters had all married men two years younger than them. This is unusual – typically men tend to be about two years older than the women they marry. Even though the average marriage age has gotten older over the last few decades, husbands are still on average two years older than their wives.

That marriage was interesting. Darlene managed to estrange her entire set of in-laws from both herself and her husband at the wedding. She claimed they took a comment out of context, but in retrospect I doubt it. I think she may have engineered the falling out. Darlene was a funny bird. If she didn't like what she was hearing in a conversation, she would just up and leave. Regardless of whether it was a family gathering or a telephone call. She'd later act as if it had never happened. Another clue.

Mary's mom was the eldest of three sisters. Her mom's mom—Mary's maternal grandmother— was an ugly woman personality-wise. She was so horrible to live with that her three daughters all left home between the ages of 14 and 16. The middle daughter was a school teacher and never married. From what little I saw of her, it appeared as if she was very withdrawn and meek. The youngest daughter was a bit of a feisty woman, like Mary. This aunt of Mary's was divorced, as was the aunt's daughter.

Mary remembered her maternal grandmother as always seeming frail and ill, and saying things like, "Now bring your poor grandmother some tea." The grandfather spent a month away at a time working in the mines, and he would drink an entire quart of spirits when he got home. I might get drunk, too, if I came home to a witch after a month of hard labour. He died a nasty death of emphysema. This was a blessing, considering the alternative was living with his wife. More clues, more things tucked away.

At one point Gordon left his mother's basement apartment and moved to the other end of the province. He had met a nice single mother there. At 39 or so, it was great that Gordon had finally met someone. From what I can gather, Gordon and his fiancé were afraid of Gordon's mother's reaction to his marrying a single mother, since his mother was Catholic. Their concerns were justified—she wasn't particularly nice to her new daughter-in-law at the wedding. As it turned out, it had nothing to do with religion.

Interestingly, shortly after Gordon moved out, Darlene and her husband moved into the basement apartment. Darlene was worried about her mother being lonely. It seems that Darlene felt guilty about her mother being all alone. There's the guilt thing again. Clue.

Mary's strange behaviour continued. When we had our sons baptized, the family, priest, and friends came over to our house for refreshments afterward. Then Mary pulled a Darlene. Nobody could figure out what triggered it. She went up to our bedroom and refused to come out. It's slightly embarrassing having your wife act like a spoiled child with guests over. "Sorry, Father. My wife has the emotional maturity of a three-year-old. And that's one of her better points."

Mary could seem like a reasonable person one-on-one, but she often would change when others were around. Just like the Three Stooges hyuk-hyuk slaps to the back of the head.

Once, Mary took the kids out of province to visit her family. Since Mary did the finances, she asked me to log my expenses while she was gone. This seemed like a reasonable request, so I did. I played non-contact hockey a couple of evenings a week as part of my military physical fitness program. After one of these games, the guys and I went out for a beer. I bought a round that cost me $20.

Mom and Elizabeth drove Mary and the kids back home from the airport in Halifax. Shortly after she came in the house, Mary looked at the expenses. She asked about the $20, and I told her what it was. She then, in front of Mom and Elizabeth, stated in a loud, ugly voice, "You should be ashamed of yourself for drinking the clothes off your children's backs!" I was a little shocked, to say the least. Here we (me, actually) had just paid for her trip out of province. Yet she was berating me in front of my mother and sister over $20. Elizabeth, who saw what was happening, said, "Nice guilt trip."

Mary actually smiled and replied, "Thank you," pleased with herself. She hadn't realized that Elizabeth was being slightly sarcastic.

Another time when Mom and Elizabeth were visiting for a week, I planned to go out for an evening hockey game. I still had to stay in shape. I didn't think this was a big deal, since Mary and Mom and Elizabeth all knew one another. I thought they got along fairly well, but perhaps guys are dense in this regard. For some reason, Mary didn't want me to go, and said so in front of Mom and Elizabeth. She gave me her look that said, "I've asked you, so do as you're told."

So I said I was going to hockey. When I went to leave, my wallet wasn't where I usually left it. I needed it, as it contained my military identification card. I had to have this to be allowed on base to get to the arena. When I asked Mary if she knew where my wallet was, she said that she had hidden it. She admitted this in front of Mom and Elizabeth!

More emotional terrorism. Do what I want or I'll create a big scene in front of your family. I'll make everyone miserable. Wanting to spare Mom and Elizabeth, I asked Mary if I could have a word with her in our bedroom. With a look that could kill, I pointed my finger straight at her and told her that she was going to tell me where she hid my wallet right fucking now.

She glared at me angrily, but after a moment's hesitation she told me. I don't think she expected to be put in her place. Snake bites tiger.

Mary, it is safe to say, was manipulative and controlling. She had a sense of entitlement, as she felt she could do as she pleased in some regards. She had a lack of empathy, as she was incapable of understanding or caring about how I felt. I understand this in retrospect. At the time, all I understood was that the part of Mary's brain that should tell her when she was really pissing me off didn't work right. In fact, it often didn't work at all.

Remember those attributes: manipulative and controlling, a sense of entitlement, and lack of empathy. They became crucial to unraveling the puzzle later on.

Another disturbing incident occurred around late winter, 1997. Mary seemed angry for a period of weeks and claimed to have "fifth's disease." For me, fifth's disease is what strikes me after there are only 8 oz left in my 40 oz bottle of whisky. My version can be very painful. However, for everyone else, I gather that after mumps, measles, chicken pox, and something else, they ran out of names for childhood diseases. So they just called the fifth one "fifth." Rather makes sense. Mary claimed it was going around, and said she was having serious joint pain.

Strangely, she never saw a doctor for this. Nor did I hear of anyone else getting it at the time. She never had a rash, either. A mysterious medical condition with no verifiable symptoms, and she wouldn't go see a doctor "as there was nothing they could do." Hmmm...

I wasn't aware of her bogus illness from earlier in the marriage at the time. Also, my mind hadn't made the connection to her nasty grandmother's appearing 'frail and ill.' In retrospect, I believe there was nothing actually wrong with Mary. She was again faking being ill.

My mind sensed there was a pattern, but it didn't have enough to pin it down. More things tucked away for future processing.

It was during Mary's 'struggle' with fifth's disease that Hillary, who was not yet seven, snuck out of the house one day. Mary was changing Hugh and later claimed she was in too much discomfort to check on the sound of the front door opening. Hillary had slipped her boots on and went outside for a walk. It was late winter, not too cold, but there was still snow on the ground. Hillary went out without putting a coat on. No big deal, no hypothermia, no polar bear attacks.

Or so I thought.

A few months later, I came home from work for lunch one sunny day. Mary came out to meet me in the driveway, sobbing in distress. Someone, whom we later learned was the lady across the street, had called the child protection service.

Women. You've got to love them.

The neighbour had alleged that Mary was a negligent mother. She cited, amongst other things, Hillary's having been allowed to go out in winter with no coat. The investigation found no support for the allegations. This woman was a bit of a crackpot, and had previously made questionable sexual harassment allegations against a respectable school principal.

What didn't make sense was how Mary was devastated by this. Some crackpot woman makes ludicrous accusations, there's an investigation, and the allegations are found to be bogus. I couldn't fathom why this was such a big deal. Clue.

It got worse when Leslie informed Mary that a couple of women were gossiping about the affair. Mary was livid. She wanted blood. I ended up getting a lawyer to write curt letters to the women, which stopped them. For someone who went to church regularly, Mary didn't seem to have yet figured out the forgiveness part. Jesus said what?!

Here's some advice to married men: don't tell your vindictive wife that she's being vindictive. I did, and boy did I ever hear about it. I was so mean and insensitive, hurting her when she most needed support. She was the violated one, blah blah blah. Another mega guilt trip from Mary the righteous and wounded one. The pattern kept building.

For his first two years in school, we had put Hugh in a French immersion program. About halfway through Grade 1, the principal asked to speak to us. Only us meant me, as I was the one who dealt with the school. Mary didn't like doing this.

The principal (i.e., headmaster)—a kind and experienced educator—explained that he did English work with the French immersion kids. He didn't want them falling behind in English. He said that he was seeing something with Hugh in both English and French. Hugh had some sort of learning disability that the principal couldn't put his finger on. All the principal knew was that, based upon his 30+ years as an educator, something was going on with Hugh.

With the importance I placed on education, this was an issue with Hugh that stayed in the back of my mind. It, too, became important later.

As if there wasn't enough to be concerned about, there was another serious issue regarding Mary. Perhaps it was fortunate that I was ignorant of it for many years. My mother wasn't. She understood far better than I had and recognized far earlier than I had that something was wrong with Mary.

Hillary was born at the 95th percentile for height and weight, and stayed there during growth as a child. When she was in elementary school, our family doctor noticed that Hillary had developed a slight scoliosis (a sideways bend) in her lower spine. This was likely due to her rapid growth. Mary was adamant that we watch Hillary for posture to ensure she didn't worsen her condition.

Hillary was referred to a Halifax, Nova Scotia specialist. (State of Maine, up one, right one. If you see *Anne of Green Gables*, you took a wrong turn somewhere.) The appointment occurred while I was away on a short deployment. Mom came from Halifax to help Mary out. What's really strange is that Mary asked Mom to take Hillary to her specialist appointment. Mary claimed that she needed to stay with Hugh and Leo.

It's subtle, but there's something just wrong with this. Mom had had three kids, so she was well qualified to look after two young boys. Mary was a former military Nursing Officer. Why wouldn't she go to her own daughter's specialist appointment?

Wasn't that also kind of arrogant and insensitive of Mary? Her mother-in-law drives an hour and a half to help out, then Mary asked her to drive an hour and a half back to the same city for a grandchild's specialist appointment. After this, she had to drive an hour and a half to get her grandchild back, only to have to drive herself home (another hour and a half) to Halifax. Mary doubled Mom's driving inconvenience, and thought nothing of it.

There's the sense of entitlement and lack of empathy again. And more, as it turned out.

The specialist assessed that it was a minor scoliosis, no problem, nothing needed to be done. Mom spoke to the specialist alone briefly after he had seen Hillary. Mom described how Mary was instilling the idea in Hillary that her condition was bad enough to be concerned about. The specialist said that what Mary was doing was bad. She was needlessly worrying Hillary.

Mom tried to warn me about this, but I didn't understand. It seemed to me that Mary, an ex-nurse, was just being cautious. Mary ignored the specialist and asked our family doctor if he'd prescribe physio "just as a precaution, as it couldn't hurt." The doctor agreed, not understanding what was going on. Mary had caused Hugh's and then Leo's insomnia so they would need her. She had provoked me to the point where she could be my 'victim.' Now she had created an imaginary reason for Hillary to need her care and oversight, too.

I had by this time come to understand that Mary needed the kids to need her to some extent, but I had no concept of how serious an issue this was. I wish I'd paid more attention to Mom. Moms are so much more than clean underwear police.

I ended up spending eight years at the same base doing three different jobs in succession. I was happy with this long stay. I wanted to minimize postings with moves, so the kids could have geographic stability. I never accepted any geographical posting without first discussing this with Mary, as I considered moving both a family matter and a professional matter.

I then spent a year on the Canadian Forces Aerospace Systems Course (ASC) in Winnipeg, Manitoba. Winnipeg is a three-hour drive north of Grand Forks, North Dakota. Known as the divorce course, this was an intensive, multi-subject course taught at a master's degree level. It was like drinking from a firehose, depending upon your academic background. As an example, one lecture (not course— one *lecture*) was an introduction to differential equations, and the next lecture was an introduction to Laplace transforms. In that universe, one plus one does not equal two. This was to warm us up for control theory, in which you can learn the arcane mathematics of how a toilet works (feedback loops), amongst other things.

The whole family went to Winnipeg for that year. Since I knew I'd be posted back to the same base, we rented our house out. That way the kids would move back to the same familiar home out east. The moves to and from would have minimal impact on them.

Though it was tough, ASC was a great learning experience. Like my time with the Army, I wouldn't want to do it again, but I was a better man for having done it. ASC prepares RCAF officers for many possible duties. One is to function as a liaison between the regular military and its defence scientists. We had been taught mathematics, science, and technology, and how to conduct and publish research. Thus, we could act as defacto translators for the people in uniform and the people with the 100 pound brains.

Around this time, I was made a Member of the Order of Military Merit. Amongst other reasons, I had contributed to my community's tactical body of knowledge. I have a respectable ability in tactical analysis, as some odious women were to later learn. My professional specialty included potentially dealing with nuclear ballistic missile submarines—strategic thinking wasn't exactly foreign to me, either.

We moved back to the east coast and our same home after ASC. Things were a little different than before. Our kids were getting a little older and were less dependent upon us. In a couple of years, Leo would be going off to school, the last of the three kids.

With some encouragement, I convinced Mary to enter a two-year computer programming diploma program at a local community college when Leo would be starting school. Mary would have been all alone at home if she didn't have something to do. By going back to school, Mary would still have the summers off when the kids were off. Hopefully, she'd have a good education to exploit when she eventually went back to the work force.

It was a rigorous program. One of the instructors had a Ph. D, and the others weren't slouches. Mary eventually went, but the pattern of negativity was the same as with the income tax preparation business. At first she said that she would never get accepted. Once she got accepted, she said she would never pass. She then made pretty much straight 100's on virtually every test and assignment.

Every time she came back in glee with her latest 100%, she'd refer to her course rubric and do some stupid calculation. "If I get 60% on this test, and can get 60% on my assignments, I can still pass with an 80% final mark!" I kept telling her that she was nuts—she was going to keep getting 100s. I didn't realize that she was again manipulating me to feed her ego. That level of understanding was still several years away.

Mary did work hard, perhaps too hard. When I came home from work, I took care of the kids and helped with their homework. Mary came home from school and did her school work. I helped prepare supper—Mary was a better cook than I—, and I usually did the after-supper cleaning. This allowed Mary to get back to her school work. I did all the bedtime stories, snacks, and getting the kids to bed. I hadn't expected Mary to need to do so much work, with her intelligence and her siblings' academic pedigrees. However, she was bound and determined to excel, even with her false protests of insecurity.

Since I had suggested she go back to school, I felt obliged to support her. Those were two long and tiring years for me. I still had this inconvenient thing called a job with which we paid the mortgage, put food on the table, and paid Mary's tuition.

When Mary graduated, she won a significant academic award for her performance. I was actually looking forward to her helping out and taking her turn putting the boys to bed. That dream didn't last long. The first few times she tried putting the boys to bed, she got angry and started shouting at them. They weren't being bad. They were just being boys and playing around a bit. Each time I had to go in and take over before Mary had a hissy-fit melt-down. It didn't take very long before I was again the only bedtime parent. Emotional terrorism—do what I want or I'll hurt the kids and the family.

Morris, Leslie, and their three daughters had moved away by this time. Small-town east coast was a great place to raise a young family. However, with our friends gone, the kids getting older, and Hugh's learning dysfunction, we started to feel as if we had outgrown the place.

I had a chance in 2003 to get a fantastic posting back in Winnipeg, Manitoba. We'd been there only three years before, when I was on the Aerospace Systems Course. Thus, it would be a bit of a known quantity for the kids. Mary would just have graduated and would have hopefully had better chances of finding a job there. After discussing it with Mary, I accepted the posting.

The RCAF had decided that it needed something that was, in effect, an applied think tank. I was part of a team that translated high-level command guidance into the RCAF Welfare Centre (not the real name). The Welfare Centre's job was to figure out how to keep our guys—tons of them—who'd been screwed in divorce from having to go on welfare to survive. It was a challenging and exciting task, and I worked with some great guys doing it.

I know myself better than I did when I was in Grade 12. Many of us do. If I had to pick a different life path that matched my natural strengths, I'd probably choose life as a university academic in something like math. I love thinking, and I love teaching. However, I also loved spanking nuclear attack submarines, as it turned out. The Welfare Centre was a really good fit for me. Sadly, things didn't get better in Winnipeg.

Quite the opposite, in fact.

3
Decline & Fall

Words have no power to impress the mind without the exquisite horror of their reality.
— EDGAR ALLEN POE

I had scouted out schools for the kids before going to Winnipeg. I found a great Catholic elementary school for the boys in a nice, modest neighborhood. It was free as long as your family was part of the parish. For Hillary, I found a reasonably prestigious all-girls school that I could afford.

Mary had no luck finding a programming job. The high-tech sector meltdown happened just before she graduated. She eventually got jobs with two federal government departments. I wrote all her resumes and cover letters, because I was "better at it."

I really enjoyed my job. The original intent was that the Welfare Centre would be formed in Winnipeg. If Winnipeg proved to be a good fit for the family, the RCAF's operational headquarters was there, as was an RCAF base. It would have been easy to stay there for an extended number of years, which Mary and I had discussed.

Hugh's learning dysfunction became even more apparent. He was quite intelligent and a voracious reader. He was in Grade 4 and simply devouring the fantastic *Redwall* series of children's books. Scholastic.com lists the grade level equivalent as 7.8. He was almost at a Grade 8 level of reading.

His spelling, however, was terrible. He could misspell the same word three different times in the same paragraph and not realize it. His teacher gave her students a practice spelling test of 15 Grade 4-level words every Monday. The students then had all week to memorize the words' spellings for the real spelling test on Friday. It was an excellent way of teaching spelling.

Hugh would typically get four or five out of 15 on each practice test. I would work with him every night to memorize three or four of the words, so that when we got to Friday he was ready for the test. He'd typically get 11 or 12 out of 15. I think he scored 15 out of 15 only once. However, by the start of the next week he'd still be misspelling the same words he'd just learned. Or rather, hadn't learned.

The school's resource teacher did extra work with Hugh, which did nothing. All anyone could ever tell me was that Hugh had a "non-verbal learning disability." That's education babble that means, "We haven't a clue what's wrong, but we don't want to admit it."

One day I read a newspaper article about a place in Toronto called the Arrowsmith School. Bingo. If you have a child with a learning disability and your school is useless (sadly, too many are), I recommend you visit *www. arrowsmithschool.org.*

The story of the school's founder (Dr. Barbara Arrowsmith, Ph.D., real name) is great, but I won't repeat it in great detail here. In a nutshell, she was inspired by the work of Russian neuropsychologist A.R. Luria (real name). Luria was able to equate injuries to certain parts of the brain with specific cognitive impairments. Arrowsmith then mated Luria's work with American psychologist Mark Rosenzweig's (real name) work on neuroplasticity—our brains can continue to learn, even in adulthood.

Arrowsmith developed sets of specific brain exercises for Luria's set of brain dysfunctions, which she refined. These exercises target the weak region(s) of the brain to fix the learning dysfunction. The theory made so much sense to my logical mind.

Based on the website's descriptions, it was pretty obvious to me that Hugh had something called Motor Symbol Sequencing (MSS) learning dysfunction. It turns out that this is one of the more common dysfunctions, and it is one of the hardest to correct. I finally had a name for what plagued Hugh, no thanks to public education. Your tax dollars hard at work.

Or not.

When I contacted Arrowsmith, I discovered that I could get Hugh into an every second Saturday MSS weekend program. It would require him doing about 45 minutes of brain exercises every evening.

Ontario became a higher priority than Winnipeg.

Leo had his challenges in school as well, but they weren't academic. Leo's problem was bullying. One big kid in his Grade 2 class had decided that Leo was going to be his primary victim. Leo refused to defend himself, because he'd get in trouble.

The school had a "zero tolerance" policy about fighting. It didn't matter who started the fight. Both kids got detention with the principal. Leo refused to fight back—he was a good kid who was doing what the principal told him. The bully didn't care about the detention. Sitting in the office isn't like getting the strap. So he kept beating on Leo, and then was rewarded with time off from class.

Good intentions can lead to stupid policies. That should be a mantra for everyone.

I explained to Leo that he had to defend himself. I told him point blank to ignore the principal on this issue. The principal was wrong. "Leave the principal to me," I said. (I politely took care of that little issue.) I told Leo that the same thing would happen to him (detention) regardless of whether or not he fought back. So why not fight back? If he didn't fight back, the bullying would never stop. If he did, it would.

I saw the gears start to turn. Leo wasn't just a good kid; he was a smart one, too.

To help Leo out, I got him into a good kung fu school with a great kids' program. Leo did surprisingly well in his first big martial arts tournament, wining gold medals in forms and the gentle touch-sparring for his young age group. This gave him a big boost in self-confidence. It didn't take Leo too long before he straightened the bully out.

I'd also reinforced the kung fu school's strong ethics with Leo. Only in self-defence or the defence of others, never more force than is necessary, etc. The bully then tried picking on other kids. After a couple of more wallops, he quickly learned that Leo wasn't going to let him get away with that either.

And, boys being boys, it wasn't too long before the bully and Leo were on friendly terms. He just needed Leo to lay a little love on him. Man love, that is. The five-fingered kind.

I'm sure many parents have had to deal with similar learning dysfunctions and bullying problems. It wasn't anything that I couldn't handle, and it was I who was handling it. Mary didn't get involved with the schooling too much, other than ensuring the kids did their homework. Although it always seemed to be me who was the one helping them with it. "Because you're better at it."

After the first year back in Winnipeg, we drove out west for a family vacation in 2004. My sister Ann and her husband lived in Calgary, Alberta. We visited them and did a little camping in the Rockies. We then visited Mary's sister Rebecca and her family in Edmonton, Alberta.

Rebecca was a charming professional woman. She was the model of what the 'modern' woman is supposed to be: an accomplished professional woman married to an accomplished professional man with 2.0 kids. She often seemed to be ever so slightly exasperated with her husband Ken for no real reason. Ken was a great guy.

It was a fun family visit, but there were a couple of strange things that stood out in my mind. The first happened when Rebecca was recounting some family events from early in their childhood. She all of a sudden said, "I think we grew up in an abusive household," to Mary. There was a brief pause while a strange look passed between them. Mary replied, "Oh, I don't think so." Then the topic abruptly changed.

What the hell was that all about? It came out of nowhere, and suddenly it's like let's pretend it never happened. Had there been sexual abuse? Weird. Clue.

The other thing that stood out to me was Rebecca asking Mary if she remembered their mother storming out of the house when they were young. Mary didn't. Rebecca related how, on several occasions, their mother had loudly announced that she was leaving. She would then storm out the front door. Rebecca would ask their father, "Aren't you going after her, Daddy?" He'd say something like, "Aw, let her go," as if it was a relief she was gone. Rebecca had to goad their father into going after their mother.

Weird. I again made another promise to myself. If Mary ever tried such an immature stunt with me, I wouldn't go after her. Good bye.

Leo and Hugh brought challenges to our (my) life while we were in Winnipeg. Hillary, however, brought the biggest challenge.

It started when we discovered that Hillary was also being bullied. A small group of girls were sending her threatening notes. Nothing as bad as what Leo had to endure, although perhaps things are different for girls. Once I became aware of this, I contacted the school immediately. Unlike the boys' school, Hillary's school contacted the offending girls' parents and put a stop to it immediately.

It was shortly after this that Hillary started to develop mysterious stomach pains, which appeared to be so severe that she couldn't go to school. With two working parents, this is a problem. Despite Mary's having been a nurse, it was always me who had to speak with our family doctor. Just like it was always me who had to deal with the school and the homework and assignments. "Because you're better at it."

Nothing our doctor tried had any effect. Hillary's episodes went from being a few days long to eventually being weeks long. It was tough, but I managed to help her pass her second year at the girls' school. It had fairly high academic standards, yet Hillary was intelligent. With help, she made it. Hillary's stomach was bad enough that she underwent an exploratory upper gastrointestinal scope done under full anesthetic. There was nothing wrong.

Our family doctor also had Hillary assessed by a specialist for her sco-liosis. This was the second time Hillary had seen a specialist for this. I was very surprised when the specialist said that it was minor and not an issue at all. I'd been influenced by Mary's repeated 'concern' over this non-existent problem.

Mary's unpredictable behaviour continued. She could be angry at the kids one moment, and then get angry at me the next for being 'mean' to them. Other times she could seem normal.

Another incident really stands out in my mind. One day Mary, from out of the blue, told me that she thought I had problems with my relationship with Hillary. Where the hell did that come from? When I pressed her for details, she remained vague. The same sort of vague back when she claimed she couldn't take care of Hillary, but couldn't explain why.

Mary thought it would be a good idea for me to read *Reviving Ophelia*, a book about how devastating life is for girls. It was part of the

Oh-Our-Vaginas-All-Hurt book movement. What's interesting is that Mary had never read the book herself.

So, Mary can't tell me what she thinks my problem is as a parent, and recommends a book she's never read?! Just a little bit grandiose as a parent, don't you think? An important clue, but a subtle one. Just like with my mother and sisters, Mary was trying to undermine my relationship with Hillary. And if she was doing it to me, you can bet she was doing it to Hillary, too. There's a word for it, but that comes later.

The building in which my team was working also housed the School of Aerospace Studies, which had a library. As it turned out, they had a copy of *Reviving Ophelia*, so I did eventually read it. The only major point I took from it—other than everyone's vagina hurt—was that girls need loving but firm dads. This supposedly gives the girls something solid to anchor on in the stormy lives they all lead.

Boo hoo, all our girls are drowning.

I may not have been a perfect dad, but I'm nothing if not loving and firm. I had a great relationship with Hillary. When I told Mary this, she sort of let me know she didn't believe it. She clearly felt I had a problem—Mary was great at leaving things unsaid and communicating by innuendo. As I was to later learn, she was devastatingly effective in this regard.

The RCAF decided after a year and a half to place its new Welfare Centre at Canadian Forces Base (CFB) Backwater,* Ontario. Our family hadn't quite found its groove in Winnipeg, with the bullying, the learning issues, and the stomach problems. Backwater would have given Hugh a chance at Arrowsmith, as well as allowed me to continue with developing an institution that I was committed to. After discussing this with Mary, I asked to be posted to Backwater to be with the Welfare Centre in the summer of 2005.

Another bonus to Backwater is that it was within a few hours' drive from Ottawa, where my parents lived. My sister Elizabeth and her family lived there, and I had aunts, uncles, and cousins on Dad's side there, too. It was by far the largest single concentration of family on either side of the family.

I believe it was around this time (or shortly thereafter) that Mary and I discussed the posting *after* Backwater. This is actually normal for military families. You need to plan ahead so as to minimize any potential impact on your kids' schooling. We were moving to the Backwater area in 2005, and

---

* Not the real name.

Hillary was going into Grade 10. Postings are normally three or four years long, so the summer of 2008 would have been the best time if we had to move again. Hillary would have been graduating from high school, and Hugh would have been just entering high school that fall, so he'd have to change schools anyway. Leo had always adjusted well to the moves, so we weren't concerned about him.

Neither Mary nor I wanted to go back to Winnipeg. No other place with family appealed to us, so Ottawa seemed to be the only real option, and a good one at that. There are plenty of military jobs there. It isn't difficult to stay in Ottawa for the last few tours of your career. It's like the Pentagon and Washington D.C. if you're an American. Mary would have better job prospects there, too.

So, we left Winnipeg with the intention of staying in the Backwater area for three years, after which we would go to Ottawa. We chose to live in Krakton, which is within 30 minutes of Backwater by car. Krakton was larger than Backwater, and it had more amenities for the kids.

Life was looking reasonably good back in the summer of '05. Hillary's stomach hadn't troubled her all summer. (It didn't the previous summer either.) Perhaps it was the stress of the all-girls school that had been causing the stomach problems. She would be graduating in three years and would hopefully go off to university. Hugh would have the chance to get to Arrowsmith School and finally get some competent help in addressing his learning dysfunction. Leo would do fine; he always did. The boys had an easy 10 minute walk to their Catholic school, Grades 1 to 8. Hillary's high school seemed new and nice. I had a job I truly enjoyed, working with great people. And in three years, we'd likely move to Ottawa and settle down near my family for good.

It didn't take long after school started for Hillary's stomach problems to come back with a vengeance. Krakton had a shortage of doctors, so it was hours waiting with her at the local clinic to try some other medication in desperation. As before, Hillary began missing extended periods of school. As always, it was never Mary the ex-nurse who took Hillary to the clinic. It was always me.

I was also the one who negotiated with Hillary's school to reduce her workload, get her back into classes, and help her catch up with homework and assignments. Come to think of it, *Mary did nothing to help Hillary get back to school.* Not ever.

One day, her sister Rebecca passed on to Mary that we were "probably dealing with stomach migraines." Even though Rebecca is a medical specialist, her specialty has absolutely nothing to with stomachs or neurology or migraines. Why would she express such a crackpot diagnosis without ever having seen the patient? This was another blind alley we went down in a useless attempt to deal with Hillary's problems.

I was also concerned about Hillary's socialization. School is important in this regard, too. I wasn't just constantly encouraging Hillary to do school work. I would also try to get her out of the house to see her friends. This always seemed to make her feel better. Strangely, Hillary could be fine all weekend with her friends, yet have crippling stomach pains come Monday morning. Hmmm...

It was around this time that I learned that Rebecca's daughter Melanie had been having serious medical problems for some years. Instead of stomach pains, for which there is no confirmatory test, Melanie had migraines (wicked headaches). For which there is also no confirmatory test. I wish I had known then of Mary's having faked being ill before. I also wish I had put this together with Mary's less-than-pleasant grandmother always seeming 'frail' and 'ill.' I eventually did, but too late.

Melanie had missed copious amounts of school due to migraines. Or 'migraines.' It turns out that, like Hillary, Melanie always got better during the summer. Let's see, what is particular about the summer? 1) The sun shines more than in the winter, and 2) There's no school.

As with Hillary and medications, no medication ever really worked for Melanie. Things even got worse. Eventually, Melanie was diagnosed with migraine, seasonal affective disorder (SAD), and fibromyalgia.

What's even more astounding was that her doctors eventually found a single drug that actually worked for all of Melanie's symptoms: Prozac. Yes, put the wee lass on happy beans and she magically gets better. Rebecca probably still believes the migraine, SAD, and fibromyalgia 'diagnosis.'

It was around this time that Mary was dismayed to learn that Rebecca and Ken were getting divorced. She'd talk to Rebecca on the phone and then come tell me that the divorce happened because of something that happened to Ken when he was young. Then there'd be another call later, and then it would be Ken's fault because he had stopped loving Rebecca. It didn't take too long for me to recognize that the fault would change, but it was always Ken's.

Apparently Saint Rebecca had tried hard to save the marriage, getting herself and Ken to try different therapists. I thought this was rubbish. It sounded to me like Rebecca was dragging Ken around to different therapists instead of accepting her part in the problems. Therapist shopping. I wisely kept this to myself.

After some delay, being busy with work and Hillary's problems, I got Hugh into the Arrowsmith program. As I suspected, he was formally assessed as having severe MSS. Every second Saturday morning we drove the couple of hours to Toronto for his class and interim assessments. We'd always stop on the way back for a treat at New York Fries. It was poutine— fries, cheese curds, and gravy. If you haven't tried it, it's worth risking a heart attack for. Almost every evening I made certain that Hugh did his 45 or so minutes of brain exercises. These were mentally tiring for Hugh, so I had to be firm with his doing it. Man love—it's what fathers were made for.

I had informed Hugh's pleasant little school about his Motor Symbol Sequencing learning dysfunction and his remedial brain exercises. I had to pay for Arrowsmith out of my own pocket. The Government of Ontario couldn't afford this. It had already wasted too much of the tax payers' money buying their votes from them.

Hugh's school insisted on having him assessed by their own school board expert. This expert was so exceptional that she was able to identify all the symptoms that I already knew about. Unlike Arrowsmith, though, she couldn't tell me what the name of the problem was, its nature, or how to fix it.

When Ontario schools don't know how to help a student, they create something called an individual education plan, or IEP. It's their way of pre-tending that they know how to help a student when they don't. Hugh's IEP included stuff like him being given extra time for exams and the like.

I was candid with Hugh's principal and teacher regarding Arrowsmith. My reasoning was simple: if we didn't correct the problem, it would never go away. Better to get it done then as opposed to continuing to ignore it, and have Hugh continue to under-perform at education. The longer we delayed solving the problem, the harder it would be for Hugh at higher levels.

I even had the Arrowsmith school write a letter to Hugh's school explaining the nature of his MSS work. I had no qualms about sending in a note with Hugh saying that I had excused him from his homework if he was too tired from doing Arrowsmith. Sometimes the school would contradict its own IEP. The teacher would say she had to see some assignment in order for Hugh to demonstrate enough proficiency to pass. Which is why they made the IEP in the first place. So he wouldn't have to do meaningless assignments that got in the way of fixing his learning dysfunction. In fairness, though, Hugh's school was generally good about the issue.

What's interesting is Mary's role in all of this. She almost never took Hugh to Arrowsmith, unless I was away on a business trip and the weather was nice. Mary always made sure to know what the boys' homework was. She also made certain that I was the one who helped them get it done if help was needed—"You explain it better than I do." She didn't like it when I excused Hugh from his home work. She finally confessed that it was "different for mothers:" it looks bad on the mother when the homework isn't done, which were pretty much her exact words.

There it was. Mary didn't care about Hugh's learning dysfunction. Not one single bit. All she really cared about was how she looked as a mother. That's why she always ensured that the boys' homework was done (with my help). So she would look good as a mother. Big clue in hindsight.

Leo was virtually a problem-free child. He did well in school and eventually found a good martial arts club. Supreme Ultimate Grandmaster Phu Manchew's School of the Forbidden Drunken White Lotus Style of Red-Hot Iron Fist Internal Kung Fu.™ Future bullies beware. Your man-love awaits.

Mary wasn't getting out of the home much, but it wasn't for my lack of effort. I suggested she try yoga or something else for self-interest and to meet people. No dice. When I encouraged her to look for computer-related jobs, she said there was no point. Everyone wanted database programming skills, which her program hadn't taught. When I encouraged her to upgrade her education, she said there was no point. She seemed to want to be the victim of circumstances. Another clue.

Always another clue.

Mary had one infrequent habit that I could never fathom. Not only did she need to have the kids need her, Mary occasionally *had* to worry about money. While we weren't wealthy, we'd done well by buying our first home early. We had about $120,000 in home equity, relatively little non-mortgage debt, and we always paid off our credit card balance every month. I also had a stable career with a good pension.

I couldn't fathom why Mary would seek to be reassured about money. Especially given her understanding of taxes and personal finance, and her likelihood of employment when we got to Ottawa.

This is when I made the mistake of trying to reassure her by seeking professional investment advice. The financial adviser recommended getting a home equity line of credit to get the money to make mutual fund investments. I repeatedly asked Mary if she didn't want to do this, and she never said no. I would have been happy to stick with our home as our sole investment.

We ended up having to promise another financial institution we'd bring our mortgage to them when it came due in order to get the line of credit. So we did it.

After our second year in Krakton, Hugh had improved to 'only' moderately severe MSS. This was significant, as it was the first time in his life he'd made any progress with his learning dysfunction. Hillary's stomach episodes, though, were getting worse. Except for the summer. She also had a major stomach episode just before she was to start driver's education, and we lost the $500 course fees. I was trying to get her to become independent; life seemed to always conspire against me.

Only it wasn't life that was conspiring against me.

There was another incident a bit like the *Reviving Ophelia* one. I had stopped wrestling with the boys at bedtime. Hugh was getting too old and strong. Instead of playing with dad, there was a danger of it becoming a dominance issue. Since I had always wrestled with both of them, I didn't want to wrestle only with Leo and exclude Hugh.

Mary felt the need to speak to me about it. "You don't wrestle with the boys like you used to." It was almost an accusation. There was an innuendo of "You don't love the boys anymore?" that came with it. I explained to Mary that there was a risk of it becoming a dominance thing with Hugh. I explained that I didn't want to exclude Hugh by only wrestling with Leo. From the look on her face, it was clear that Mary didn't believe me. She had to believe I didn't love the kids as much as she did.

Leo eventually made me a coupon for a free wrestle with him. I was touched, and did end up wrestling with him a few times when Hugh was out playing with friends.

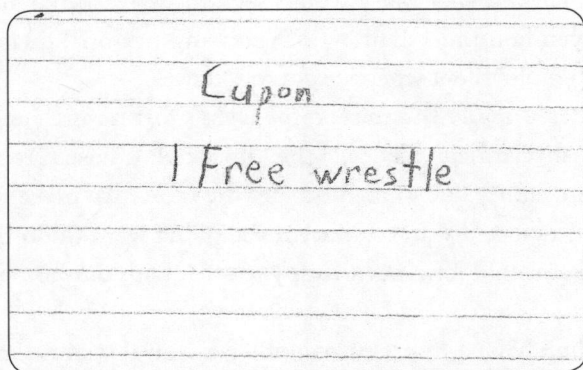

> Cupon
>
> 1 Free wrestle

"Cupon" from 9-year-old Leo

Mary had developed a new and disturbing problem by the spring of 2007. She'd starting playing the kids' video games, especially one called *Animal Crossing*. When I say playing, I mean as in all day long. *Animal Crossing* is the sort of game that little girls around 9 or 10 years old might like. I was amazed that Mary wasn't the slightest bit embarrassed about playing a kids' game.

I was concerned that perhaps she was slightly down about not getting a computer programming job. I'd come home from work and the same breakfast dishes were still in the kitchen sink. It must have been too much for her to put them in the dishwasher. Although I'd always pitched in with the housework, I tried doing even more.

Her response was to do even less, and to play even more. That damn law of unintended consequences!

I thought that maybe going camping might help. It would certainly get her away from the computer games. We had also camped around the east coast with the kids when they were old enough. I thought it might bring back fond memories.

I coordinated with Elizabeth, and we arranged to vacation together in cabins on a lake between Krakton and Ottawa. It turns out that the cabins were a lot nicer in the brochures than in reality. This didn't excuse Mary's condescending or demeaning comments to me in front of the kids or my sister's family.

This was the worst incident. Elizabeth has two kids, an older boy and a younger girl. Her son and daughter are almost a year older each than Hugh and Leo. One morning when Elizabeth and I were discussing joint breakfasts, she mentioned that her daughter Marie would never eat eggs with soft yolks. In fact, she jokingly said that she would give me $50 if I could get Marie to eat them.

Poor Elizabeth underestimated her older brother. Perhaps she didn't know of my illustrious academic pedigree. So, I went to Marie on the sly and offered her $25 if she would eat just one little cooked egg with a soft yolk. After a moment's thought, she said yes.

The next morning we had a joint family breakfast. I told my young niece in no uncertain terms that Uncle Michael was making her a soft-cooked egg. She was going to eat it, and that was that. Elizabeth looked on in amusement at my apparent folly.

Elizabeth's amusement turned to stunned disbelief when her daughter gobbled down the egg. I turned to Elizabeth, held out my hand, and awaited my $50. When Elizabeth had given me the money, I immediately turned to her daughter and said, "Here you go," giving her $25.

Elizabeth has a great sense of humour. She recognized that she'd been had, and thought that it was outrageously funny.

Mary, however, thought differently. She immediately got angry and said something like, "I wish you were that nice to your own kids! You would have smacked them on the back of the head and forced them to choke it down." Right in front of our kids and my sister's family. Just like the "drinking the shirts off the kids' backs" episode.

If I had said anything to Mary, she would have been ugly to everyone and ruined both families' vacation. More emotional terrorism. So I gritted my teeth and said nothing.

There is another good example of what Mary could be like when someone didn't behave the way she wanted. It happened not too long after getting back from camping. I made a comment one day to Mary in front of the kids as to our being middle aged. Mary replied to the effect that no, we were *young*. She used her this-is-how-it-shall-be sort of tone. As if she'd tolerate no discussion on the issue.

I was getting pretty fed up with her by this point, and I decided that I wasn't going to be bullied into dropping the subject. I said that it was simple:

up to 30, you're young; 30 to 60, you're middle aged; over 60, you're old. Easy thirds, more or less. Then I pointed out that Mary was turning 45 years old in a few months. We were middle aged.

Mary said that we were *YOUNG* in that sort of voice that warned I was in danger of really pissing her off. Happy to oblige, just this once. So I pointed out that Hillary was 17 and that we were old enough to be grandparents, for goodness sake. We had to be middle aged.

Well, that did it. She clenched her fists, scrunched her face, and stomped her foot three times to emphasize as she shouted "WE! (foot stomp)—ARE!! (foot stomp)—YOUNG!!! (foot stomp)." Right in front of the kids. I was married to a woman with the emotional maturity of a two-year-old. This is why I had taught the kids to placate their mother. I knew these sorts of episodes are what would have otherwise resulted.

As bad as things were, they were about to get a whole lot worse.

Everything I had tried to do to help Mary with her preoccupation with childish video games failed. Mary was not the sort of woman whom you could have a mature conversation with regarding her behaviour. You can't have a mature conversation with a two-year-old child. When the kids' school started in the fall of 2007, Mary had a lot of free time, even with Hillary often at home. Sadly, Mary discovered MMORPGs.

MMORPG stands for massively multiplayer online role playing game. They're imaginary internet game worlds where tons of people join teams, groups, clans, or something else and play make believe. I recall it starting with *Fallen Sword* and then progressing to *Samurai of Legend*. Harmless kids' games.

Only it wasn't harmless with Mary. It quickly became an all-out obsession. She'd sit at the computer playing for extended periods. There's a technique called "grinding," where a player repeatedly 'slays' monsters to build up experience points. Mary had it down to a science. Click, click, click went the mouse, and she had slain a Sap Sucking Swamp Spirit. Seconds later it was click, click, click on the same spots on the screen, and down went the Shaggy-Bottomed Slime Troll.

She did this for hours and hours and hours. She stopped coming out of the computer room to eat supper with the family. She stopped doing any house work whatsoever, except laundry (not folding, nor putting it away). The laundry room was between the computer room and the main bathroom.

She stopped buying groceries or making supper for the kids. At one point she ranked 40ᵗʰ out of nearly 10,000 players in one of her games. After only a couple of months of playing every waking moment, she was in the top half percent of all players.

She was so engrossed and excited about her games. What really amazed me was that she completely did not care that she was more or less abandoning the family.

Mary and I used to watch movies at home some evenings when she wasn't playing, which became a rare event. We'd sometimes have a bottle of wine when we did this. I am a larger guy. Mary was around average height and weight. I understand that the male metabolism is better at processing alcohol than is the female metabolism. Yet even with my size and gender advantages, Mary always insisted that she had to drink half the bottle of wine. Otherwise it was unfair to her. It was just another way in which she was a victim, and I was the victimizer. In her mind, of course. Only in her mind.

One ugly incident happened about a month after the boys had gone back to school. We'd watched a movie, and I was locking up the house as Mary went to the bedroom. She must have had more to drink than I realized. When I got to the bedroom, Mary was hunched over the toilet in our small ensuite bathroom. She didn't vomit, but she clearly felt ill.

I wasn't upset that she'd had a bit too much to drink. What she started saying did upset me, after I asked her if there was anything that I could do to help. She replied by shouting that, to me, she was "just another hole to fuck."

Not the nicest thing that a wife can say to a husband. She continued shouting it as loudly as she could for the next twenty minutes. Her voice was hoarse by the end. I do not know how the boys or Hillary didn't hear this disgraceful tirade from their drunken mother. I can only hope they slept through it.

The next day Mary had acted as if nothing had even happened. Let's all play ostrich. Let's stick our heads in the sand.

Mary was also going through menopause during this period. She was not yet 45 years old—the women going through her family entered menopause early. Menopause and the video game addiction were threatening to kill the physical intimacy in our marriage. When I tried to talk to Mary about this, I literally got the talk-to-the-hand gesture as she looked away. "Bring me some red wine and chocolate, and we'll talk about it." Talk about condescending. "I will condescend to have conjugal relations with you, husband, but I have to get half-loaded first. And make that good dark chocolate, you lout."

So, like any red-blooded male, I went to the liquor store. Better than a gorilla suit. Mary was to later accuse me of getting her drunk so I could have sex with her. I don't know what I did in my previous life to deserve Mary in this one, but it mustn't have been good.

Mary's addiction threatened to affect my work. I had to go to Germany for a week in October, 2007. I was taking a course at the NATO School there. Mary's addiction was bad enough that I did not trust her to look after the kids by herself. So I arranged to have my mother come stay and give Mary a hand. I hadn't told Mom about how bad things were. I was hoping that Mary would be too embarrassed to play video games constantly with her mother-in-law there.

Boy, was I wrong. Mom saw how bad it was. Mary was feeding the kids soup and apples most of the time. Hugh was hungry enough that he was eating six or eight apples a day. Dad came down to visit, too, and both he and Mom couldn't believe how Mary ignored them and let Mom do most of the housework while Mary played her video games.

My sister Ann and her husband had also visited while I was away, and they also saw what had happened to Mary and the family.

It is no exaggeration to say that Mary spent every waking hour on the computer. On the worst day that I witnessed, she started playing when she woke up at 7:00 a.m. She played non-stop until 4:00 a.m. *the next morning.* 21 straight hours. I was always going to bed by myself to the sound of Mary furiously pounding on keys in the room next door. I'd wake up briefly when she finally came to bed, usually between 2:00 a.m. and 4:00 a.m.

Mom also noted how Mary made zero effort to get Hillary off to school. We had, in the previous year, gotten Hillary to see a psychiatrist. This psychiatrist didn't put any label on Hillary's condition, but said it was very important that Hillary go to school every day, no matter how bad she felt.

It wasn't too long after this before Hillary suddenly developed 'insomnia,' making it impossible for her to follow the psychiatrist's instructions. I had to get up and leave the house early to get to work, so it was Mary's job to get Hillary out the door. Mary couldn't be bothered.

Melanie had migraines, seasonal affective disorder, and fibromyalgia. So she couldn't go to school. Hillary had 'stomach migraines' and insomnia. So she couldn't go to school either. Hmmm...

Mary was so engrossed in her games that she completely forgot about my fall 2007 birthday. The kids certainly didn't know about it. This was the first time Mary had ever forgotten anyone's birthday. When I mentioned to her that it was my birthday, she laughed and asked me to buy some steaks and red wine. She would then make me a birthday supper. Only she couldn't be bothered to get off the computer to do it. So I made myself my own birthday supper.

Happy birthday to me. Happy birthday to me. Happy birthday, dear me. Happy birthday to me. Thank me. I'm welcome.

By November 2007, the kids were starting to complain to me that they could never get any computer time for games, interest, or homework. Mary was always on it. I was a little slow one morning getting ready for work. I usually left the home before the kids left for school. This particular morning, the boys were goofing around a bit while getting ready to leave. Mary came out of the computer room—they had interrupted her early morning playing—and was really ugly to them. Hugh in particular. I could see the hurt on his face.

Hugh got in trouble at school that day for swatting some kid in the face. Hugh *never* got in trouble for fighting. This was clearly due to Mary's ugliness as a mother that morning. I knew that it was past the point where I had to intervene in her addiction. I wanted expert guidance as to how to go about this. Mary could be ugly at the drop of a hat. I knew she was going to be Medusa ugly over her addiction.

Mary actually ended up making Medusa seem kind of attractive, after all was said and done.

I discovered that the Canadian Armed Forces Base in Backwater had professional counselors for families. I made an appointment to see one in early December. I explained to the kids that their mother had an addiction problem, and that I was going to get professional help for her. I told them that it wasn't their mother's fault, not to say anything to her, and to not get upset about the computer. I was very careful to preserve her image in their eyes. This is something that I cannot say that Mary ever did for me.

When I saw the addictions counselor in early December 2007, I told him everything that was going on. He said that the addiction sounded very serious, and that Mary should see a psychologist. The base had one on contract. The addictions counselor also warned me that this could be a very ugly period. As if I hadn't already figured that one out! He recommended that I wait until after Christmas to try to intervene. It would probably ruin the kids' Christmas if I had tried to intervene right away.

I decided to wait. I was fed up with Mary by this point. I wouldn't have minded at all if she packed her bags and left. However, I was concerned for the kids. For this and out of loyalty, I resolved to try and help Mary. I also spoke to the boys' principal, to let her know that we were dealing with a problem at home. I wanted to know if Mary's addiction was further affecting the boys' education.

Christmas 2007 was a disaster. I had work to contend with. I had Hillary's medical problems and her schooling to contend with. I had Hugh's Arrowsmith to contend with. I had Mary's addiction to contend with. As if that wasn't enough, I was doing virtually all of the housework and helping the kids with their homework.

I was so busy that I missed an appointment with our financial adviser. I was going to sell the mutual funds and get out of the market. Had I sold then, we would have saved $4,000 on losses that we eventually took.

I realized almost too late that Mary was so lost in her stupid game world that she had done nothing to prepare for Christmas. I had to scramble to buy gifts and get a turkey and all of that stuff. With all that I had on my plate and the limited time, my gift selections weren't the best. Mary had done this stuff for the previous several years; she normally enjoyed it.

I bought Mary a couple of nice sweaters from her favourite shop for her Christmas gift, hoping this might help cheer her up. She was able to tear herself away from the computer on Christmas morning long enough for the opening of presents. She actually belittled my gifts to her in front of the kids, as well as some of the kids' gifts too.

In retrospect, our marriage died that Christmas morning. Stone cold dead. It would take a few more months before I'd understand and accept this, however.

After the presents, Mary went back to the computer with a glass of wine. I went and got the turkey prepared and in the oven, and then I cleaned up. When the turkey was ready, I took it out of the oven and went to get Mary. She was the gravy expert in the family. Surprisingly, she wasn't at the computer.

I found her in our bed, passed out drunk from the wine. Merry Christmas, indeed.

Hillary and I tried to make gravy from the turkey drippings, but we'd never done this before. Eventually, Mary came out—still drunk—and started to make joking comments about our gravy incompetence. When Hillary got out the digital camera, Mary started hamming it up like she was the life of the party. She kept insisting Hillary take her picture, and was doing immature things like sticking her bottom out for a great bum photo shot.

In short, my drunken wife was acting like a drunken idiot in front of the kids on Christmas day. If I had said anything, Mary would have been miserable and ruined Christmas for the kids. I still have copies of those pictures. It doesn't amaze me that Mary was oblivious to how disgusted I was with her behaviour. That part of her brain never did work right.

Merry Christmas to me. Merry Christmas to me. Merry Christmas, dear me. Merry Christmas to me.

I did nothing until shortly after New Year's Day, when I placed a brochure about addiction on the computer keyboard one morning. She wasn't impressed when she found it, nor did she like my suggesting that she had a problem. It was the you're-displeasing-me-so-stop-before-I-get-really-pissed-off sort of look.

I also emailed my family to let them know what was going on. With my parents having been over during the previous October, this wasn't a surprise to them.

By the second week in January, Mary started to let the kids have the computer for a bit after supper. It was as if she was trying to prove that there was no problem. Yet she was still up all night playing. One night, she came to bed at 4:00 a.m., waking me up in the process. I couldn't get back to sleep and ended up taking a nap after work the next day as a result. Mary made a disparaging comment about my having a nap, as if she was in no way responsible. She also made a show of doing housework when I came home from work. However, from the state of the house, it was clear that she had been playing games all day.

A week later, Mary became quite belligerent towards me. She had learned that I had spoken to the kids before Christmas about her addiction and my seeing a counselor. Mary accused me of being the cause of Hillary's medical problems because of this. This was utter nonsense—these problems had started years before. When I say "belligerent," I mean that she was using language like "Fucking asshole!" and "It's always my (Mary's) fucking fault!" She made sure to shout this loud enough so that everyone in the house could hear her. She wanted the kids to know. She always did.

Mary also threatened to leave the home. Again, it was loud enough for the kids to hear anywhere in the house. Just like her mother. I wasn't falling for that trick. What I wanted to say was, "Let me help you book your flight out. Is Antarctica too far?" However, I didn't for the kids' sake. I merely asked her where she would go. She wasn't expecting that, and didn't answer.

I generally did a good job of keeping my cool. However, Mary always seemed to want to provoke a conflict, especially in front of the children. Ever the emotional terrorist—I'll demean you, and you'll take it or I'll hurt the kids.

Clearly, this was affecting the children, as much as I tried to shield them. Interestingly, towards the end of January, Hillary confided to me that she felt guilty about her mother's situation. There's the guilt thing again. Hillary thought her mother might be lonely, and suggested having one of Hugh's friends and her mother over to visit. Hillary felt she had to try and solve her mother's problems. Play date therapy for Mommy.

By this time, Mary was drinking frequently. Not getting drunk, but more in a steady, medicinal fashion. She was self-medicating to deal with her computer withdrawal agony. In giving the kids evening time on the computer, she had to reduce her computer use to 'only' 12 or so hours a day. Every day. Mary was to later falsely accuse me of stating she was an alcoholic when I mentioned this fact.

Ever the victim.

It was probably around this time that I started becoming suspicious of Hillary's medical problems. My mind had started putting the pieces of the puzzle together. One weekend, I mentioned to Mary how it was odd that Hillary was always too sick to go to school, yet could go to her friends' homes on the weekend. She'd come home Sunday evening, seemingly fine. Then, come Monday morning, Hillary would always to be too sick to go to school. It was getting to the point where I couldn't keep Hillary ahead of her school work. She was in danger of failing.

The Monday morning after I voiced my suspicion to Mary, I came out of the shower to the sound of screaming. I hurriedly threw on some clothes and went to the basement to investigate. It was coming from Hillary's bedroom (in a fully finished basement). Hillary was curled up in a ball on her bed, sobbing with grief. Mary was screaming at her to get out of bed so she could go to school. Only it was "You're getting out of that fucking bed and going to fucking school right fucking NOW!"

Not everyone is aware of how eloquent a delicate flower can be at times.

I went straight to Hillary to console her. Between her heaving sobs, she managed to get out, "I feel so guilty," before bursting into tears again. Mary wouldn't leave, but my presence acted to silence her.

I kept the addictions counselor informed of how things were progressing. I tried my best to act according to his advice. Around this time, he suggested that having the kids on board might be the trigger Mary needed to confront her addiction. He thought that I should bring the boys in to talk with him and an experienced family counselor. I agreed, which would have meant taking the boys out of school to see them. My attempts to speak with Mary always hit a brick wall. She would say things like, "There's no point. You've already made up your mind," and, "You can't be reasoned with."

Knowing Mary, I had expected this. Denial. Ugliness. The pot calling the kettle black, so to speak.

I did take the boys out of school to see the counselors. The boys were uncomfortable—that was rather obvious. In retrospect, it did no good, and when eventually Mary found out, she went ballistic. No surprise there, either.

As much as I was fed up with Mary as a wife and a mother, I didn't quit. The kids needed a mother, despite my growing contempt for her. Around the middle of February, Mary suggested we see a marriage counselor. It was not a "her" problem, according to Mary. It was an "us" problem. It was our problem.

Our problem was that the kids and I had to live with Mary.

Right away, I knew that this was her way of denying her addiction. She was trying to deflect blame from herself. My mind saw the parallel between this and her older sister dragging her husband to different marriage counselors.

"Look how wonderful I am, valiantly trying to save our marriage." Rubbish. However, I knew this was the only way that I could get Mary to see anyone. I could only hope that we got a good counselor. Unfortunately, it turned out to be a social worker.

Just in case any social worker missed that, let me repeat it: *Unfortunately, it turned out to be a social worker.*

Mary would not condescend to find a marriage counselor. I had to do this, and the counselor had to meet with Mary's approval. I made the big mistake of suggesting we use a military social worker—her 'services' were free for me. She was a woman with a master's degree in her field.

We saw military social worker Captain Sarah Symmes-Pathetique in March and early April. After the first session, she told us she could see us "going either way." Mary couldn't grasp that I had had it with her. Mary did the "I-was-depressed, and-maybe-playing-too-much-to-escape-my-unhappiness" routine. Pure rubbish. I was there, and there was absolutely no depression. Mary couldn't understand that I wasn't falling for it.

The sympathy well had run dry Christmas morning.

Let's see—whom did the female military social worker Symmes-Pathetique believe? If you guessed me (the man), then you're way off. Military professionalism and competence clearly don't apply to social workers. Mary would do her little "I think I was depressed" act, and the social worker would cock her head and adopt a sympathetic and caring smile.

It was pathetic.

Things weren't good at home. Mary was by then bad-mouthing me in front of the kids at every opportunity, using her half-in-jest way of taking jabs at me. If I objected, she would then demean me for being unable to take a joke. There was no winning with Mary – she had to have her way.

Things had not been going well with Hillary. She had missed so much school that she was probably going to fail Grade 12. Not that this seemed to upset Mary in the slightest. This screwed up the intended move to Ottawa – we would want Hillary to repeat her final year in the same school. We couldn't afford to further stress her. However, Hugh would then have done a year at the same high school if Hillary graduated the following year. So, we'd prefer to stay put for a double-length tour in Backwater/Krakton. This would get Hugh through high school, too.

In discussion with my unit and my career manager, I expressed a desire to stay for a double-length tour. This wasn't going to be a problem. Sadly, as I look back at it, I now understand that Mary deliberately ensured that Hillary failed Grade 12. Mary engineered Hillary's failure, in part to keep us from going to Ottawa. Mary didn't want us living near my family, especially my mother and my sister. The one morning where Mary was screaming obscenities at Hillary was an exception. Mary probably thought it would make her look bad if Hillary didn't go to school that day.

Yes, Mary was that cunning and manipulative. She had absolutely no trouble exploiting the kids to suit her purposes, no matter how much it hurt them. Sadly, there are other mothers like this. The only thing I remain uncertain of is whether or not Mary understood that she was doing this. I'm still not certain, but I tend to think so. At least on some level.

Hillary was starting to become a bit of a drama queen herself. She was also starting to become confrontational with me as well. In one episode, she mentioned that she had considered suicide. She threw it in my face as if I didn't care. Like her mother, she was trying to make me feel guilty. She was also becoming rude to me in these episodes. I actually got upset to the point of being angry with her once—I was under so much stress. It wasn't long after this that I realized that it was Mary who was provoking Hillary into the confrontational episodes.

There were no further upset moments with Hillary after that. I knew it wasn't her fault. It was her mother who was trying to engineer conflict between Hillary and me.

Mary's prolonged, obnoxious behaviour finally drove me to consider making an appointment to see a divorce lawyer. I couldn't stand the sight of her, not even for the kids' sake. She was unworthy to share my last name. She was unworthy to be the mother of my children.

If you're a feminist and those last statements offend you, good.

Before I actually had a chance to make the appointment, something awful happened. It was on 14 April 2008. Mary sank to a new low, which I hadn't thought possible. We were having supper. Mary had just given me her patented don't-piss-me-off, do-as-I-want tone in something she said. That was it. I'd had all I could take of her. I told her I was planning to see a divorce lawyer.

No sooner had the words come out of my mouth than I realized that I had said it in front of the kids. After all I'd done to shelter them and spare them pain of their mother's explosive nature. It was probably made worse by what I'd put up with in the marriage for their sakes. They didn't understand what living with Mary could be like. All they saw was a happy family that had tragically gone downhill in a hurry.

If the kids were very upset with my screw-up, they were truly devastated by the time Mary got through with them. As the kids ran to their bedrooms, Mary began howling in outrage. She actually screamed out—no word a lie—that she knew that sex had only been a mechanical act to me. Leo was still 11 years old when he heard his mother scream this. He was 11 years old when he probably heard his drunken mother scream out that she was just another hole to fuck, too.

Some of the other gems she screamed out for the kids to hear—it was obvious that this was her true intent—were:

- That I had no emotional commitment (I am bad);

- That her addiction wasn't the real issue; it was her 'unhappiness' with the marriage for the last six years (not her fault, feel sorry for her, and I am bad);

- That I was abandoning the kids (I am evil);

- That she knew that I was divorcing her to separate her from the kids (I am evil); and

- That I was cruel to the kids (I am so bad that I am evil).

Mary kept herself between me and the kids so I couldn't go speak to them. She actually gave me a double-handed shove/hit to the chest to keep me away from them. I felt so badly for having hurt the kids' feelings that I couldn't muster the energy to counter her rabid campaign of hatred and lies. I was exhausted from Mary's abuse, her addiction, the kids' problems, and my ensuing workload. I was devastated by my mistake. I was numb.

We were to have our next marriage counseling session in slightly over a week. I said I wanted to think about things and would let her know at the next session what my decision would be.

I was soon to learn that all those weird and ugly aspects to Mary's personality and behaviour had a name: *narcissism*. By then, it was far too late, for she was about to get even uglier.

Much uglier.

4
Mirror

Nothing is easier than self-deceit. For what each
man wishes, that he also believes to be true.

— DEMOSTHENES

What I am about to describe is what I understand narcissism to be. It is grounded in 19 years of detailed exposure to it. When you think about it, this is a significant experience base upon which to hang theory. My description is also based on my military-analytical type of thinking. Theory is useful only so long as it explains observations. I don't ignore reality. My interpretation of narcissism is also based on the professional and academic works that I have read.

The names in this chapter are real, other than for my family.

When I first became aware that Mary's weird behaviour might be due to narcissism, I began to read up on it. One psychiatrist's bible, so to speak, is the *Diagnostic and Statistics Manual*, or DSM. It is used for diagnosing mental disorders, and is updated about every 10 years or so. At the time, the current version was the DSM-IV TR. The "IV" part is the Roman numeral denoting the fourth edition. The "TR" was for "Text Revised."

According to the DSM-IV TR, Narcissistic Personality Disorder is defined as:

> A pervasive pattern of grandiosity (in fantasy or behaviour), need for admiration, and lack of empathy, beginning by early adulthood and present in a variety of contexts, as indicated by five (or more) of the following:
>
> 1. Has a grandiose sense of self-importance
>
> 2. Is preoccupied with fantasies of unlimited success, power, brilliance, beauty, or ideal love
>
> 3. Believes that he or she is "special" and unique and can only be understood by, or should associate with, other special or high-status people (or institutions)
>
> 4. Requires excessive admiration
>
> 5. Has a sense of entitlement (i.e., unreasonable expectations of especially favorable treatment or automatic compliance with his or her expectations)
>
> 6. Is interpersonally exploitative (i.e., takes advantage of others to achieve his or her own ends)
>
> 7. Lacks empathy, is unwilling to recognize or identify with the feelings and needs of others
>
> 8. Is often envious of others or believes others are envious of him or her
>
> 9. Shows arrogant, haughty behaviour or attitudes

There's more to an official diagnosis than merely displaying five or more of these nine traits, but this is a good starting point. These DSM criteria can give the false impression that someone either is a narcissist or isn't a narcissist. The criteria for the diagnosis are actually somewhat arbitrary.

Narcissism is not like being pregnant. You can't be a little bit pregnant. However, you can be a little bit narcissistic. Many of us are. Those who are not narcissistic are the most righteous and spiritual of people—think of Jesus, Buddha, Gandhi, or Mother Theresa. At the extreme other end of the spectrum are people like Adolf Hitler and Alexander the Great.

I've found another good list of the traits that a narcissist can display. It comes from the Hare Psychopathy Checklist Factor One—Aggressive Narcissism. Just realize that these traits can be very subtle if the person is only slightly narcissistic versus being a full-blown psychopath:

- Glibness/superficial charm

- Grandiose sense of self-worth

- Pathological lying

- Cunning/manipulative

- Lack of remorse or guilt

- Shallow affect (genuine emotion is short-lived and egocentric)

- Callousness; lack of empathy

- Failure to accept responsibility for own actions

When I tried applying the DSM's criteria to Mary, they didn't quite fit. Yet it wasn't a square-peg-in-a-round-hole, either. They sort of fit, but not quite. Some of the theory-type articles concerning the nature of narcissism that I had read—its causes and nature—really rang true, though. So on the one hand, I had the DSM-IV TR suggesting that it wasn't really narcissism. On the other hand, I had the theory suggesting that it was.

It didn't take long in my research before I came across the concept of covert narcissism. Bingo. I finally had the key to the puzzle that my mind had been sensing for nearly 20 years. All of a sudden, everything fell into place.

Before I get too deeply into narcissism, I have to mention Otto Kernberg and Heinz Kohut. They were two giants in the field of narcissism theory. In the 1970's, they both independently came to the realization that there was a second kind of narcissism. This is known as *covert* narcissism. As a result, experts often refer to the official DSM kind of narcissism as *overt* narcissism. I'll explain the covert-overt thing shortly. For now, I'll just go over the general aspects that apply to both.

The term "narcissism" apparently comes from just before 1900. Experts trying to fathom abnormal behaviour recognized an intuitive similarity to the myth of Narcissus. I don't think that experts have paid enough attention to this myth for an unorthodox reason: the book *Hamlet's Mill*. Its authors, two scholars, argue that certain myths around the world can be traced back to what I'll say is an original proto-myth. This proto-myth, they claim, contains accurate information regarding precessional astronomy.

Precession deals with the slow wobble of the Earth's rotational axis about the centre of the Earth. When I say slow, I mean on the order of 25,800 years. *Hamlet's Mill* causes problems for regular academics, which is why they reject it. For some ancient civilization in pre-history to have understood this, they must have been disturbingly advanced. However, history says there wasn't any such civilization.

Perhaps instead, history should say that there must have been such a civilization.

So, when I read about the myth of *Narcissus*, I kept an open mind. I was open to the possibility that it was a metaphor for actual knowledge. (If you've been out of school for a while, a metaphor is when something is used in writing to represent something else.) This may have been knowledge sufficiently important that it had to be encoded in myth to preserve it through the ages.

Or maybe it was just a silly story. Who knows?

Some would immediately dismiss this concept of myth as metaphor. These skeptics should read *The Origin Map: Discovery of a Prehistoric, Megalithic, Astrophysical Map and Structure of the Universe*. Written by Thomas Brophy, Ph.D., it suggests that at one point in the distant past humanity may have known more about science and the universe than we do now. Much more.

Let's look at my very condensed rendition of Ovid's version of the *Narcissus* myth (1899 'ish translation by Henry T. Riley, M.A.):

> *The river god Cephisus ravished the nymph Liriope. She later gave birth to an exceptionally beautiful son named Narcissus. Liriope was concerned about her son, so she consulted the blind seer Tiresias regarding Narcissus' future. Tireias prophesied that Narcissus would live to an old age if he never recognized himself.*

By the time Narcissus had turned 16, all the girls and youths in his town were in love with the handsome young hero. Yet Narcissus haughtily spurned them all.

One day, when Narcissus was hunting stags, a Nymph named Echo spied him and immediately fell in love. She longed to speak to him. However, she had been made mute in a special way that only allowed her to reply in the same words that had been spoken to her.

Echo followed Narcissus. Hearing footsteps, Narcissus shouted, "Who's there?", only to have Echo reply, "Who's there?" This repeated itself until Echo revealed herself and went to embrace Narcissus, who pulled away and vainly rejected her.

Echo, heartbroken, spent the rest of her days withering away, until only her voice remained. Nemesis, goddess of retribution, heard Echo's lamentations and doomed Narcissus as a punishment.

Narcissus later came across a gentle stream and bent to drink from it. As he did, he gazed upon his reflection and immediately fell in love with it. After pining away for some time, he eventually came to realize he was seeing a reflection of himself. The angst of knowing he could never actually love the perfect person he saw— himself—was intense. Narcissus proclaimed to the surrounding trees, "Was ever, O, ye woods! any one more fatally in love?"

When his tears of sorrow fell into the gentle waters and disturbed his own reflected image, Narcissus destroyed himself in a fit of rage.

The bodiless Echo came upon Narcissus as he died and felt pity and sorrow for him. Narcissus' soul was sent to the darkest hell, and where his body had withered away the narcissus flower grew.

Hopefully no classics scholar suffers a heart attack due to my attempt at condensing Ovid. Fit of apoplexy, foaming at the mouth, and all that. Harrumph!

Let's treat this as a metaphor, and see what results when we try to analyze the myth. To do this, we have to start with the obvious. Narcissus was a seriously messed up kid. His psychological problems go very deep, to the core of his existence. These problems, as Narcissus himself alludes, relate to his fatally destructive inability to love himself.

Look at the parents. They're not the usual sort. Having a god as a father? How can dad not be grandiose? He doesn't sound like he had much to do with raising his son. Probably had more important godly things to do than deal with his own child.

Mom seems a little weird too. A nymph? This might be where Narcissus' beauty came from. Aren't nymphs supposed to be vain, concerned about their physical beauty, and very sexually active? Why was she so worried about Narcissus' future? It seems to be more than a normal level of motherly concern. If mothers are supposed to be caring, this mother seems to be grandiose in a feminine way. She cares more than a regular mom. Perhaps more than is healthy.

And what's with this if-he-never-recognizes-himself bit? That's certainly odd.

In fact, it would appear as if the myth is saying that both (or either of) father and mother contribute to making a Narcissus. Just in different ways. One is under-involved and grandiose in a masculine way (father). The other is over-involved and grandiose in a feminine way (mother).

What about Echo? The myth seems to say that to love a Narcissus is to not have a voice. You can only repeat back to your Narcissus what he or she says. If you reveal your true self, Narcissus will reject you. And the question itself is haunting—"Who's there?"

Who indeed? The question goes to the very core of Narcissus' existence as a person.

The Nemesis part is uncomfortable. It seems to suggest that the outcome for a Narcissus is a foregone conclusion. It is a doom. The tragedy is already written at the tender age of 16. Interestingly, even the best clinicians find adult narcissists notoriously difficult if not impossible to treat.

Now consider Narcissus at the stream. This is vivid imagery. He falls in love with his reflection, not his real self. This is like the part with Echo. Only, instead of verbal reflections off of Echo, it is now visual reflections off the water. Echo is a verbal mirror; the water is a visual mirror. Mirroring would appear to be profoundly important. Interestingly, "mirroring" is indeed a term used by experts in the field of narcissism.

When Narcissus' tears disturb his reflected image, he self-destructs in a major fit of rage. This would seem to suggest that disturbing the reflected image of himself (the one that Narcissus has fallen in love with) exposes him to the full fury of his inability to love his true self. If the myth is indeed a metaphor, this is at its very heart. Because of his parents, Narcissus cannot truly love himself. He can only love his beautiful, superficial image reflected back to him. When that reflection is disturbed, it sets off a self-destructive rage.

Yet Echo still has pity for him. Is the white flower—all that remains of Narcissus— nothing but a sad reminder of this doom?

The myth appears to give significant insight into narcissism, as we shall further see. Maybe there is something to the myth as metaphor after all.

Experts know that narcissism can be inter-generational. It is somehow passed from parent to child. This seems consistent with the myth. Experts have also determined that unconscious shame is at the core of narcissism. This isn't obvious, but as we shall soon see, it makes sense.

We are reminded of Narcissus, as narcissists can display unhealthy self-love on the surface. However, the opposite is true. Deep down, these people cannot truly love themselves in a decent, meaningful, and spiritual way. A way in which they can see themselves for who they truly are—warts and all—and peacefully accept themselves.

I should point out that some experts refer to this healthy sort of self-love as "healthy narcissism." This is silly. Can you imagine if your family doctor said to you, "You have healthy cancer. Your cells are dividing properly."? You'd probably think that your doctor is a bit of a twit. You'd be right— cancer is, by its nature, decidedly unhealthy. It's the same with narcissism. It cannot, by definition, ever be healthy.

Due to unconscious shame about themselves (which I'll get to shortly), narcissists develop a protective false self. Most people have an intuitive understanding of "self." For example, they know what *myself, yourself,* or being *self-conscious* mean, even if they can't give explicit definitions. Let's simply say that a *self* is the sum of everything that makes a person that person, be it genetic, life experiences, family, or whatever.

A false self is how a narcissist wants (and needs!) to perceive himself or herself, *and to be perceived by others*. A narcissist's mind will unknowingly create a grandiose false self to protect against the terribly painful exposure to the intense shame of their real self. The grandiose false self is a denial or contradiction of the unlovable true self. Narcissists are doomed to be actors on the stage of life, playing the parts of their false selves.

You can think of this false self in terms of a department store mannequin. It is artificial and hollow. Hidden inside is an immature, terrified true self. Anything that threatens to break through the false self (the mannequin) and expose the true self to reality is unconsciously terrifying. Thus, fear joins shame at the core of narcissism. At least, this is my experience.

It seems this was Narcissus' experience too.

This is just like the myth as metaphor. For a narcissist to recognize his (or her) self, it means his false self must have been penetrated. The hollow mannequin of his false self has been broken (or is under threat of breaking), and the narcissist is helpless against exposure to intense shame and fear. It is fatal for a narcissist to come to recognize his or her *true* self—just like the myth.

What I saw from Mary has led me to suspect that experts may not fully appreciate the significance of mirroring. As a teaser, this was also reinforced during my inquiry into feminism. Dr. James F. Masterson, in his book *Search for the Real Self*, describes mirroring as reinforcing feedback. Dr. Masterson writes:

> *The narcissist looks to others in his environment, and to the environment itself— clothes, car, home, office—to reflect his exaggerated sense of importance and perfection.*

My experience suggests that even this highly respected expert hasn't quite gone far enough. Despite the many patients he's obviously seen and studied over his long career, I suspect he's never actually lived with one for 19 years. I did. I also doubt that Dr. Masterson tried my *Hamlet's Mill* approach to examining the myth. That would be most unorthodox for such a respected expert.

Mirroring is the essential aspect of the narcissist's outward behaviour. It is not enough for a narcissist to believe in their false self. They must constantly have the reinforcing feedback of others that supports this false self. Narcissists will go to extreme lengths to create their own delusional mirrors. If they didn't, life would truthfully reflect who they really are. They would *recognize* their true self. They would be exposed to the excruciating truth of being unable to love themselves.

Thus, narcissists tend to manipulate and control people for a reason—to maintain a stable mirror for themselves. Not so much a physical mirror as a conceptual one. And, like the wicked queen in *Snow White*, their magic mirror must always tell them they are the fairest in the land (or whatever else they want to believe). If it doesn't, they get very ugly very quickly.

Experts also refer to the reinforcing feedback of others as narcissistic supply. Mirroring is thus also the act of obtaining narcissistic supply. If something happens to threaten a narcissist's mirror (and thus the false self), it is called a narcissistic injury. The narcissist's response is called narcissistic rage. Just as with Narcissus—he destroyed himself in a rage.

There's the myth again.

A narcissist is pathologically driven to create his or her mirror. The world of the narcissist *must* reflect what the narcissist needs to be 'true' about her or his false self. This is a crucial point to remember—I cannot emphasize it enough. This is why narcissists are manipulative and controlling. There is no length to which a serious narcissist won't go to protect his or her mirror. The survival of the false self depends upon the narcissist's mirror.

This becomes especially dangerous when a group of narcissists share a part of the same mirror. This relates to something Sigmund Freud referred to as *introjection,* and becomes important in *Book Two.*

It should thus not be surprising to learn that a narcissist's mind distorts the truth. Their minds will twist events and facts to build the mirror that supports the false self. And they will twist the truth for others, too. Narcissists will lie, deceive, and manipulate. They will use words with twisted meanings that others don't perceive. In terms of lying, Freud called this "thaumaturgy"—magic words. The narcissist says it and then magically insists it is true just for having said it. They can make up lies on the spot, if necessary (even if they blatantly contradict something they said earlier).

Just like when feminists say or write things, and then furiously insist they are magically true.

(In fact, Mary used to do this, and could even contradict a previous statement she had made. When I challenged her—"But I thought you said..."—, she'd just deny ever having made the previous statement that she had just contradicted. She'd seem so certain that I would almost at times wonder if I wasn't going crazy.)

Narcissism, then, can also be viewed as the corruption of truth. It not only does corrupt the truth, it *must* corrupt the truth. This is important to remember. Narcissism must corrupt the truth. Narcissists can be the most deceptive of liars; they can believe their own lies and so seem most sincere and passionate.

Since a narcissist recognizing his or her (true) self can lead to self-destruction, it's not surprising that narcissists have to defend against this. Their false self is constantly under siege from reality and truth. Mary's emotional terrorism—her holding the kids' and the family's happiness hostage—acted in this way. It helped protect her grandiose delusion of being an exceptional mother.

There are other ways that narcissists protect themselves against narcissistic injuries to their false selves. These are known as narcissistic defences. There is one narcissistic defence that is particularly insidious: projection.

An excellent introductory book on narcissism is Sandy Hotchkiss' *Why is it Always About You? The Seven Deadly Sins of Narcissism*. Here are Hotchkiss' insightful words on projection:

> *In addition to magical thinking, there are other, more hurtful ways that narcissists distort reality. The most toxic of these is a process whereby they transfer to someone else whatever evokes shameful feelings in themselves. What psychologists call "projection," I have re-named shame-dumping, a common phenomenon in narcissistic families.*

Back when we were living in Winnipeg, my efforts to deal with Hillary's 'stomach problems' would have provoked shame in Mary. She needed to be a great parent, and above all else better than me. Only I was the one who was dealing with Hillary's problems, not Mary. Mary would have been envious of my relationship with Hillary, as hers would seem inferior by comparison.

Mary would have needed to undermine this threat to her mirror and thus her false self.

So Mary projected her shame onto me. Then, in her mind, it wasn't she who had relationship issues with Hillary. It was me. It was shameful that I had relationship problems with our daughter. There was Mary, the GREAT MOTHER, helping inferior me with my inferior parenting problems. Mary needed me to believe this as well. She needed me to be part of her mirror.

Had I not been secure and thought she was being absurd, Mary may have planted a seed of doubt in my mind. Those narcissistic seeds can blossom very quickly if one isn't secure (which I was) and aware of the danger (which I wasn't). Mary must have been acting in the same way behind my back to undermine my relationship with Hillary. She would have been poisoning Hillary with doubt.

Understanding projection is easy when you think of this expression: "That's the pot calling the kettle black." Do you know someone who is a bit of a hypocrite? You might be looking at narcissistic projection. It can be subtle. Does your spouse try to make you feel guilty for taking the last of something in the fridge, yet she or he never hesitates to do so? When someone tries to make you feel guilty for bogus or trivial reasons, you may be the victim of projection.

This would explain Mary's having gotten angry at the kids, and then her getting angry at me for being 'mean' to them when I calmed things down. She was the one who had been mean to them, and she HAD to be the superior parent to me (grandiosity). My calming things down would have been doubly shameful to her, given her behaviour. So she projected her shame onto me. It was then me who should have been ashamed for being mean to the kids instead of her. In 'protecting' the kids from me, she was again superior (in her own mind) to me as a parent.

Interestingly, Hotchkiss' excellent book also has a chapter entitled "*Narcissism and Addiction: The Shame Connection.*" Mary's addiction had nothing to do with depression. It was caused by her narcissism.

As it will come in handy later on, I have to mention "splitting." With narcissists, this can mean different things. One is the split representation of objects. This simply means that narcissists tend to see things in black and white terms. Either things or people are good or they are bad (mostly bad, as the narcissist tends to view things negatively). There is also splitting of the ego, a concept pioneered by Otto Kernberg. This gets into deep psycho-analysis/psychology. In layman's terms, it's where a person cuts himself or herself off from a part of their true self.

Splitting of the ego can be a very bad thing.

Living with a narcissist—wife, husband, parent, friend, or co-worker—can be a challenge if not a nightmare. To compensate for unconscious feelings of lack of worth and inferiority, they compensate with the grandiose false self. This tends to be "I'm great" or "I'm better than you." However, it can be *implied* by their words and actions instead of actually being said. It can be quite subtle.

Grandiosity can also manifest in the negative sense. If the narcissist has to be better than you, you have to be worse than the narcissist. Thus, they will tend to be negative about you or things associated with you. They will try to belittle you or bring you down. They presume to judge you or to assess your actions or accomplishments. Again, this can be very subtle. It can be through innuendo, through tone of voice, or through things left unsaid. It can be implied, but not actually stated.

Since narcissism is inter-generational, the intense unconscious shame and fear must tend to come from narcissistic parents. Let's think about this.

New parents are often amazed to discover what little learning machines their children are. Children suck in information and knowledge like little self-programming vacuums. Their developing brains have self-replicating logic circuits that we still don't fully understand. When we think of infants and children this way, it isn't hard to see how narcissism becomes inter-generational. The shame and fear aspects become apparent too.

Let's adopt this kids-are-little-subconscious-logic-machines point of view. Suppose a child feels like he's been abandoned by his parents, especially a mother, at a young age. His developing mind would subconsciously conclude that they or she didn't love him. Which then leads to the conclusion that he isn't worthy of love.

You must be pretty worthless if even your own mother doesn't love you. You're so worthless that you can't help but feel ashamed of yourself. You are unworthy to be loved, and you feel alone and terrified. Potentially, all subconsciously.

Even if the child doesn't feel abandoned, having a narcissistic mother can still have a similar effect. Mary's black moods as a 'victim' if the kids didn't behave as she needed are a great example. It's called conditional love—the narcissist can only 'love' people when they behave as is needed to support his or her mirror.

What does a child's mind conclude if Mom only loves him conditionally? It sees that he can only be loved when he behaves a certain way. It's clear that he isn't loved for who he really is. He is only loved *for what he does.* Unworthy of mother's unconditional love. Shame. And fear. She won't love me if I don't behave. She'll be mean to me or make me feel guilty.

An overt narcissistic mother might go back to work as soon as possible and foist the infant off on a nanny or relative. She'll spend far more of her time and energy feeding her own narcissistic grandiosity by getting ahead professionally than she will loving her child (which she can't truly do). The message and the effect are likely the same.

This is what I believe happened to Mary's niece, Melanie. (Rebecca's narcissistic personality would also explain her marriage breakdown—no matter what the fault was, it was never hers. Yeah, right.)

I suspect that even with an emotionally healthy mother, if she goes back to work shortly after giving birth, she causes some degree of harm to her child's developing self. I've read that infants can identify their mothers by the smell of breast milk. Even in the care of a good nanny, the message the child can take from this is still the same. I've been abandoned, if only for eight hours every day. "I used to get delicious breast milk, and now I get fake crap from a plastic bottle. I'm not worthy to be loved." Fear. Shame. Only less.

As the child grows older, a narcissistic parent still needs to be superior. They'll find ways to demean their child, if only subtly. Comments said "half in jest" always hide an emotional barb. School performance is never quite good enough, or it's the only thing that matters about the kid. It could be performance in hockey games or figure skating competitions instead. The lesson is the same. I'm not worthy of love. Shame. Fear. This is magnified when a narcissistic parent projects shame onto her children by frequently making them feel guilty. I am bad. Not worthy of love. Fear. Shame.

Or if kids rarely see their fathers, as narcissistic dad has to work 70 or 80 hours a week to get ahead. Same message. I'm not important enough for dad to spend time with me. I'm not worthy of love. Fear. Shame.

The painful if not excruciating shame, the sense of worthlessness, and the fear of being unloved and unlovable take root deep within the young and delicate true self. And, to varying degrees, they maim it.

. . . .

In trying to learn more about covert narcissism, I came across an important academic paper written in 1991 by Paul Wink. It was entitled "Two Faces of Narcissism." It describes the results of research into the question of whether or not there are two forms of narcissism. Interestingly, Wink did not use the terms overt and covert. Wink instead used the terms Grandiosity-Exhibitionism and Vulnerability-Sensitivity.

Wink did find evidence to support the idea that there are two forms of narcissism. Vulnerability-Sensitivity is a great way to describe how a covert narcissist can appear. Their false self is such that they make you want to console or protect them, as they appear vulnerable. And they appear to be easily offended or easily have their feelings hurt—they are very sensitive, unpredictably so at times. You have to walk on eggshells around them.

Just like *sensitive* Mary, the 'delicate flower' and 'fine china.' The same *vulnerable* Mary who was always worried she would do poorly at school, and constantly needed me to tell her that she was doing brilliantly.

Wink found that there were adjectives that were unique to either overt narcissists or covert narcissists. He also found adjectives that were common to both forms of narcissism. This reinforces the belief that there is a common basis to these two forms narcissism. Here's what Wink's research found (using our overt and covert terms):

Both Narcissists: *bossy; intolerant; cruel; argumentative; opportunistic; rebellious; conceited; arrogant; demanding; temperamental; and loud.*

Overt Narcissist Only: *aggressive; hardheaded; outspoken; restless; show-off; assertive; egotistical; determined; evasive; impulsive; and self-centered.*

Covert Narcissist Only: *worrying; emotional; defensive; anxious; tense; complaining; dissatisfied; and moody.*

It was at this point that I had my first big insight. Overt and covert forms of narcissism are *gender forms of narcissism*. Not only are they gender forms, they are literally narcissistic corruptions of the way men and women socialize, as described in the book *Men are from Mars, Women are from Venus.* Thus, I feel that Wink's insightful adjectives are better rendered as follows:

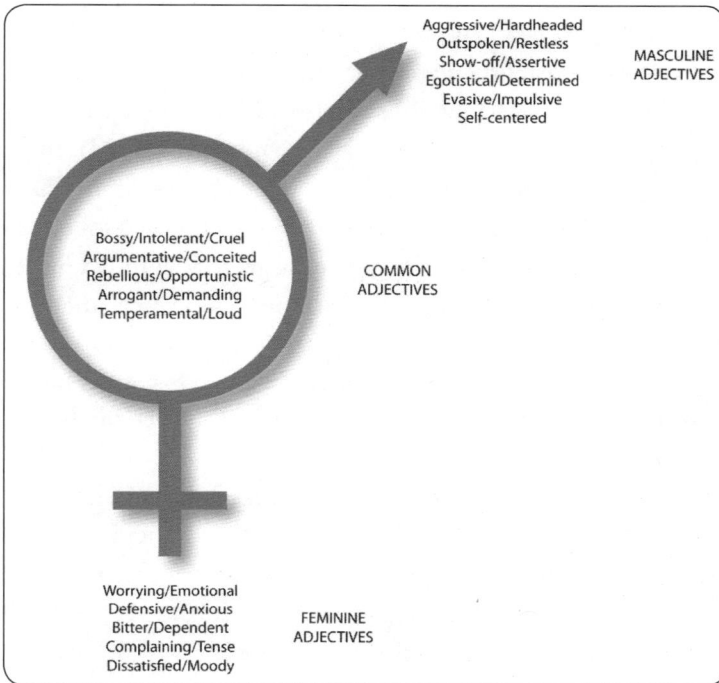

Aggressive/Hardheaded
Outspoken/Restless
Show-off/Assertive
Egotistical/Determined
Evasive/Impulsive
Self-centered

MASCULINE
ADJECTIVES

Bossy/Intolerant/Cruel
Argumentative/Conceited
Rebellious/Opportunistic
Arrogant/Demanding
Temperamental/Loud

COMMON
ADJECTIVES

Worrying/Emotional
Defensive/Anxious
Bitter/Dependent
Complaining/Tense
Dissatisfied/Moody

FEMININE
ADJECTIVES

Mars & Venus was written by John Gray, Ph.D. It is based on his many years of observing couples in therapy, and it was a huge best seller. It was a best seller because men and women recognize the inherent truth of Gray's observations. What Gray said made so much sense. It was intuitive.

The most important part of Gray's work—I'll use my own interpretation of it—is that male socialization stresses independence in achieving some outcome. Females, on the other hand, socialize by stressing mutual support. Thus, for women, relationships tend to be more important than the outcomes. (Or, perhaps, for women it is the relationship that is the true outcome.) Gray observed that about 10 percent of women socialize as men typically do. He likewise observed that about 10 percent of men socialize as women typically do.

Experts have never figured out why their research tends to find that there are more male narcissists than female narcissists. The answer is simple: they are likely only looking at overt narcissism. They are only looking at the masculine form of narcissism. Of course they're going to find that more men are narcissists if they only examine the masculine form. If they understood covert narcissism, they'd likely find a different answer.

With overt narcissism, the narcissist seeks attention in the form of admiration for his masculine virtues. This can be for his wealth, power, strength, military brilliance, genius (which can lead to academic fraud), role as protector, saviour, etc. It can be subtle: admiration for his being an inspirational leader; a person who takes care of the weak and downtrodden; protector of the environment (e.g., Climategate); or a great athlete (hopped up on performance-enhancing drugs). This exploits masculine independence socialization.

If you ever hear of a public figure concerned about his or her 'legacy,' you can almost bet there is some degree of narcissism. Overt narcissism, most likely.

A covert narcissist, on the other hand, will tend to seek attention in the form of sympathy, caring, or concern. She needs to believe herself to be a victim of varying degrees, or be self-sacrificing and supremely dedicated, or vulnerable and concerned. Because of mirroring, she needs others to believe that she needs such emotional support. She can and will manipulate to make herself a victim or to be in need of sympathy appear to be 'true.' This exploits feminine mutual support socialization, and perhaps the traditional masculine role of protector or provider.

I've noticed that there appears to be a bit of an unconscious male bias in understanding narcissism. The most obvious way relates to grandiosity. What makes a man appear great is not necessarily what makes a woman appear great.

Since most women will be mothers in their lifetimes, how would a narcissistic woman behave in being a mother?

If she was the more likely covert narcissist, she would want to be seen as a great mom. Perhaps even the "super mom," scheduling an incredible number of events into her kids' daily lives—the piano lessons, the karate club, ballet lesson, etc. "Look at me, what a great mom I am!" is her implied message.

Rest assured, she'll have her husband running all over the place to ensure the kids get to the game or the lessons. She'll make sure he helps them with their homework and helps out in the house. All while making him feel guilty should he ever object. After all, look at all *her* sacrifices for the kids and family! He doesn't care about the kids and family as much as *she* does. (Not that she really loves him or cares about him—his only real purpose is to bring home a paycheck and support her mirror.)

If the family didn't pseudo-worship her, she'd also want to be seen as a victim too. She'd be the hard working mom who wasn't appreciated. She'd be the woman who makes her husband feel guilty for leaving her at home with the kids all day, ignoring that he works hard to put bread on the table. She'd be the one who made her kids feel guilty for being ungrateful for all her hard work.

Oh, the sacrifices she makes! Just ask her.

She might also work outside the home. Like a female bully, she'll subtly backstab the people who threaten her mirror. She may go to her boss or her boss' boss and express her "concerns" in private. She'll try to bring people on her "team" by taking them into her confidence. She'll work to undermine relationships in the office. "I think it's great that you get along with Greg, but..." and something subtly negative. Always something nice followed with "but." She'll be familiar with people higher up, claiming that she "doesn't believe in rank or calling people Mr. or Mrs." They may think she's friendly, but it's really her narcissistic grandiosity: she's equal to them if they're on a first name basis, and better than others who use Mr., Mrs., Sir, or Madam for higher management.

She'll try to end run her boss and do things directly for the next boss up. She'll wait until a weekly meeting to ambush a peer with a "question." What she's really trying to do is create the impression that her co-worker should have done something and didn't. Or she will want to seem to be in charge and a leader, and be "worried" that something will go wrong if someone doesn't do something (they're bad) or we don't follow her advice (she's great).

There is some truth to her anxieties, though, but in a different way. If work doesn't go well, her mirror of being the lynchpin of the operation may waver. She's terrified of this. One mirror as the Super Mom, another as the anchor of the office. She works so hard to build and sustain them; yet they are still so fragile.

While she may be very hard working and competent, she will poison her work environment. Her boss or boss' boss may love her, and some co-workers may too. Others who aren't on "her team" are ostracized. She is the wolf who tries to end-run the pack hierarchy and ingratiate herself with the alpha male leader. She will not hesitate to exploit company grievance procedures or make harassment complaints, if necessary, to attack someone who is a threat to her mirror. She can provoke others to anger while appearing to be the sensitive victim, afraid. She is cunning and manipulative; she needs to control the office. She will appear to be vulnerable, sensitive, and concerned as required to achieve this end.

Covert narcissism also provides a perfect explanation for some mysterious conditions that even experts admit they don't fully understand. To consider this, we need to refer to an exceptional book by Professor of Psychiatry Dr. Marc D. Feldman, M.D.: *Playing Sick? Untangling the Web of Munchausen Syndrome, Munchausen by Proxy, Malingering, and Factitious Disorder.*

Let's say that a woman is a covert narcissist. She pathologically craves attention in the form of sympathy. What better way to get such attention than by being sick? So, her false self is a sick woman. Due to mirroring, it isn't enough that she believes this herself. She needs others to believe this, *especially medical professionals*. If the doctors and nurses believe she's sick, then it must be 'true.' So she manipulates and deceives them to build the mirror for her false self. She can believe her own deception to some extent, and so is an exceptional liar.

This behaviour, which we predict, strongly corresponds to factitious disorder. With factitious disorder, a person is aware (on some level, at least) that she is feigning her malady (or harming herself to create symptoms), but she may not be aware of why she is doing it. The motives are emotional in nature.

Munchausen syndrome is factitious disorder in its most extreme form. These poor individuals make being ill the centre of their existence. They tend to keep moving to re-invent themselves as desperately sick individuals. Here we see some logical inconsistency in official terminology. A *disorder* (in the sense that I am using the term) is the something that is wrong with an individual. However, a *syndrome* is a cluster of symptoms normally seen together.

If Munchausen is the extreme form of factitious, then we might think that one of the two terms should change. Either it should be factitious syndrome, or Munchausen disorder. I think they should be both syndromes, in that there is a common underlying cause.

Interestingly, Dr. Feldman's experience is that the majority of people afflicted with factitious disorder are women. He writes that in the majority of cases, the person suffers the additional mental disorder of the *borderline* personality. This is a personality disorder that is recognized to be related to narcissism—they are both disorders of the self.

My interpretation of the borderline personality is based upon my interpretation of narcissism. They are both related, so I assess that they share a similar underlying, unconscious basis. What is subtly different is what results from this. The narcissist, in a sense, has a pathological fantasy about herself (the false self). I believe that the borderline woman, on the other hand, pathologically needs to create a fantasy about her life. One avoids painful feelings by having a false self. Similarly, the other avoids painful feelings by to some extent having a false life.

The borderline compensates for her intense unconscious feelings of inadequacy, which may be linked to abandonment fears, by living in a bit of a fairy tale. This can be a good fairy tale (which denies her unconscious pain), or it can be a sad fairy tale (which is an outlet for her unconscious pain). Or perhaps these are masculine and feminine forms, akin to overt and covert narcissism. Like the narcissist who is driven to make her false self appear 'true,' the borderline is similarly driven to make her fairy tale life or world seem 'true.' Instead of compensating with a false self, the borderline vests her sense of self in a false surrounding. Like the narcissist, she needs the reinforcing feedback of others.

This may appear subtle or even innocuous. The mildly borderline woman may be driven to have the perfect dinner party, the perfect home, the perfect outfit, or the perfect family Christmas. She can compensate for her unconscious feelings of inferiority by needing to live in her tiny perfect world. If something in her perfect little world isn't so perfect, it exposes her to her own painful, unconscious feelings.

Given the feminine emphasis on relationships, the borderline's man can be central to her fairytale. She needs him to be her Prince Charming in some way. She will be thrilled at his successes or perceived virtues, even minor ones. Yet perceived faults, errors, or imperfection— even trivial ones—can trigger the equivalent to a narcissistic injury. She splits her objects—her man is either good or bad, depending upon how his behaviour supports her fairy tale at any given moment. She is constantly yet unconsciously judging him in everything he does. One moment he's good, but the next he could be bad. She idealizes him or devalues him; yet he remains the same person. He can't understand why he is constantly being judged. Her emotions are a bit of a Russian Roulette to him.

Prince Charming's forgetting to take out the garbage on occasion can become a huge deal, as she can no longer "trust him." Or perhaps her bank account has gotten too low (not part of the fairy tale), so she then perceives she is getting "ripped off" in the financial arrangement with her boyfriend (projection).

What has really happened is that her fantasy has been broached, like the narcissist's false self. She reacts accordingly.

If other areas of her fairy tale are failing—at work, for example—, she can still take it out on Prince Charming. She could need to rid herself of such exposure to her unconscious feelings by perceiving that he wasn't contributing enough to the housework, for example. To make this 'true,' she might go on a cleaning rampage. See?—he doesn't support me around the house. I do all the work. Her fairy tale has turned negative. Even though he may do laundry, wash the dishes, and clean toilets.

According to Dr. Marsha Linehan's 1993 biosocial theory of borderline personality development, borderlines have three broader emotional traits. They have a heightened emotional sensitivity to life's events and issues. They have an inability to deal with these heightened and at times intense emotional responses. And, they are slower than normal to return to a normal emotional baseline.

This is a technical way of saying "drama queen."

Dr. Feldman informs us that often women who suffer from factitious disorder also display *pseudologia fantastica*. Pseudologia fantastica is basically when a person weaves some aggrandized story about themselves, even if there is a small basis in truth it. A pseudologue might have tragic deaths or illnesses in the family—or so she tells her confidante(s). Dr. Feldman states that one-quarter of pseudologues feign illness, too (factitious). Indeed, pseudologia fantastica may be the primary aspect to some individuals, and factitious behaviour the secondary.

If my interpretation of borderline and narcissism has some basis in reality, then Dr. Feldman's observations raise some interesting possibilities. Pseudologia fantastica would then be a (or even the) fundamental aspect of the borderline personality's behaviour. Pseudologia fantastica appears to be what I describe as the borderline's fairy tale. This in turn would suggest that feigning sickness for emotional reasons should be considered factitious syndrome and not disorder. We might expect to see a mixture of covert narcissism and borderline in these individuals. Covert narcissism causes faking illness; borderline causes pseudologia fantastica. The relative mixture of factitious and fairytale may be an indication of the relative mixture of (likely covert) narcissism and borderline.

Narcissism and/or borderline are the cause(s); factitious / Munchausen are the results.

It isn't hard to imagine how masculine overt narcissism might also be a factor. Let's consider an overt narcissistic man. In one sense, his deep-seated sense of being unworthy of love and being ashamed of himself might lead to a logical (and unconscious) conclusion: there is something fundamentally wrong with him as a person. Given this ever-present unconscious feeling, it doesn't take much imagination to see how this might "bleed" into his conscious narcissistic mind.

If this happens, such a man might feel that there had to be something wrong with him, but *physically* wrong. This is his false self. Since he is an overt, masculine sort of person, he would take action to address the 'problem.' He would be super-proactive in educating himself and then constantly seeking the specialists he needed to treat his 'condition.' Pure mirroring—his false self is the permanently ill person. If / when he was exposed in a particular situation, he would move on. New location, new doctors, new sympathetic and admiring friends, possibly new condition(s).

Same unrelenting cause: narcissism. If there was also pseudologia fantastica, we might also suspect borderline.

I won't address malingering, which is when someone consciously fakes being ill for some material reason (e.g., a prisoner trying to get away from other prisoners, insurance fraud, soldier getting out of combat, etc.). That leaves Munchausen by proxy, and it's a nasty one. As Dr. Feldman correctly points outs, Munchausen by proxy is not a mental disorder. It is a very serious form of child abuse, and it is too often fatal. As Dr. Feldman says:

> The typically female perpetrators who engage in Munchausen by proxy also play sick, but cruelly use the bodies of others—usually young children—to meet their needs to be perceived as virtuous, indefatigable caregivers who merit our respect and compassion.

It's almost as if Dr. Feldman was writing specifically for this book. This screams of the covert narcissist's false self and mirroring. It is narcissistic grandiosity in its feminine form.

Most of what I have read only uses the term "Munchausen" by proxy. However, if we were being technically correct, we should distinguish between it and factitious disorder (or syndrome) by proxy in less serious cases. I'll use Munchausen by proxy as the generic term for simplicity.

Let's imagine a woman who is a mother and who is also a serious covert narcissist. She pathologically craves attention in the form of sympathy, or compassion in Dr. Feldman's words. Yet she also has serious issues with her narcissistic grandiosity. She needs to believe that she is an exceptional mother. She desperately needs others to believe this too (she can't be her own mirror). She needs her narcissistic mirror to reflect this back to her.

So how can this woman be a grandiose super-mom and still get tons of attention in the form of sympathy and compassion? By having a very sick kid that she is so devoted to. Only she doesn't have one. So what does she do? *She makes one.* Build the mirror. Munchausen by proxy child abuse is easily explained by mother's covert narcissistic grandiosity and mirroring. Our concept of covert narcissism fits perfectly with Dr. Feldman's words:

> The majority of MBP perpetrators are women, most often mothers, who induce illness in children or subject them to painful medical procedures in a quest for emotional satisfaction, such as attention from and control over others.

Regarding one specific case, Dr. Feldman wrote:

> By devoting her [the mother's] life to "helping" her "sick" child, she could, in the eyes of the world, be a nurturing, martyr-like mother, unlike her own abusive mother.

Again, Dr. Feldman's observations fit our concept of covert narcissism like a glove. This strongly suggests feminine narcissistic grandiosity and mirroring. We also see a hint of the inter-generational aspect to suspected covert narcissism in this example as well.

Like Mary with Hugh's sleeping, the covert narcissistic mother is a bit of a feral animal perpetrating Munchausen by proxy. She is driven by a deep, dark pathology. She lacks empathy, so she can't *really* care about her children. She can, however, be very convincing to the contrary. Like Mary, if the narcissism is milder, mother can merely encourage the child to believe he or she is ill. "Are you all right? Are you *sure* you're all right? You look sick to me. Does your stomach hurt?" Started young enough, the child starts to doubt himself or herself.

There is a yearning in mummy's voice. Every child wants to make mummy happy, and when her child says he or she feels ill, mummy is happy. The child becomes uncertain, too. Mummy keeps asking me if something is wrong, so there must be. Over time, what is normal becomes perceived as sick by the child. The child is subconsciously afraid that mummy won't love him if he isn't sick. He is probably right. It is conditional love, conditional on his being ill and needing mummy. A *folie a deux*, as they say. A shared delusion.

Stomach migraines—pure bloody rubbish! At least it was in our case. They seemed to go away whenever Hillary stayed elsewhere. With Munchausen by proxy, this is known as a positive separation test.

As Dr. Feldman informs us, these mothers can also fake their kid's medical tests. For example, a mother can put a drop of her own menstrual blood in her child's urine sample. A good number of these women have some sort of medical or healthcare background.

Mary was a former nurse.

Some women cause serious physical harm to their child. Some mothers go too far and tragically kill their children. The ultimate in sympathy—a grieving mother. Other children are harmed by unnecessary medical treatment. Hillary didn't need drugs and an upper gastrointestinal scope. This was child abuse.

If you want to know how serious and pervasive the problem is, Dr. Feldman says it best:

A small body of statistics is available for MBP, and the data are staggering: For instance, the estimated mortality rate is 9 to 10 percent, making it perhaps the most lethal form of child abuse. Mothers are the perpetrators in around 75 percent of the cases, with females such as grandmothers, babysitters, foster mothers, and stepmothers comprising most of the remaining 25 percent; fathers and other men account for fewer than 25 cases (less than 3 percent) in the literature.

Covert narcissism explains the gender disparity. A feminine form of narcissism explains why mostly women perpetrate Munchausen by proxy. The logic is too powerful to ignore.

Dr. Feldman also gives us another very important clue that we are likely dealing with serious covert narcissism in cases of Munchausen by proxy. Even when confronted with irrefutable video evidence of them harming their child, some of these women cannot admit to it. They cannot allow themselves to believe the truth. Just like Narcissus, it would be fatal for them to recognize themselves. It would destroy their false selves as exceptionally caring moms of 'sick' kids. It would expose them to excruciating feelings of shame, worthlessness, and being unlovable.

As Dr. Feldman writes:

When confirmed perpetrators are confronted with video evidence, they may claim that "this is the first time" they've ever engaged in this behaviour; alternatively, they may try to explain away suffocation as "cuddling" or tampering with IV lines as "just straightening out the tubing."

A tragic case that made the news recently is worth considering. On 11 January 2013, the *National Post* website ran an article by Aly Thomson. It was entitled: "'Super mom' who starved one-year-old daughter sentenced to two years in jail." In that case, mother Susan Elizabeth MacDonnell starved her adopted daughter for a prolonged period. When the girl was hospitalized as a result, MacDonnell tampered with her feeding tube.

The forensic psychiatrist in the case, Dr. Grainne Neilson, testified "that MacDonnell deprived her daughter of food in an attempt to showcase her devotion as a mother." This appears to be consistent with mirroring and covert narcissism. Dr. Neilson diagnosed factitious disorder by proxy. Dr. Neilson testified that MacDonnell had: a borderline personality disorder, several anti-social traits, and was a pathological liar.

I don't have the credentials to dispute dedicated professionals like Dr. Feldman or Dr. Neilson when it comes to borderline personalities and Munchausen by proxy. Indeed, this appears to be conventional wisdom in their fields. However, what they have observed and discussed appears to me to be a perfect fit for covert narcissism. I find that covert narcissism provides a stronger theoretical explanation for this form of child abuse than does borderline. However, if there was pseudologia fantastica too, this would then suggest either borderline or both.

Perhaps experts need to consider the differential diagnosis between borderline and covert narcissism. Furthermore, experts should be alive to the possibility that borderline, too, has masculine and feminine forms. There may be common borderline traits and gender-specific, *Mars-Venus* traits too.

There is one further bit from Dr. Feldman that is very important to my story (*Book Two*). Dr. Feldman has formally proposed the concepts of *factitious victimization* and *factitious heroism*. I believe these correspond to my covert-overt or feminine-masculine narcissistic false selves. Obviously, Dr. Feldman approaches such behaviour from his area of expertise versus from my perspective of narcissism.

In fairness, please recall that he is an expert, whereas I am not.

It is Dr. Feldman's concept of factitious heroism that is important to my story. It comes into play a little later on. An example of factitious heroism might be a fireman who actually commits arson so he can 'discover' the fire and heroically battle the blaze by himself until the fire department arrives to put it out. Whether one adopts Dr. Feldman's interpretation or mine doesn't matter. What is important is that it is a fact that some men disturbingly engineer the circumstances needed for them to be 'heroes.' Instead of playing sick, these individuals sadly play hero.

Fibromyalgia is another mysterious medical condition that is potentially explained by covert narcissism. It is a medical disorder characterized by chronic widespread pain and a heightened and painful response to pressure. There are other symptoms. Interestingly, it disproportionately strikes females by a 9 to 1 ratio over males.

My, my. Doesn't this seem to fit Gray's 10 percent of men who socialize like Venusians rather nicely? Since women Venusians outnumber men who socialize like Venusians by a 9 to 1 ratio, we might expect to find the same ratio amongst covert narcissists.

Covert narcissism fits fibromyalgia like a glove.

Fibromyalgia is a diagnosis of exclusion. I think this is fancy medical speak for "we don't know what this is, so let's make up a name. We don't want to look silly."

Neurologists tend to believe that fibromyalgia is a neurological disorder. However, when you talk to nurses who deal with fibromyalgia patients, you might get a different story. Nurses are mostly women, and women are generally better at seeing through female deception. Some nurses see fibromyalgia patients as needy and manipulative women. This fits perfectly with what covert narcissism is.

It is possible that fibromyalgia is not a legitimate disorder in and of itself. It is perhaps an unrecognized form of factitious disorder (or syndrome). At its core, it could be covert narcissism. It seems to make far too much sense for it not to be.

Interestingly, this gender interpretation of narcissism, mirroring, and projection can also explain school bullies. Male bullies tend to intimidate their victims and provoke fear by either beating up on them, threatening to beat up on them, or at least physically controlling and dominating them. Female bullies can be physically violent, but they tend to be more emotional bullies. They'll work to ostracize their victims and make them the outcast slut. They are also apt to manipulate others to do what they want done; they can act indirectly. By any measure, these behaviours are still controlling and dominating.

If we consider *Mars*, courage is a virtue we associate with men. Fear and cowardice are sort of the opposites of this. So, if you're afraid, this is shameful for a male. A school boy who is a narcissist would obviously have unconscious issues with shame and fear. He is unworthy of love, afraid, and ashamed. How does the narcissist boy defend against this?

He projects the shame of his fear onto his victim. Again, here's where I believe that experts haven't quite appreciated just how powerful mirroring (combined with projection) really is. It isn't enough for the bully to simply believe that it's some other boy who is the one who is afraid (the mirror).

The bully needs to see and feel this reflected in the victim boy's fearful words and actions. It is the victim boy who should then feel the shame of being afraid. The bully needs this narcissistic supply. The bully needs to build his mirror. He bullies the other boy to make that boy afraid. His victim's response, and to a lesser extent that of the other boys, is the male bully's narcissistic mirror.

Now think about *Venus*. Girls socialize by mutual dependence. They support one another. So let's say that one of the girls is a narcissist. She has deep unconscious fear of being unworthy of love and associated shame. How does this female narcissist defend against this shame?

She projects onto her victim. The bully will act to ostracize her victim. She will whisper behind her back, spread lies about her, write nasty things on the girls' bathroom walls about her, and leave nasty notes for her to find. (This is probably even worse in the age of internet cyber-bullying.) The bully will turn the others against the victim girl. The bully builds her mirror—see, it is the victim whom none of the other girls like, not me. This is bad for a girl, so she should be ashamed of herself for being rejected. The bully needs this narcissistic supply. The bully needs to build her mirror. Her victim's emotional response, and perhaps even more that of the other girls, is the bully's narcissistic mirror.

The reason that male and female bullies tend to keep bullying is explained by narcissism. Bullying provides only temporary relief. The shame is always there, lurking beneath the conscious mind. Depending upon the age and severity, narcissists have no other way of getting relief from the shame.

For an excellent short article on the more subtle female bullying, read Ditta M. Oliker's, Ph.D., "Bullying in the Female World."* While the author doesn't discuss narcissism, she does note the covert nature of the female bully's aggression. She also mentions mirroring within a peer group. Her description of the bullying leader of a female group is that of a "Queen Bee."

Oliker's descriptions of a female bully are too close to a covert narcissist for it to be a coincidence. Also, Oliker's mechanics of female bullying seem an awful lot like the covert narcissist woman at the workplace.

Since narcissism can be or is inter-generational, let's make a prediction. I'll bet that if you ask school principals, they will tell you that *bullies tend to*

* http://www.psychologytoday.com/blog/the-long-reach-child-hood/201109/bullying-in-the-female-world (31 March 2013)

have problem parents. This only makes sense. One or both of the parents of the bully are likely to be narcissists themselves. Thus, to be told that their kid was a bully would cause a narcissistic injury. It would imply that they were bad or inferior parents (yes!). Thus, their minds would corrupt the truth to the principal/school being mean and picking on their kid. They would become, to some extent, hostile to the idea that there was something wrong with their kid's behaviour.

If you're out there principals, let us know.

· · · · · · ·

After some thought, there's another case that I have to discuss: that of American Susan Smith. Born in 1971, Smith phoned police in October of 1994 to report that an African-American man had carjacked her car with her two sons still in it. What had actually happened was that Smith let her car roll into a lake with her two young sons trapped in it, so she could get rid of them.

They were getting in the way of her love life.

Apparently, her defence psychiatrist diagnosed Smith with dependent personality disorder (DPD). I understand that Smith's birth father committed suicide when she was six, and she was sexually abused by a step-father as a teenager. She had made a couple of suicide attempts as well.

Dependent personality disorder is a personality disorder where a person has an all-encompassing psychological dependence upon other people. It seems to affect females more than males.

Hmmmm....

What disturbs me about this – beyond the boys' tragic deaths, of course—is that DPD sounds an awful lot like Mary's behaviour at certain times. Those times where she absolutely had to be vulnerable and manipulate me for sympathy. She'd normally be this super-well organized individual, and then she'd suddenly be like this little girl looking for daddy's comfort.

There's something almost Freudian with this. Sexual abuse?

Regardless, this suggests one of two possibilities to me. The first is that Mary had what's referred to as co-morbidity. That is, she had both covert narcissism and DPD. The other—and this makes more sense to me—is that DPD isn't a genuine disorder unto itself. DPD could be a manifestation of (or a subset of) covert narcissism.

Susan Smith was highly cunning and manipulative. She was a pathological liar. She severely lacked empathy, in that she killed her own sons in cold blood. She was grandiose in an indirect, feminine way – such a caring, vulnerable, and sensitive mother. She "played the race card," a horrible thing to do anywhere, especially in the US. Oh, those darn car-jacking black men! Yet she was charming too, in that she made people sympathize with her plight and agony.

Sounds like a feminine form of narcissism to me.

. . . .

At the risk of putting the cart slightly before the horse, we can now consider parental alienation. Covert narcissism explains parental alienation, although it isn't the only explanation. Feminists adamantly deny that parental alienation even exists. Just like the tobacco companies denied that smoking causes lung cancer. Just like Holocaust deniers deny that 6,000,000 Jews were murdered in World War Two concentration camps.

Feminists are pathologically driven to corrupt the truth about alienation. There is a pattern building here, but it will have to wait for awhile.

So what is parental alienation? This is actually a slightly tricky question, as it gets into custody disputes and legal definitions and so on. I'll save the formal definition until after a little background. For now, let's just say that it's one parent turning a child against the other parent. It is an utterly horrid thing to do to a child and to the other parent.

And narcissistic women are particularly good at it.

Dr. Barbara Jo Fidler, Ph.D., is a Toronto psychologist. She is also a past president of the Ontario branch of the Association of Family and Conciliatory Courts (AFCC). Nicholas Bala is a distinguished professor of law at Queen's University. Together they wrote a special guest editors' editorial notes article for the January 2010 edition of AFCC's *Family Court Review* professional journal.

According to Dr. Fidler and Professor Bala, the concept of parental alienation was identified as early as 1949 by psychoanalyst Wilhelm Reich. Psychoanalysis is the Sigmund Freud stuff—ego and psyche and all that. Alienation is thus nothing new—professionals have known about it for over 60 years. Reich wrote that divorced parents with certain personality types would defend against "narcissistic injury by fighting for custody of the child and defaming the partner in an effort to rob the other parent of the pleasure of the child."

Much later, in 1980, researchers Wallerstein and Kelley described an "unholy alliance between a narcissistically enraged parent and a particularly vulnerable older child or adolescent." Together this pair "wage battle to hurt and punish the other parent."

There were others who considered the phenomenon. However, it was the late Dr. Richard Gardner who, in 1985, introduced the term "parental alienation syndrome" or PAS for short. The year is important. Feminism was exploding at the time in terms of its fundamentally perverting society and justice.

To me, it seems that there were two aspects to Dr. Gardner's work that outraged feminists. The first was Dr. Gardner's early observation that it was more women doing this horrible thing to children and ex-husbands. The second was his recommended treatment protocol. In severe enough cases, Dr. Gardner recommended switching custody from the offending parent to the victim parent. In essence, he was recommending that a lot of abusive mothers (and, in fairness, some abusive fathers, too) lose custody of their children for what they were doing to them.

Even to this day, feminist academics, lawyers, judges, and activists work to deny the existence of parental alienation. They work to suppress any progress whatsoever in acknowledging that the problem even exists, let alone remedying it. If you haven't guessed it already, I'll explain why in a later chapter. It came as the result of another beautiful and eloquent insight.

To avoid confusion, from now on I'll refer to the offending parent as the *alienator*. She (or he) is the one who alienates the kids from the other parent. The victim parent I'll refer to as the *target parent*. He (or she) is the target of the alienator's campaign of alienation.

Dr. Amy Baker, Ph.D., is a New York City research psychologist. She is one of a cadre of experts who are world authorities in the field of parental alienation. In particular, Dr. Baker conducted ground-breaking research that confirmed what clinicians and theorists in the field had long maintained: alienation has extremely harmful and *life-long* consequences for victim children.

Dr. Baker also gained tremendous insight into what goes into a campaign of alienation. She did this by studying adults who had been alienated as children.

Dr. Baker came to Krakton, Ontario in October of 2009 to testify at my divorce trial. She then had 20 years of post-Ph.D. experience. After her credentials were established, the judge found that Dr. Baker was "qualified as an expert in parent/child relationships and parental alienation syndrome." Dr. Baker gave sworn oral testimony, submitted a sworn affidavit, and was cross-examined.

Her evidence was too good, which is probably why it had to be criminally suppressed by feminist judge Larrisa Lyon-Hoare. (Lyon-Hoare comes in *Book Two*. It just keeps getting better.)

There is an indirect link between Dr. Fidler and Dr. Baker. In the 2009 Canadian case of *A.G.L. v. K.B.D.*, Dr. Fidler testified as an expert witness. Dr. Fidler's testimony included her citing the research of Dr. Baker. This was accepted by Madam Justice McWatt of Ontario Superior Court of Justice. Justice McWatt wrote at paragraph 91 of her decision:

> As a result, I accept the evidence of Dr. Fidler in relation to conclusions about the parties' family by 2000. And, I accept her evidence about the concept and qualities of child alienation and its effect on families.

Here are two more important paragraphs from that decision:

> [97] Dr. Fidler testified that long-term research by Amy Baker on adults who were alienated from a parent as a child suffered depression in 70 percent of the individuals studied. Two-thirds of the same population became divorced themselves—a quarter of that group more than once. The adults talked to researchers about interpersonal problems, dysfunctional managing of their lives and difficulties trusting other people. One-third were reported to have substance abuse problems. Fifty percent of this group in this study became alienated from their own children.

> [98] Dr. Fidler also testified that the study in question found that the bulk of those involved had wished that "someone had called

them on their strong wishes and statements not to see the other parent", but that they could not do it themselves. They could not reverse their public stance against the alienated parent, but wished someone else would make the decision for them that they had to see that parent. This way, the child could "save face".

At my divorce trial, Dr. Baker's evidence was about alienation in general, not as it applied to our case. Dr. Baker was clear that parental alienation is when a parent manipulates a child to reject the other parent. It is a form of emotional child abuse. This was expressed in language that was virtually identical to the crucial definitions in Ontario's *Child and Family Services Act.* That means that parental alienation is emotional child abuse in the Province of Ontario in accordance with the Rule of Law. This is true regardless of what feminists or judges who are influenced by feminism say.

The law is clear in its interpretation: *children must be protected from alienators.* Feminists can deny and suppress all they want. What they are truly doing is supporting serious child abuse and undermining justice, human rights, and the Rule of Law.

(Feminists are controlling, manipulative, lack empathy, and are pathological liars. Too many of them are judges.)

If a child rejects a parent for legitimate reasons or for reasons other than alienation, then that child is *estranged* from that parent. However, if the other parent influenced the child to reject a parent, then the child has been *alienated* from the target parent. It is conceivable that a child can be both alienated and estranged from a parent.

Dr. Baker also presented expert evidence that parental alienation is quite, quite comparable to cult programming from the perspective of the psychology involved. Cult programming is obviously another term for brainwashing. This has a precedent in Canadian law. In the 1987 case of *Tremblay v. Tremblay,* Madame Justice Trussler of the Court of Queen's Bench of Alberta wrote:

I start with the premise that a parent has the right to see his or her children and is only to be deprived of that right if he or she has abused or neglected the children. Likewise, and more important, a child has a right to the love, care and guidance of a parent. To be denied that right by the other parent without sufficient justification, such as abuse or neglect, is, in itself, a form of child abuse.

> *... I also concluded as a result of the 14th January hearing that the children were essentially being brainwashed by their mother with respect to their father and she was attempting to instill in them an unwanted fear of the father.*

It's obvious that Justice Trussler was dealing with a case of alienation and cult-programming. She didn't have access to the professional language of today. However, this wise judge clearly understood what was happening. So, parental alienation has been legally accepted as cult-programming child abuse in Canada since 1987. Dr. Baker's expert research and evidence in 2009 merely confirmed what was already known in Canadian law for over 20 years.

Based upon my experience and Dr. Baker's expert evidence, I now define parental alienation as:

> *Emotional child abuse **as defined in child protection law**, in which a parent (or another adult) effectively cult-programs or attempts to effectively cult-program a child to reject the other parent (or another meaningful adult) via manipulative strategies and techniques.*

Most people tend to think that younger children are most vulnerable to alienation. My understanding is that research suggests this isn't true. Children are most vulnerable when they approach or enter their teenage years. They are just starting to think independently, but lack the ability to perceive that they are being manipulated. As a result, they become cult programmed but believe they are thinking independently. At this point, they have taken up the alienator's cause. Serious psychological harm is already occurring.

I've taken 17 of Dr. Baker's most prevalent alienating strategies and put them in the following table. I've indicated if I witnessed them or I can reasonably infer that Mary employed them.

Strategy	My case?
badmouthing the targeted parent	YES
limiting the child's contact with the targeted parent	YES
interfering with communication between the child and the targeted parent	YES
limiting mention and photographs of the targeted parent	YES
withdrawal of love/expressions of anger if the child indicates positive feelings for the targeted parent	YES
telling the child that the targeted parent does not love him or her	YES
creating the impression that the targeted parent is dangerous	YES
withholding medical, social, academic information from the targeted parent and keeping the targeted parent's name off of such records	YES
cultivating dependency	YES
confiding in the child	YES
asking the child to spy on the targeted parent	YES
referring to the targeted parent by his/her first name	YES
forcing the child to choose between his/her parents	YES
forcing the child to reject the targeted parent	YES
referring to the step-parent as "Mom" or "Dad" and encouraging the child to do the same	NOT APPLICABLE
asking the child to keep secrets from the targeted parent	YES
changing the child's name to remove any association with the targeted parent	NO

Mary's alienation of our children from me was rabid. It was virtually an all-out assault to cult program our children to reject me. It was severe and unrelenting. Thank God it wasn't so severe that Mary changed the boys' last name to her maiden family name.

That would have been Russ Williams bad. (I'll discuss his case in *Book Two*.)

Here's something else to consider. It comes from alienation expert Dr. Richard Warshak, Ph.D. Dr. Fidler and Prof. Bala also cite Dr. Warshak's research. In his superb book *Divorce Poison* (2nd ed.), Dr. Warshak writes :

> *If your spouse manipulates the children to blame you for the divorce, or to believe that you have abandoned them, affection can dissolve overnight as their distress and hurt feelings are channeled into hatred.*

And

> *By now it should be clear that a close relationship with your child offers no guarantee against alienation.*

I can attest to this. Kids you've loved and cherished their whole lives can be turned against you with stunning speed and ease. Even within a few days. You can be almost helpless to stop it on your own. Intervention in suspected cases of parental alienation child abuse must be swift and decisive.

Tragically, it is not in the Matriarchy of Ontario, Canada.

What can be worse for a target parent is that it is so, so easy for unsuspecting bystanders to help the alienator. These unsuspecting other adults will not believe that kids can reject a loving parent so readily. These bystanders will wonder, what did he (or she) *really* do to be rejected by his (or her) kids? So these bystanders are deceived too, and become part of the alienator's mirror.

Mary's rabid alienation of the children makes perfect sense from a covert narcissism / mirroring point of view. She needed to be a superior parent to me (covert/feminine grandiosity). She especially needed the kids, above everyone else, to believe this (narcissistic supply, mirroring). So the truth of her addiction had to be corrupted in her mind into her being 'depressed' (victim, covert narcissism) due to an 'unhappy marriage.'

Boo, hoo—poor Mary.

When I had had enough and was going to divorce her, this was a staggering blow to her false self. It threatened to destroy her mirror and her false self along with it. She had to alienate the children to preserve her mirror.

Here's why. If she hadn't, the kids would have continued to have healthy, loving relationships with me. This would have meant that I am a good parent and pretty much a decent fellow. This, in turn, would have meant that a good father and a decent fellow couldn't stand to live with her anymore. And not just any ordinary decent chap, but a Catholic one. Catholics don't believe in divorce.

This, in turn, would have suggested that there was something so bad, so wrong about Mary, that it would even drive a decent Catholic man of 42 years to divorce her. That threatened to expose her to a huge amount of shame. Admitting to her addiction and negligence as a mother would also have been hugely shameful. As a narcissist, she was exquisitely sensitive to even a miniscule amount of shame.

To protect herself from the shame, her mind had to pervert the truth. She hadn't been addicted and been a cruddy mother and wife. She had been 'escaping an unhealthy marriage' and was 'depressed.' I hadn't divorced her for legitimate reasons; I was 'abandoning' her and the family. She had valiantly tried to save the marriage, but to no avail due to her cad ex-husband.

It must be true—see, the kids believe it!

Mary's story was all a narcissistic lie. Mary caused it to be 'true.' She caused the kids to believe it. Just as the Munchausen by proxy covert narcissist causes her 'sick' child to be 'true.' Marriage counseling was a way to deflect blame (and shame) from her addiction onto me. Feel sorry for me—I was depressed. What sort of cad won't feel sorry for a depressed wife?

Only it wasn't depression; it was 'depression.' Which is to say, it was covert narcissism.

This was pretty much like her older sister Rebecca, dragging her poor, unsuspecting husband to several marriage counselors. "Look how valiantly I am trying to save our marriage!—'our' problems must be his fault." This was Rebecca's implied message. This was what she needed her mirror to reflect. Admire my noble efforts.

Of course, marriage counselors and social workers can eat this up: hook, line, and sinker. At least, they certainly did in my case.

There is another way to consider Mary's alienation of the children. Mary would also have had intense subconscious fear that the children would have preferred me if they knew she was a deadbeat addict of a mom. She would be terrified that she wouldn't have the kids to admire her and sympathize with her. They were the ultimate foundation of her grandiose feminine mirror. She couldn't risk letting me have any relationship with them. She had to maintain control. She alienated the kids and at the same time projected the shame of her actions onto me. In Mary's victim eyes, I had alienated the kids from myself, due to the mean things that I had done to her.

As it turned out, Mary's victim mirror became part of a bigger feminist victim mirror.

. . . .

I am not a psychiatrist. Nor am I a psychologist, nor a psychoanalyst. I don't pretend to be. I don't expect experts to trip all over themselves in a mad rush to modify the DSM because of what I have written. However, I lived with the milder narcissistic personality traits of my ex-wife for almost 20 years. As she was below the threshold for a major personality disorder, I was able to see the subtleties of how narcissism manifests in a woman. I had access to data on narcissism, if you will, that wasn't generally available to people who work in this field.

This is one of the reasons why I have included the autobiographical portions of this book. I couldn't find anything in the literature on narcissism that describes, in everyday language, what covert narcissism really is, or how it manifests. It does not appear to be well understood.

Given that I may have had unique data or information that would be of use to experts, I thought it best to capture it. I wanted to stimulate expert interest in covert narcissism, and how it might relate to borderline. I wanted to show how interpreting covert narcissism as a feminine form of narcissism could explain so much that is presently not understood. If covert narcissism is indeed behind Munchausen by proxy, kids are being harmed, maimed, and killed by it. Munchausen by proxy must be stopped. To be stopped, it must first be understood.

Every time I consider narcissism, I see the unappreciated significance of mirroring. I cannot help but think that there might be some truth to the myth as metaphor. Little did I know, after my lawyer suggested narcissism to me, that another narcissistic mirror, and a great big one at that, was going to reveal its ugly self.

Mirror, mirror, on the wall...

Courts of InJustice

5
Maelstrom

From the deepest desires often come the deadliest hate.
—SOCRATES

When Mary was the center of attention in the right sort of way, she glowed. She radiated happiness. She exuded sublime joy. She beamed. It's a look that now tips me off to when someone is in their narcissistic glory. When they are high on narcissistic supply.

Mary was like that the day after I mentioned I was seeing a divorce lawyer. She was beside herself with joy as she went about the house 'consoling' the kids after her previous night's fireworks. It was just like with Hugh's sleep, though. Mary had done as much as she could to worsen the pain and suffering of the kids. So they would need her, feeding her sick ego. Build the mirror.

The next two weeks were a bit of a blur for me. I still had to work, unlike Mary. I was exhausted and at an emotional low. Mary remained constantly abusive towards me at home, making certain the kids heard every bit of it. I stayed in contact with the counselors from the base. I mentioned to them that I was starting to see the same behaviour from Hillary that Mary typically displayed. I'm glad I didn't think that things couldn't have gotten worse, because they did.

Much worse.

I also kept my family in-the-loop as to what was happening. My sister Ann emailed me back to describe what she had seen at our house the previous October, when I was in Germany:

> When Kevin [Ann's husband] and I visited in Oct [2007] I will tell you I was shocked and Kevin was shocked too. I could see things were very bad in your house. I couldn't believe Mary on the computer. I thought there was something really wrong there. The house was not clean at all and she wasn't even working. Hillary wasn't going to school and I had a feeling Mary was playing a bit part in nurturing that problem. I didn't want to say anything and make you feel bad. Why couldn't Hillary or Mary even clean the downstairs for company? I would have been mortified to have company come and have my house that dirty. You were working your ass off and NOTHING is being done while you are at work.

It didn't take long for the base counselors to warn me: "Take care of yourself." Like protecting the king in chess, if I fell apart, I couldn't protect the kids from Mary. It was good advice that I took to heart. The kids always came first, though. Always.

On the 21st of April, as if things weren't bad enough, I got a real shocker of an email from my sister Elizabeth, the nurse:

> ...suggest you google Munchausen by proxy. I believe that Hillary's medical problems have been caused directly by Mary and her need for attention and validation, and to provide herself with a companion... Mary is manipulative and abusive—she bad mouths you behind your back and to your face, and picks away at your self-esteem to belittle you and make you small.

Great. Just what I needed. Concerns about possibly the most lethal form of child abuse (although I hadn't researched this yet). Mom emailed me two days later with similar suspicions:

One thing is odd though. One day, I am talking to Elizabeth and she tells me that she's wondering if Mary might have Munchausen by proxy. Elizabeth didn't know, but 10 days before she told me that, I had bought a book on that exact subject as I wondered too. That is God's honest truth. That shook me. I wasn't 100% sure after reading the book, was it or wasn't it?

Things were going from bad to worse on a daily basis.

We went to see our social work marriage counselor for the last time. I had decided that I'd rather spend the rest of eternity in hell than another day with Mary. This being the lesser of two evils, of course. However, I wanted another adult around when I said this. Hopefully, this would keep Mary from blowing a gasket. The kids wouldn't be around, either.

So when Captain Sarah Symmes-Pathetique—the fool—asked us how it was going, I said I wanted a divorce. I could see Mary's face contort in the effort it took her to suppress her rage. Symmes-Pathetique the social worker was too biased to see what was actually going on. I could see that the she was only full of sympathy and concern for Mary, the woman. The good captain couldn't care less about how I felt—I was just a man.

Mary the Vindictive One was not about to waste a golden opportunity. She said Hillary was angry with me about the divorce, and asked Captain Social Worker if Hillary *had* to speak to me if she didn't want to. The good Captain, brimming with sympathy for Mary, said of course not. With a smile, no less.

If it is not already obvious, I have come to rather dislike social workers. By the end of this book and its sequel, you'll understand why.

What Captain Social Worker did was play right into the hands of Mary the Great Narcissistic Manipulator. I knew that Mary was on the verge of exploding, and if I said anything it would only lead to a fight. Same old emotional terrorism. Mary was dead silent on the drive home, but she made up for it as soon as we arrived. She made a point of saying out loud (so the kids could hear her, again) that the social worker had said that Hillary didn't have to speak to me if she didn't want to.

This quickly changed to "the social worker said that Hillary didn't have to speak to Dad." Mary omitted the "if she doesn't want to" part. Within about two days, this changed to "the social worker said that Hillary shouldn't speak to Dad." Mary informed me that I would have to go through her to speak to Hillary. It had taken Mary perhaps two or maybe three days before she had completely isolated me from Hillary, who refused to speak to me or be with me.

Mary had the advantage of being at home all day with Hillary, while I had to go to work to support the family. God only knows what Mary was saying behind my back, given what she would say to my face (for the kids to hear). Small wonder that in one of my emails to Ann, I expressed my concern about Mary's campaign to isolate me from the kids.

To give you an idea of what I was living with, here are a couple of gems from a single day. When I went to get into the shower one morning to get ready for work, Mary ambushed me and started to ask me accusatory questions. Always loud enough for the kids to hear. She was trying to start a fight when I didn't have time to defend myself. When I told her I would be willing to discuss things with her after work, she accused me of not wanting to talk with her.

Yet when I came home from work, Mary refused to talk to me about these very same issues. This way, her morning accusations were 'true,' as I had 'refused' to talk with her about them.

The abuse never stopped. In a later episode, Mary suddenly decided that our deck needed staining. This came from out of the blue. So, in front of the kids, Mary tried to shame me into staining the deck. She said "it's man's work." Look kids—Daddy isn't doing his work to help out in the house. Mary was projecting the shame of her lack of house work onto me, and using this to help alienate the kids from me.

I had my first meeting with my lawyer on 25 April 2008. The male addiction and family counselors that I had been seeing weren't allowed to recommend a lawyer to me. So they casually mentioned that some people were very happy with local lawyer Daphne Dockett. One of the counselors even suggested it would be good to have a female lawyer. His reasoning was that the courts were so biased against men that it would look good if a woman lawyer took up my case.

Wrong! Our courts are way beyond "so biased." Our courts have been fundamentally perverted into courts of injustice.

There is something that I have to declare before I can go further. In law, what you discuss with your lawyer is sacred. It can't be used in court. This is referred to as "solicitor-client privilege." However, a person can waive this privilege, although it supposedly is a bad idea.

If a person starts blabbing about what was said between them and their lawyer, this can be equally bad. In the eyes of the law, this can be considered as someone in effect having waived privilege. Then, anything discussed between them and their lawyer becomes fair game.

There is no way that I can tell my story without revealing some of what went on between my lawyer and me. I am only doing so to let the truth of the matter be known. For the record, I do not waive solicitor-client privilege, neither explicitly nor implicitly.

The first meeting with Daphne was a sort of getting-to-know-one-another affair. I got the basics of how it should ideally go, and the general fees. I don't know if Daphne completely believed me at first when I told her what was going on. However, I don't blame her. Lawyers have to sort out if their prospective clients are actually the people they claim to be. I'm sure many lawyers have been lied to by clients, and my story may have seemed a bit extreme at first.

It only took a couple of visits for Daphne to suggest that Mary sounded narcissistic. Munchausen by proxy, parental alienation, and now narcissism. At least I finally had a name for Mary's twisted nature.

Mary couldn't do enough to keep herself between the kids and me. She asked me not to watch their favourite TV shows with them, as it was "her special time" with them. She also never let up with the badmouthing, always so the kids could hear.

Once I was folding laundry, something that Mary hadn't done in the better part of a year. She asked me, "When did you decide to start helping out in the house?" Unbelievable. When I mentioned that her statement was a bit much given her lack of contribution starting the prior fall, she had a response. "Did it ever occur to you that I was clinically depressed?" More guilt (projection), more ducking responsibility for her own actions. I'm pretty sure she got her 'clinically depressed' diagnosis long-distance from her sister Rebecca. The same sister who made the quack long-distance diagnosis of Hillary's 'stomach migraines.'

Remember the 'depressed' bit.

We hadn't been to church in over a year. It was a combination of things. Mary's addiction, my workload and exhaustion, and the crummy Krakton parish we had ended up with. We felt like ghosts. No one spoke to us. The only thing we ever got from the parish was a once-a-year receipt for charitable donations. Just give us money every week for our new church and shut up, thank you very much.

Didn't Saint Mary decide one day (27 April) that she would start taking *her* kids to church again—without me. When I told her in no uncertain terms that this wouldn't happen without me, she almost lost control and hit me. She then tried to blame me, saying that I "knew how to push her buttons." She also accused me again of trying to separate her from the kids. Again the pot calls the kettle black. Projection at its very finest.

I emailed Dad to tell him of the divorce, Mary's worsening abuse, and how Mary had effectively isolated Hillary from me. I didn't know of alienation at that point. I wrote that Mary's divide-and-conquer tactics were very effective, as Hillary was working on her brothers.

Mom and Dad had previously volunteered to take Hillary for the summer. The hope was that a change of scenery might help her get herself back on her feet. I had to tell Dad that Mary said that Hillary now didn't want to spend time with him and Mom that summer. According to Mary, of course. I also let Dad know that Mary was trying to lay guilt trips on me to no avail, which angered her.

That actually makes sense from a narcissism point of view. Her shame projection repeatedly failed. As well, Mary needed to believe that I was the villain. To build her mirror, she would try to provoke fights with me. Then, I would be the bad guy that she wanted me to be. Though I hadn't yet come to appreciate narcissism and mirroring, I intuitively understood that she was trying to provoke fights. Thus, I didn't rise to her provocations.

However, this caused her narcissistic injury. She needed the feedback of an angry me, only she wasn't getting it. Her mirror didn't reflect what she wanted it to, and *this upset her even more.*

Mary and I were still sleeping in the same bed. Like hell was I going to give up my bed for the likes of that abusive woman. It wasn't a big deal, as we were almost sleeping in shifts. I'd go to bed whenever, wake up briefly when she came in from computer gaming, and later get up for work while she was fast asleep.

That night, I awoke to the sound of Mary furiously pounding on the keyboard in the next room. I glanced at my bedside clock to see that it was 4:30

a.m. I then heard an obviously tired Hillary telling her mother that she was going to bed. I didn't hear Mary get off the computer until shortly after 5:00 a.m.

Yep. Mary wasn't addicted. No siree. Just ask her. And it was rather obvious what the source of Hillary's 'insomnia' was: being Mommy's best friend, and having an excuse not to go to school.

So I got up that morning, quietly got showered so as to not wake the addict (who was going to lead *her* kids to salvation that morning, Hallelujah!), and walked the dog.

The dog. I haven't mentioned that story, either. Just as Mary *had* to worry about money on occasion, she also *had* to worry about Hugh. Only it wasn't sincere, genuine concern. I know that now. If she actually cared about Hugh, she would have supported his Arrowsmith.

What Mary cared about was *seeming* like she cared about and was worried about Hugh, so she could get sympathy. So she could seem like a caring, worried, vulnerable mother. One day, about a year earlier, Mary out of the blue suddenly became concerned (again) about Hugh. About his socialization, specifically, even though he seemed to be doing all right with friends. Mary thought it would be a good idea for Hugh to get a pet.

I went to the local animal shelter and got Hugh a two-year-old mutt. Hugh jokingly called him Lord Muttington McWoof the 7th, or something like that. I didn't get the mutt before again consulting Mary. The thing is, she couldn't exactly say, "I wasn't serious. I was only manipulating you for sympathy." As Mary didn't object, we got a family pet. Just as with the investments—I didn't understand that she was manipulating me for sympathy.

Anyhow, I walked the dog and then waited to go to church. And waited. And waited.

It is a bit shameful to make such a display of taking *your* kids to church, only to play kids' video games until 5:00 a.m. and then sleep through the holy gathering. Sure enough, Mary projected her shame onto me by being ugly, trying to make me feel guilty, accusing me of being the cause of Hillary's failing school, blah-blah-blah, etc., etc. Par for the course.

Hillary's cult-programming had been brutally quick and effective. Later that day, she phoned my father and swore him to secrecy. After Dad agreed, Hillary spent the next 40 minutes vilifying me to my own father. The only reason I know is that Mom overheard Dad's half of the conversation. Just in case Dad needed her, of course. Like when she read my college mail. True to his word, Dad has never spoken to me about that telephone call.

Like Mary, when she had tried to undermine my relationships with Mom and my sisters. Like when a female bully tries to ostracize her victim. Hillary was clearly feeling unconscious shame about herself and how she was treating me. So she projected it onto me as female bullies do. In the same way that she was acting as a proxy alienator for her mother, by manipulating the boys to reject me, Hillary was manipulating my father to reject me, too. Pure female bullying.

It didn't work.

That was me. Major Michael M. McConaughey: Member of the Order of Military Merit and family slut. This from the daughter I had always loved, snuggled, hugged, tickled, read to, played with, and striven for nearly five years to keep from failing out of school.

Welcome to the brutal world of parental alienation and inter-generational covert narcissism.

Around this time, Mary mentioned that she was taking Hillary to a walk-in clinic for Hillary's 'depression.' Mary told me that parents weren't allowed to speak to the clinic—they only spoke to teens. Yet when I checked with Elizabeth, she said this was rubbish. It was my right as a parent to have input. Besides, any decent counselor would want to meet the parents to get at least an impression of them.

Mary was lying to me, again. She was building her mirror, trying to deceive some unsuspecting counselor of the truth. "Hillary had been depressed due to her father's abandoning the family. It's his fault that she's failed Grade 12." If the counselor believed it, then it must be 'true.' There was also the I-am-such-a-great-mother grandiosity. "Look how great and caring I am, taking my daughter to counseling to counter the harm her father caused." She didn't want me screwing up her web of self-deceit by telling the truth.

Pure narcissistic mirroring. Just like factitious disorder—if the doctor believes that I am sick, it must be 'true.' I contacted the clinic and gave them my side of the story. This started a month or two of cat-and-mouse. I would learn that Mary was taking Hillary or the boys to some counselor, so I would have to contact the counselor and explain how Mary was using him or her. This is what I had to worry about in my spare time, as I still had this little thing called a job to do during the day. Someone had to pay the mortgage and the bills, and it sure as hell wasn't Mary.

In hindsight, I can see that Mary was cult-programming the kids to believe that I was trying to take them away from her. She had openly said this to me—loudly enough for the kids to hear, of course. She was really speaking to them, obviously. I can only imagine what she was saying behind my back, either directly or through innuendo, tone of voice, and things left unspoken (her triple specialty). This was clearly alienation from a covert narcissist: Dad is evil; I am a victim, so protect me from him.

It was also projection. She was alienating the kids from their loving and devoted father. She had to do this to protect her narcissistic mirror. Yet it was a despicable and shameful act. So, to rid herself of the intense shame, she projected it onto me. I was thus trying to take them from her and turn them against her (but not really). This was an added bonus, as it greatly helped in the alienation. It set me up for failure in trying to protect the kids. The rational actions that an unsuspecting father or mother take to counter alienation and protect his or her children *can actually work to make things worse.*

It should be evident by now that narcissism and the dynamics of parental alienation can be somewhat complex. The experts in the field—the best psychiatrists, clinical psychologists, and psychoanalysts—understand this stuff. Too many social workers and too many judges do not. An obsessed alienator is constantly devising traps and lose-lose situations for the other parent. It is extremely difficult to counter an obsessed alienator without expert help.

Sadly, our society doesn't help target parents protect their children from alienation. Quite the opposite, in fact. Ontario, Canada supports and helps perpetrate this form of child abuse. Especially when mother is the alienator.

Enthusiastically, actually, when mother is the alienator.

Things came to a head on 30 April. I had been keeping the boys' school principal advised on an intermittent basis so the school could monitor the boys to ensure their education wasn't suffering. I'd also done some preliminary internet reading on Munchausen by proxy, which was very sobering.

I received a cryptic email or voicemail—I don't remember which—to contact the school principal. She'd said it was information that she didn't want to put in an email. I phoned her and received some disturbing news. The principal knew there were problems at home, so she had told the boys' teachers to let her know if the boys' behaviour became abnormal. Leo's teacher had seen something weird that day that had raised flags.

Leo was the boy who had learned to overcome bullies by taking kung fu. He wasn't a "macho" guy, nor was he a wimp. He was a secure, decent, normal boy. Yet that day, he'd come to school looking very different. For the first time ever, he had his hair all done up with mousse in a very effeminate (womanish) style. He was wearing a flaming pink shirt with wide white cuffs and collar, whereas he always had worn a t-shirt, like every other boy.

So the principal had Leo come in and have a little chat. It seems that Leo had only gone to school dressed like a girl on a dare from Hillary. Only Hillary was her mother's cult-slave by this point. Not surprisingly, Leo also said that his mother knew about it, too.

This was getting too weird. I was really worried that Mary was about to go off the deep end. That is, if she hadn't already. After a check on the internet, I learned that Ontario's child protection agencies were called Children's Aid Societies. CAS for short. The CAS that I was supposed to deal with was the Pasties CAS. It was based where we lived—Krakton.

I called the CAS and spoke to a Ms. Mindy Moorecock. It was like ho, hum, thanks for reporting. No, we're not going to do anything. Nothing I said seemed to make any impression on this woman.

Sorry to have bothered you. I was only worried that my kids were in danger. I'm surprised Pasties CAS, to add insult to injury, hadn't used a 1-900 number as their hotline. Then I would have had to pay to have Moorecock pretend to be interested in me, too.

For the record, here are parts of what Ms. Moorecock wrote in her actual Pasties CAS case notes about my call:

> ... *Michael expressed his concerns Mary was suffering from Munchausen* [by proxy] *and believed the children to be at risk. Michael advised he has spoken to doctors on the Backwater base who agree Mary displays symptoms of this disorder. A family member who is a nurse has also suggested this.... Michael asked for a CAS worker to attend the home and assess whether Mary has this disorder.* **I advised Michael a psychiatrist and medical professionals were the only persons able to make such a diagnosis.**

I added the bold. Remember: this Pasties CAS worker admitted to me that psychiatric and medical professional help is required in Munchausen by proxy child abuse cases. Despite this, no amount of pleading could get me CAS help. They weren't interested.

They could not have cared less.

I left work right after that phone call and got home shortly after the boys had arrived. It was surreal—I could feel it as soon as I entered the home. Our house was a split- or bi-level, which is also known as a raised ranch. From the entrance, you could either go up or down a half flight of stairs. Hillary was at the bottom of the basement stairs, as if on sentry duty. I asked her where her Mom was. She replied that Mom was in the basement bathroom with Leo.

That in itself was weird. Hillary's standing at the bottom of the stairs was weird. Her expression was weird. Her attitude was weird.

I went into the bathroom, and the weird, surreal nature of the moment didn't get any better. Mary was sitting on the side of the tub. Leo was on her lap, with his shirt off. There were a couple of tears running down his face, but he wasn't sobbing. In fact, he wasn't even crying. It's almost as if he thought that he was supposed to be sad and cry, but he couldn't understand why. Have to make Mom happy, and nothing makes Mom happier than when the kids need her.

Mary had that sick look of narcissistic happiness on her face. She was in a moment of narcissistic glory. She glowed. When I asked what was going on, Mary informed me that Leo was upset because the principal had told him about the divorce. Because I had told the school this. Only this was utter rubbish, as I later confirmed with the principal that she had never mentioned the divorce. Mary had planted this via suggestion to Leo, one of her favourite tricks. Just like convincing the kids they were ill. Hence, Leo's forced tears.

This is what my sick, deranged, estranged narcissistic wife had done. Via her manipulative proxy Hillary, Mary had sent Leo to school looking like a girl. The boys would make fun of him, and then she could console him. And blame it on me. Only it worked better than planned, as Leo had been called in to speak with the principal.

What does a man do when his deranged wife is doing sick things to his kids' minds? I had called Pasties CAS. As it turned out, I had to by law. It is known as a duty to report that a child is in need of protection.

It was the worst thing I could have possibly done.

Suddenly, Mary declared that my presence was bothering Leo and told me to leave. Like hell was I going to leave that sick woman alone with Leo. I told her that I thought it was best that I stay. Mary picked Leo up and literally said that she was taking him behind locked doors, so I couldn't be with him. She pushed past me with Leo in her arms. I didn't try to stop her, but to say that I was alarmed would be an understatement.

She went upstairs and took him into the master bedroom, which locked from the inside. I called out from the living room that if she didn't come out immediately, I was calling the police. She didn't, so I did. I called 911. Mary had obviously heard me, as she stormed out of the bedroom and in an ugly voice demanded to know who I was phoning. She tried to grab the phone out of my hand just as the 911 operator answered. I asked the operator to send the police for a domestic disturbance.

Hillary and Hugh went to huddle with Leo on our bed. I stayed with them, as there was no way I was letting Mary get near the kids without me. However, in acting to protect the kids, I had fallen into Mary's alienation trap. She'd been cult programming them to believe that I was trying to take them away from her (the victim). She'd projected her alienation onto me. In her behaving in such a deranged fashion that I had to call 911, it must have seemed to the kids that this was exactly what I was doing. They were beside themselves with grief and crying. Hillary and Hugh were screaming obscenities at me. I tried to calm them in response, with little apparent effect.

The police didn't take too long to get there. As a military guy, I have a lot of time for cops. They have a difficult and thankless job, and they generally do it well. I think any cop reading this will understand how difficult domestic calls can be. They'll also understand that as a military guy, I'm going to tell it like it was. There's nothing personal in this.

The three young Royal Krakton Constabulary officers who showed up acted professionally. They were also biased, and they unknowingly aided and abetted serious child abuse. It wasn't their fault. They tried their best in a difficult situation. Their training and policies didn't just fail them, they forced them to fail. These poor guys had no clue what they were dealing with. They were also abandoned by the reprehensible Pasties CAS.

The first thing they did was to separate Mary and me, to get each side of the story independently. Okay, that made sense. Only I was the one who called 911—why did I have to leave the house and wait on the front step for the neighbours to stare at? There was an immediate and obvious bias against me, *because I was a man.*

I told the cops what was going on, and I asked to speak to Pasties CAS. I ended up calling them from the front step and nearly begged them to send someone. Pasties CAS couldn't be bothered to send someone to a 911 emergency call.

If someone from that CAS ever tells you they care about children, don't believe them. When you go to their website and see pictures of happy, smiling children, understand what you are seeing: propaganda. I know the truth; I experienced it first-hand.

The officers couldn't sort this out, so they defaulted to the "you're the man, so be the bigger person and leave the home," routine. Let's see—I have valid reason to be concerned that my estranged wife is so deranged that: a) I am certainly being alienated from my children; and b) I might even be dealing with Munchausen by proxy, likely the most lethal form of child abuse.

And your solution is that I be "the bigger person" and leave the home?! Are you serious?!

These guys were dealing with a situation that was way over their heads. They obviously had been given sexist, feminist-influenced policy for domestic calls. They had no immediate access to an expert psychologist. They'd had no proper training for what they had been called to deal with.

In my opinion, these police officers were victims of a failure of leadership at the Royal Krakton Constabulary. Unlike the horrid women of the Pasties CAS whom I was soon to deal with, these cops acted in good faith and to the best of their abilities in a tough situation. I don't think anything less of them because of it. They had a professional attitude, and it showed. As professionals, they'll understand my being candid as to how they screwed up. Professionals accept this—it's nothing personal.

I respectfully refused to leave my own home, and explained why—I was legitimately concerned that Mary was a threat to the kids. There was no way

I was going to leave the kids alone with her that night. At the same time, I could see through my front door's window that Mary was laughing, smiling, joking, and getting along famously with the cop who was in the house. Mary's new best friend, it seemed.

Had the cops had the proper training, they would have realized that this was very wrong. An emotionally healthy woman should have continued to be genuinely upset in those circumstances. A narcissistic one, however, would have been tickled pink. The cops bought her story, whatever it was, so she was overjoyed. Hello, and welcome to my mirror; thank you very much.

The lead cop, at a bit of a loss as to what to do, called back to the station. Whomever he spoke to gave him the plan. The police let me back into my own home and sat Mary and me down. He politely read us the riot act. We were to sleep in separate bedrooms and not speak to one another until the next day.

Saint Mary immediately volunteered to move into the spare bedroom. To show the cops that she was the bigger person. She neglected to mention that this was where the computer was and that she was addicted to it. As they were about done, Mary told the cops that the kids were angry with me. She asked them if the kids had to speak with me if they didn't want to.

The lead cop didn't understand what Mary was up to. It was just like with that biased fool of a military social worker. So the cop said no, the kids didn't have to speak to me. He didn't understand that Mary was manipulating him as an authority figure. She would use his words against the kids, just like she used the social worker's. Mary would justify telling the kids not to speak to me by saying the cops had said so.

Mary was an expert at manipulating and exploiting authority figures to alienate.

I wish somebody had told these guys that abused kids often side with their abusive parent and not the good one. Or that kids are more likely to be abused by their mothers than their fathers. The cops eventually left. True to my word, I didn't say anything to Mary that evening. Like the liar she was, she took a few digs at me that night. The cops weren't around to see the real her.

The next day I got an email from Elizabeth. She suggested I look up something called parental alienation. There was a name for what Mary was doing! Elizabeth also mentioned that Hillary had deleted the email account that Elizabeth's daughter Marie used to email Hillary. Hillary was rejecting not only me, but my family as well. As it turns out, this is a common aspect to alienation. It is called the "spread" of alienation—it tends to spread to the target parent's other family members. It started to happen with Hugh as well.

Then, something triggered my memory. Sometime in the preceding weeks, Mary had mentioned that she had made Hillary an appointment to see our family doctor for sleeping pills. We'd managed to get a family doctor a little while previously. I hadn't thought much about it at the time, but then I suddenly remembered the time Hillary had thrown the "I've thought about suicide" thing right in my face, as if I didn't care.

I didn't know if the sleeping pills were a major Munchausen by proxy event waiting to happen or not. I'd seen Mary encourage Leo to think he was upset. I'd seen how she programmed the kids to think I was trying to take them away from her. I'd seen Mary manipulate authority figures to help in her campaign of alienation.

It took very little imagination to conceive of this scenario: Mary gets Hillary sleeping pills (Mary was an expert at manipulating doctors with her 'concern'); Mary keeps harping about her 'concern' to Hillary regarding Hillary's 'depression' (due to me) and the possibility of suicide; Hillary overdoses on sleeping pills due to Mary's subliminal suggestions; Saint Mary, Patron Saint of Mothers, 'saves' Hillary; Hillary's nearly successful suicide is my fault.

Only, as Dr. Feldman knows all too well, sometimes these things don't work out as intended.

I couldn't take the chance that this was what was happening. I ended up waiting two hours without an appointment to see our doctor. I think I was successful in getting my message across—our doctor wasn't a native English speaker. The next day, Mary and Hillary came back from the doctor's office with no sleeping pills. Mary looked a little weird.

It was tough trying to deal with what was going on. Even experts find Munchausen by proxy a difficult thing to deal with. Try possibly dealing with it as a parent while being rabidly alienated from the kids you are trying to help. With authority figures helping your estranged wife and no outside expert help. After you've been exhausted by months of abuse and lack of help at home. While you have to work full time to pay the bills.

It was an emotional meat grinder, especially since the kids being harmed were my own.

Having pre-empted the sleeping pills, I next thought about how to stop Mary from harming the kids if she really was that far gone. It's not as if Pasties CAS cared about serious child abuse. The best that I could come up with was to write Mary an email in which I clearly stated that she had estranged the children from me. Therefore, she had exclusive influence over them and was now solely responsible for any harm that might befall them. Perhaps she wouldn't try to harm them if she felt she would be held responsible for it. That would look bad. That would be shameful.

I'll probably never know if I did indeed prevent an engineered suicide attempt or some other harm from befalling Hillary. Maybe it was all rubbish, but I'll say one thing: I'd rather live with this uncertainty than knowing that I had failed to prevent it.

When I asked about Hillary's friends, Mary let slip that they had had a falling out. I could see from the look on Mary's face that she had intended to keep me ignorant of this. For a while before the 911 incident, Mary had started to go out with Hillary and her friends to places like the mall. It was pathetic—a 45-year-old woman hanging out with high school girls. I now understand that Mary was working to cause a rift between Hillary and her friends. Mary wanted Hillary all to herself.

Mary refused to move the computer out of *her* bedroom when I asked her to, stating that she had never agreed to this. Yet she didn't have any problem with leaving her clothes in my bedroom, and going in and out when I wasn't around.

None of the kids were talking to me by now. Hillary would lead them out of a room whenever I entered. I might get a couple of words from Leo if the others weren't around. I came out of my bedroom one evening when Mary was making supper for them. She'd started doing work once she began her rabid campaign of alienation in earnest. When the kids wouldn't answer me when I spoke to them, Mary said the police said they didn't have to speak to me.

There it was again. Only the day before, I had accused Mary to her face about her alienating the kids from me. As I expected, she denied it. Liars will be liars. So I gave Mary a withering look after her last police comment.

She immediately knew that I had caught her alienating the children. So she suddenly said, "The police said they didn't have to speak to me either if they didn't want to." Only they hadn't said it. Lying as she went along. Freudian thaumaturgy: if your mirror needs it, just say it. That makes it 'true.'

The next week, Hillary appeared to be well enough to go to school, but never did. I had become an outcast in my own home. A pariah. As usual, things kept going from bad to worse. At some point, Mary had let me know that she had spoken to the school and arranged for Hillary to repeat Grade 12. Hillary had never failed while I was an influence in her life. Never.

During the night of 3 May, Empress Mary came to a decision. The next day, I went to check my emails on our computer when Mary was out of her room. Only I couldn't, as she had password-protected the computer from anyone other than herself. When I later asked her about it, she told me that she would let me have access to an account—which didn't have access to my existing email, as it turned out. She refused to re-instate my computer 'privileges,' since Her Majesty had decided it was her computer.

Oh, that wonderful narcissistic sense of entitlement.

I told Mary that she could have put her personal information on a memory stick if she was worried about privacy. She replied that she "hadn't thought of it." Sure—someone who achieves academic excellence in a formal computer programming diploma can't think to use a memory stick.

This escalation was a big concern for me. I'd read that in some serious cases of alienation, the offending parent actually abducts the kids. Pasties CAS didn't give a rat's ass about the child abuse, so I was on my own. My father had expressed concern about my vulnerability to the home equity line of credit that I had set up to placate Mary. It was something that was already on my mind, as if I didn't have enough.

I knew Mary. I wasn't surprised that she felt she could lock me out of our computer, with no regard for how I felt about it. It was only a matter of time before she did the same with the line of credit. I didn't know how deranged she actually was—I didn't know if there was a possibility of child abduction, and I wasn't about to take a chance.

For the first time ever in our marriage, I segregated our finances. I got a new bank account with my own credit card—we'd only ever had joint cards. I canceled my old ones—Mary could get her own damn cards. I then sold off the stupid investments with the extra $4,000 loss thanks to Mary.

Actually, all the loss was thanks to Mary. I then drew down our joint line of credit, leaving only $1,000 to withdraw.

I accounted for every dollar that I took out of that account. I used it to pay off our existing credit card balance. I'd discovered that computer addict Mary hadn't been paying Leo's karate instructor, so I paid off that $500 debt too. I brought a $10,000 certified cheque to Mary's lawyer, so Mary couldn't play the victim routine of being left penniless with no lawyer. I also used some of it to pay mental health experts trying to help the kids.

I knew that I was in danger of being portrayed as manipulative and controlling. Yet I really had no alternative. I was protecting the kids and me from Mary. It was she who was manipulating and controlling.

I wasn't putting up with Mary's tyranny. The next day, I took our computer to a friend who was technology-savvy. He had to re-install the Microsoft Windows operating system to get past what Mary had done. Thanks to him, I was able to copy all of my emails, digital photos, and financial files onto a memory stick. I knew she would probably try to deprive me of them again if I didn't have my own copies.

When I came home for lunch, Mary flew out of the house to confront me like a crack addict hunting her next fix. She was livid. She hated not being in absolute control of things, or being defied.

A big problem for terrorists is that when they kill their hostages, they have no leverage. In Mary's rabid campaign to alienate the kids, she'd basically started shooting her hostages. She couldn't understand that the family dynamic had changed. In her openly harming the kids, I was set free from her.

Livid Mary tried to make me feel guilty for what I'd done. Hah! Like that was going to work. This, of course, made her angrier. When narcissistic projection fails, the mirror starts to crack. She tried the guilt trip of "How-can-I-pay-the-bills-without-the-computer?" routine. As if one day without a computer was going to damn the family to bankruptcy and eternal poverty. Sometimes, narcissists don't think when they project—it can be desperation guilt-tripping.

That's when I told her about the finances, and how I would be paying the bills myself. Instead of letting her do it by herself, as it had been. I also told her about the line of credit, and how I was going to account for every cent.

Mary went berserk. She ran into the house screaming, "Daddy's taken all the money, kids! He's leaving us bereft!" It was clear that she'd been priming the kids for the big confrontation since discovering the missing computer. Hillary ran around the house screaming, hitting walls, and swearing. She seemed to be on the verge of a major mental breakdown. The boys went to get Leo's practice martial arts weapons to confront me with them—a hard wooden samurai sword and Filipino fighting sticks. Hugh was cursing at me, too.

I ended up being confronted at the top of the stairs and threatened by my own sons. Hillary started to address me by my first name in a very contemptuous tone. I put a stop to that immediately— she wasn't completely beyond my influence at that point.

Mary loved it. After having obviously primed the kids and then set them off when she ran in the house screaming, Mary got to diffuse the situation that she had created. Just like Hugh's sleeping, again. She was the magnificent mother calming her children who were outraged at their horribly cruel father. Another home run by the Babe Ruth of alienators.

I hope some of the Pharisees we call family judges read these words. This is the sort of crap that men divorcing narcissistic wives can be forced to endure every single day. These are the sort of mothers that these judges force children to live with when they maliciously and unlawfully deprive them of their fathers. I suspect that many high-conflict divorces involve women like Mary. Between ex-wives like this and our fundamentally biased judges, what hope is there for children and fathers?

None, really.

The next day I brought the computer back. When I spoke to Mary about moving it to neutral ground, she said that she had always been willing to do so. She made a comment about being the bigger person and not wanting to cause problems, unlike me. I couldn't keep track of all her lies and projection.

I also tried to talk to her about doing a financial handover in terms of bills to be paid, etc. She refused to talk to me about money. She gave excuses like she didn't want to talk to me, she didn't feel comfortable talking to me, and that she didn't feel safe with me.

This was the start of a definite trend—Mary always refused to speak to me about money, with a couple of minor exceptions.

This period was extremely stressful. I'd gone from seeking psychological counseling for Mary to asking the military medical authorities for some help for myself. You know it's bad when a military guy is asking to see a shrink. I was fortunate to be given an appointment to see the psychiatrist who was Chief of CF Mental Health Services, a full colonel. After I emailed him to tell him what I was dealing with, his brief response on 8 May included this:

> I must state, however, that you are suggesting that your wife is abusing your children. Have you discussed this with Children's Aid Services?

Yes, sadly.

I saw the Colonel a week later. Despite the stress, I got a reasonably clean bill of mental health. No pills, no stress leave. Fit for duty.

The weird stuff at home continued. One day, Mary tried to behave like June Cleaver, the sweet mother from the old *Leave it to Beaver* TV show. Mary was in her "Notice me! Notice me! Look how I am behaving" mode. She carried on with the kids as if nothing was wrong, reminding Hillary to return a call to my mother, and other rubbish. It was *Twilight Zone* weird. Mary couldn't maintain the act – it lasted only a few days, after which she turned ugly again.

One day (16 May), I came back from work and found all of Mary's panties hanging up to dry in the ensuite bathroom in my bedroom. It was *Apocalypse Now* Vietnam jungle sort of spooky-weird. What was that about? Was she trying to remind me what I was giving up?

Pasties CAS was taking its negligently slow time in getting to our kids' predicament. Or at least to hearing my side of the story. However, I suspect that the possibility of a CAS investigation and of a parenting capacity assessment had spooked Mary. She wanted Hillary far away from any expert who might figure things out.

Once again, as I was about to leave for work, Mary laid another surprise on me. Mary said that Hillary (who still refused to speak to me) would be going out of province to spend the summer with Mary's younger sister. The sister who would walk away from conversations or drop the phone for no reason. Well, for no reason that I understood at the time. I now know that these were responses to narcissistic injuries.

What was strange was that Mary had usually spoken negatively about her younger sister. I expressed my surprise—I told Mary that I thought she didn't like her little sister. Well, there went the outrage again, how much she cared for her younger sister, blah-blah-blah. Mary's comments had been due to narcissistic grandiosity. Mary had to be superior to her younger sister.

So there it was. Mary had undermined Hillary spending the summer with my parents. This might have helped Hilliary learn to become independent. Instead, Hillary was being hidden away where I couldn't get to her. This would keep Hillary dependent upon Mary.

I should point out that this is what my life was like each and every day. Watching Mary take the kids away from me and wondering what despicable thing she'd do next.

It was a nightmare.

The CAS intake worker that I ended up dealing with was Ms. Malyssa B. Kruël. She wasn't a nice person, and she was in no rush to see me. I didn't end up getting to speak to her until nearly a month after I first contacted Pasties CAS. When things were so bad that I called 911.

I first met Kruël—a social worker—at the Pasties CAS building in Krakton on 28 May 2008. As I described the situation, I knew from her blossoming, condescending smile that Kruël wasn't going to believe me. She seemed to be just another ignorant, arrogant, condescending feminist social worker.

These appear to be job requirements.

After I had told her what Mary had done and was doing to the kids and me, Kruël specifically asked, "Did this make you angry?"

What sort of question was that? My estranged wife was abusing the kids and teaching them to hate me. She was being emotionally abusive to me, too, and had been a deadbeat mom for around a year. I was slightly confused as to why Kruël was asking this. My response was something like, "Well, a bit at times, I suppose."

Mistake. What 'sweet' little Ms. Malyssa B. Kruël the social worker did after our meeting was write in her case notes that I had "admitted to some anger issues." For the record, I made no such admission. I had displayed considerable restraint throughout Mary's raging campaign of alienation and abuse. She's lucky she wasn't married to another man; she might not have been so lucky otherwise.

Kruël also asked me if there might be another possible reason for Mary's playing video games. I knew right away that Kruël had already spoken to Mary and had taken her side. I call a CAS to report my estranged wife's child abuse, but the woman social worker speaks to the woman child abuser first. Have to get *her* side of the story before the man has a chance to tell the truth.

To verify this suspicion, I used Mary's bogus 'clinical depression' excuse to test the waters. "Let me guess," I ventured, "she was clinically depressed." Kruël was clearly pleased that I had gotten the answer right. She missed the dry, mild sarcasm in my voice. Oh goodie! I might be able to train this stupid man after all!

The problem is, Kruël's own mandatory regulations stated that she was supposed to have spoken to me first. She was, in effect, admitting to at least incompetence, if not actual misconduct. As if this wasn't obvious enough, Kruël also mentioned all the negative things the kids had said about me. Gee, alienated kids who are cult-programmed to reject me have bad things to say about me. A documented clinical indicator. Wow, that's a surprise.

When I voiced my suspicions about Mary having a narcissistic personality, Kruël pooh-poohed me. "Oh, narcissism is in the DSM—we aren't competent to make such a diagnosis, are we?" is pretty much what she said. Tsk, tsk, you silly man – leave the thinking to us social workers.

Cripes. That's a scary thought.

Yet Kruël was also me telling me that Mary was clinically depressed. Depression is also in the DSM. So men can't identify their narcissistic child-abusing spouses, but women can miraculously self-diagnose clinical depression? Maybe Kruël used her feminist "woman's way of knowing."

The officer recruiting process that I underwent included intelligence testing. There clearly isn't any of this to get into social work. Kruël knew essentially nothing about parental alienation. She actually told me that she wasn't qualified to deal with it. This was shortly followed by her telling me she didn't think we were dealing with alienation.

That's like your doctor telling you, "I know nothing about cancer, but don't worry. I'm sure you don't have it." Yeah doc, thanks for that.

Kruël had done her condescending best to convince me that I was deluded (because I was a man). Then she started Phase Two of her devious little routine. In her obviously 'expert' opinion—incredibly, social workers tend to believe they are experts— the kids were at risk of emotional harm due to exposure to divorce conflict. So she ended her brilliant routine with words to the effect of, "So, you agree that we (CAS) should be involved?" She had laid out her great sales pitch.

Only I wasn't buying.

This was toward the end of the meeting. I was trying to fathom what the lay of the land was. I was still working with the assumption that CAS women (and women lawyers and judges) were like the great gals I generally worked with in the military. I was also exhausted and stressed by what I had been and was still dealing with at home. I made the mistake of thinking that perhaps I had failed to properly explain the situation. I couldn't grasp that anyone entrusted with child protection could be so biased, uncaring, and devoid of critical thought.

Surprise! These are mandatory requirements for social workers.

I replied that I would agree to CAS involvement *if it was to deal with the parental alienation and Munchausen by proxy.* That's called a conditional agreement: I don't agree unless the condition is met. Since Kruël admitted to incompetence regarding alienation, that condition could only be met by CAS bringing in outside psychological expertise. Which it more than refused to do, even though it had already admitted to me that this was required in such cases. Since the condition was not met, *I never gave my consent to Pasties CAS involvement.*

I couldn't convince the biased and arrogant Kruël as to what was actually going on. In my parting words, I civilly thanked her for her time, and I stated that it appeared *that we did not agree.*

I emphasize this, because it's an important point. Not only did little social worker Kruël scurry to her case notes afterwards to write that I had admitted to "anger issues." No, that wasn't enough. She also wrote that I had agreed to Pasties CAS involvement in our case.

Here is some of what Kruël wrote in her notes—these are her exact words:

> *Worker* [Ms. Malyssa B. Kruël] *advised at this time CAS concerned with children living in home with them together and that for them someone needs to leave – advised* <u>NOT</u> *CAS role to get involved in separation / custody / access however due to the*

concern for kids in this CAS feels may need to remain involved to monitor the children and their supports until concluded -

- he agreed -

... worker [Kruël] again advised <u>NOT</u> involved in separation / custody / access but concerned as environment <u>NOT</u> okay for children with them [Mary and me] living together & that was the protection concern due to emotional harm.

Advised worker [Kruël] not taking position on who had to move out at this time only that they should <u>not</u> be living together.

My, my. Kruël seemed to be going out of her way to secretly document that Pasties CAS wasn't interfering in divorce and custody. Those were her underlines in her own case notes, not mine. To abuse Shakespeare: methinks she doth protest too loudly. We're not interfering in divorce. No, sir. Not us. Wouldn't dream of it. Especially not on behalf of mother. No way. Not the women of Pasties CAS. And we especially aren't trying to interfere with child custody. No siree! This must be true, as I, Malyssa B. Kruël, have written it in my little Pasties CAS case notes.

What an absolute bloody liar.

I have a background in tactics and tactical analysis. I also have spent a career analyzing, interpreting, and following orders and regulations. It wasn't hard for me to eventually figure out why Kruël falsified her notes to state that I had agreed to Pasties CAS involvement in the divorce.

Pasties CAS willfully refused to perform its mandatory child protection functions. These are the only real reasons it existed. Thus, it had no business being involved in the divorce. Unless. A big "unless." Unless Mary and I *voluntarily consented to its involvement.*

Children's Aid Societies legally exist under a law called *The Child and Family Services Act (CFSA)*. It is not a coincidence that the *CFSA* section (s.) 27.1, under the heading "Consents," states:

*A service provider may provide a service to a person who is sixteen years of age or older **only with the person's consent,*** *except where the court orders under this Act that the service be provided to the person.*

I added the bold emphasis. To justify the purely malicious interference in our divorce, Kruël had to falsify that I had agreed to Pasties CAS involvement. Of course Mary would agree. Kruël would have let it be known that Pasties CAS would work on her behalf in the divorce. Wink, wink, nudge, nudge. Even if Kruël did not do this, Mary would want to appear to Kruël as the most devoted and caring mother. Mary would do whatever Ms. Malyssa B. Kruël, the 'expert' social worker, thought was best. Then, Kruël would think highly of Mary as a mother.

Welcome to Mary's mirror, Kruël.

Pasties CAS cannot produce any document with my signature on it saying that I consented to its involvement. There never was consent. Anything else is a lie, pure and simple.

I went back to work. Kruël's bias and treachery were still beyond my ability to digest at this point. I stayed there afterwards for four hours, crafting a substantial email to Kruël regarding: what was happening; why it was occurring; and how Mary's narcissism would result in her manipulating Kruël. I also outlined a rudimentary child care plan based on Dr. Gardner's protocol. It involved my parents and sister Elizabeth providing interim neutral grounds, as the kids knew and loved them. At least, they did before Mary worked her magic with the help of Pasties CAS.

It was a waste of four hours. I didn't have a frame of reference to appreciate the deceitful and manipulative nature of the child protection world. The feminist child protection world. I couldn't fathom how Kruël could not understand what was going on. A CAS was supposed to protect children. I'd done my preliminary reading—alienation was harmful child abuse, as was Munchasuen by proxy. Why wouldn't a child protection agency already know this?

Life at home was horrible. The kids had completely rejected me. Whenever I entered a room, Hillary would silently lead the boys out, like some sick Pied Piper. It was getting warm enough that the kids were starting to use the backyard trampoline. I could hear them laughing and playing outside my bedroom window like normal kids. Only whenever I was present, it was like a switch went off. Bang! Hard-cold silence and rejection.

The first book concerning parental alienation that I ordered was Dr. Doug Darnall's, Ph.D. (real name), *Divorce Casualties: Protecting Your Children From Parental Alienation*. I believe it was the 1st edition. Here's what I learned from Dr. Darnall:

- alienation does lasting damage to children;

- the target parent's responses can make the alienation worse;

- there is a brainwashing aspect to alienation;

- alienated children are typically unaware that they are being manipulated;

- by the time the children have come to side with the alienator, it is usually too late to prevent significant psychological damage to the children;

- alienation does life-long harm to children;

- alienation can be insidiously subtle;

- the most extreme type of alienator is an *obsessed alienator*, whose fervent goal is the complete destruction of the other parent's relationships with the children;

- research (Clawar & Rivlin, 1991) had shown that five percent of children victims become alienated beyond the point of no return (there is no form of cult deprogramming that can save them);

- once alienated, these children are lost to target parents for years to come; and

- Dr. Darnall had never encountered an alienated child who grew into an emotionally healthy adult.

Just bloody marvelous.

Was there any way that this could get worse? Even with my background, Darnall's book was a bit of a brutal read. The kids had already been badly harmed by Mary's alienation, and it was likely getting worse by the day. This harm would be life-long. There was a five percent chance that kids that I had loved since birth would forever reject me. I can't say that ignorance is bliss, but truth can be brutally unpleasant.

My fight against Mary's alienation had, until this point, been mostly instinctive. After Darnall, it was informed. It was professional. Although I was constrained by acting honourably, whereas Mary was not, I knew that I was the only hope the kids had.

I resolved to see this through until the bitter end. It remains bitter. After more than five years, it still isn't over. It won't be until I have Hillary back. I do not abandon my children, even if they abandon me.

When a narcissistic wife is in full alienating mode, every fiber of her being, her every waking thought, her every action and word, spoken and unspoken, is devoted to destroying you as a parent. She is obsessed with destroying you as a parent. Darnall's words, as sobering as they are, don't fully capture the relentless alienation barrage that target parents have to deal with. Instead of help, fathers get the local CAS. Might as well pour gasoline on a fire.

Around the beginning of June, I again accused Mary of working to alienate the kids from my family. She denied it, of course. However, she managed to find a way to simultaneously deny it *and* alienate the kids from my family. Her response—loud enough for the kids to hear, no surprise—was that she encouraged the kids' relationships with my parents *no matter what they might think of her.* Mary the perpetual victim. Dad's parents don't like me. I am a victim. Feel sorry for me. Defend me. Nanny and Poppa are bad. They are against your mother; side with me.

Mary also blamed me for the estrangement between my parents and the kids. Narcissistic projection at its finest. However, she became belligerent when I wasn't buying her BS story. How inconsiderate of me not to be part of her mirror. When she became verbally abusive, I politely informed her that I was leaving because she was being verbally abusive. I went to my bedroom.

Well, that sort of behaviour doesn't sit well with an enraged narcissistic woman. Mary just followed me into my own bedroom and began verbally abusing me while blocking the door. So I couldn't escape her again. My asking her three times to leave my bedroom had no effect. I had to wait until Mary had called me an asshole enough times (loud enough for the kids to hear) until she finally went away.

I think it was around this time that Mary betrayed something very important. When trying unsuccessfully to pick yet another fight with me, Mary at one point seemed anxious. She said that one of us had to leave the home, or the CAS might take the kids.

Ms. Malyssa Bloody Kruël. It appears as if she was inciting Mary to drive me from my home under implied threat of child apprehension. Mary certainly did not need any extra incentive, believe me. Regardless, it now seems apparent that this CAS worker was acting to incite serious child abuse. I would later learn of allegations that supported this assessment.

A couple of days later, Mary informed me that she had booked a flight for Hillary out of province for the summer. Guess who had to pay for the ticket? Her sense of entitlement again. Also, either Mary or Hillary came into my room when I was at work and stole my picture of Hillary. Speaking of pictures, Mary had taken our wedding photos off the wall without consulting me. It had to have been her—the kids wouldn't have touched them.

I had begun going to Ottawa on weekends to be with my parents. It was heartbreaking being in my house, and I needed time with people who cared about me. One Sunday when I was returning, Mary left stuff out for me to find in the living room. She had had an early birthday party for Hugh without informing me of this, so she could exclude me. It had been a bowling birthday party. Along with wrapping paper and cards, she'd left the bowling pin that Hugh got to keep with signatures from all his friends on it.

After I went to bed, Mary cleaned the kitchen and living room. By itself, this would have been a rare treat. Mary had made certain to leave the bowling pin in the middle of the kitchen island like a mini-Stonehenge. She wanted to be certain I knew: she'd excommunicated me from the family. The kids don't love you anymore. They love me.

I think my lawyer, Daphne, was starting to recognize what exactly I was dealing with. I wasn't exaggerating. She wanted to move things along. Unfortunately, narcissistic estranged wives tend to be utterly unreasonable and uncooperative. Mary continued to refuse to speak to me about money.

She seemed to think that she could buy whatever she wanted, and I had to reimburse her. She wasn't quite hoisting aboard that she would have to live within a budget, as did I. Mary actually bought a hers-and-hers double cell phone package for herself and Hillary, and expected me to pay for it.

That was like asking me to buy a beyond-line-of-sight tactical communication system for an enemy! Needless to say, I didn't pay.

Mary needed me to be the villain who had abandoned the family, including financially. If she and I agreed to a reasonable support package, this would have destroyed her victim mirror. So she'd just say things like she didn't feel comfortable discussing money with me, and then would try to lay some guilt trip on me. Which wouldn't work, so she'd get even more upset.

Daphne wanted to get an interim custody agreement done between Mary and me, so that I could get out of the house. Always the guy who has to leave. The ever delightful Kruël was pressuring me to leave the house. It started at our second meeting on 4 June, when I still foolishly thought that it was merely a matter of trying harder to explain things. Maybe she had a thick skull. Kruël was very abrupt with me, ignored what I had to say and quickly let me know it was "the opinion of the society" that one of the parents had to leave the house.

In that instant, it became blindingly obvious that this "one" parent was the male parent: me. Kruël was letting me know that I had to get out of the house. Just to be certain, I said something like, "Let me guess. It's me that you want to leave the home."

Kruël hesitated. I could see that she was trying to avoid openly admitting to what she was doing: trying to drive me from my home and the kids' lives. After she had thought about it, she replied something like, "That would be best." I was then under no illusions as to her utterly malicious involvement. I wasn't sure about the rest of Pasties CAS. I couldn't crack the code as to why Kruël was doing this. It just did not make sense.

A CAS worker must record every meeting they have with their 'clients' (i.e., victims). Kruël never recorded the existence of this brief meeting in her case notes. She wanted to leave no evidence of her treachery. She was not acting in good faith, and that is an important fact.

I had resigned myself to having lost the battle to prevent the alienation in the first place. However, losing a battle does not mean the war can't be won. On Daphne's advice, I was preparing to move out and fight this through the courts. Mary continued to refuse to discuss a financial agreement with me.

This proved to be a bit of an obstacle. Daphne told me in no uncertain terms not to move out without a financial agreement. It would be looked upon negatively by a divorce judge. (So would being a man; we're talking Canada here.) I couldn't move out. Only Kruël didn't give a damn about my circumstances, because as it turned out all she wanted to do was ensure Mary won full custody and child support.

The Women's Club: membership has its privileges.

By the 10th of June, I was having some limited discussion with Mary regarding custody. Under Daphne's lead, we had come to an informal interim custody sharing agreement through the lawyers. Mary discussed taking the boys out of province to see her mother for a couple of weeks, which I supported. Mary had started her "we must respect the boys' wishes" routine, but only their wishes not to be with me. 'Respecting' a kid's wish to reject a parent is a classic clinical identifier of an alienator, once they've turned the kid against the target parent.

When I mentioned that I wanted to be with the boys in Ottawa for Fathers' Day, Mary loudly said, "So you want to further increase the stress on the boys by making them do something they don't want to?"

Just another guilt trip—now wanting to be with my own sons was evil. When I told her that I expected her to encourage the boys to adhere to the custody schedule, Mary then said she wanted to talk to her lawyer, to see if Hugh had to visit with me. When I told her my moving out was conditional on her honouring the custody agreement, she said she wanted to speak to CAS. Mary was not happy in a big way.

Mary's lawyer was named Lisa Loveless-Hartt. She was the sort of woman who'd stick a stiletto in your back, smile coldly, and not bat an eyelash as your life slowly drained away, your eyes growing dim at the sunset of your existence. If I was a woman child abuser who was alienating my children from their father (with CAS help), Loveless-Hartt is the lawyer that I'd want for myself. I wonder how Mary came up with Ms. Loveless-Hartt's name? Could it have been that perhaps sweet Kruël gave Mary a helpful hint as to which lawyer might be a good choice for an alienator?

The next day Mary begrudgingly agreed that I could have the boys that weekend. She then mentioned that she had been taking the boys to a therapist named Doug Smith. That was the first I'd heard of it. According to Mary, he didn't want to see either me or her, just the boys. Yet another lie to keep me from telling a therapist how she was using him. Protecting her mirror— look what a caring mother I am, getting the boys help for the harm their father has caused them. Only she was the one causing harm. Now with the help of Kruël and Pasties CAS. Just like with Hugh's sleep, it was déjà vu all over again.

When I told Mary that it wasn't appropriate that she take the boys to a therapist without consulting me, she merely said that she had spoken to Kruël about it. Kruël supposedly thought it was a good idea. No surprise there—Kruël clearly didn't want Hugh and Leo to have a loving father in their lives.

I also let Mary know that since Leo's birthday was occurring during my time, I would be organizing it. I wanted to prevent her from excluding me as she did for Hugh's birthday. I didn't try to exclude her, even though she then told me that we shouldn't be together for the kids' special events. By this she meant that she should go and I shouldn't.

Hillary had, by now, been away for a few weeks. Without her acting as her mother's proxy alienator, Leo started coming back to me. I spoke to him about his birthday, which I made into a paintball party. That's an awesome birthday for most 12-year-old boys. However, Mary couldn't accept Leo having a loving relationship with me. She'd made her plan.

The 13th of June was to be my first weekend with the boys. I was planning to take them to Ottawa. Without consulting me, Mary allowed a friend to stay with Hugh until her parents came to pick her up, which would be well into my departure time. She knew she'd be out of the house, and that this would delay my departure to Ottawa, a 2.5 hour drive. After his friend finally left, Hugh refused to come with me. He was in a fit of tears. He threatened to call Kruël if I tried to make him come. He even had her card. It was clear that Kruël had been coaching the boys to contact her if I tried to have a relationship with them.

Kruël was an authority figure—her implied message was that your Dad wanting to love you was bad. She might have worded it like, "... if your father tries to force himself on you..." It doesn't matter—to a kid, the message amounts to the same thing.

Mary had made sure to be out of the house for the evening. I couldn't force Hugh to go, but I couldn't leave him alone in the state that he was in. He was in angst over the mental torture that his mother had subjected him to, both directly and indirectly through Hillary. The same mental torture being worsened by Kruël. It was 9:00 p.m. by the time Mary got back. Leo was too tired to make the drive with me. If I had taken Leo, Mary would have used that to say that I didn't care about the kids. She was diabolically effective in engineering no-win alienation situations for me.

I ended up going to Ottawa alone. Mary won that round. Or perhaps I should say that Mary and Kruël won that round.

I got a glimpse of what was coming next on 19 June. A quote from Shakespeare seems appropriate:

By the pricking of my thumbs, something wicked this way comes.

It was wicked, that's for certain. I overheard Mary talking to Leo about Hillary coming back early from out of province. This was the first that I had heard of it—Mary hadn't intended to tell me. A few days later, Daphne mailed Mary's lawyer, Loveless-Hartt, a proposed interim financial support arrangement. We never heard back from them until October. Loveless-Hartt was in no rush to see an honourable and fair interim settlement. Why should she, when the Women of Pasties CAS were on her client's side?

Just sit back, and let the Evil Sisterhood do its dirty work. Feminist social workers, lawyers, academics, and judges. By the pricking of my thumbs...

The next Friday that I was to take the boys to Ottawa (27 June), I knew that I was only going with Leo. He had continued to come back to me since Hillary had left, but Hugh was too far gone. He had needed protection from child abuse, but instead he got Kruël and Pasties CAS. Even though it was a rotten day, Mary had to take the boys to the beach. She had to make a good impression before Leo went with me. Can't have Leo going and having fun with Dad.

When I went to leave with Leo, I couldn't find my car keys. I looked for an hour before realizing what Mary had done. She had recently found part time employment at the liquor store and had gone to work. When I called and asked if Mary had taken both sets of keys, she had to "go and check." Lo and behold, yes, she had, in fact, taken both sets of keys. By 'accident,' of course. Mary couldn't even be bothered to apologize. Why should she? She had meant to do it.

So it took $30 in cabs and an hour's delay before I could leave with Leo. Out of an entire summer of supposed joint custody, all I ever got was that one single, solitary weekend with Leo.

How I treasured it. I still do.

Leo was relieved to see my parents again. He loved them, and he learned that they still loved him. Leo got to play with their new dog. He and I watched the *Napoleon Dynamite* movie on TV. We laughed. We still laugh about that movie, even today.

Sure enough, didn't Mary call and ask to speak to Leo. She couldn't leave him alone for even one evening with me. I knew she'd use the call to alienate. I also knew that if I didn't let her speak to him, she would have used that fact to alienate when Leo got home. "Daddy doesn't want me speaking to you. He doesn't want us to be together." Damned if you do, damned if you don't. So I gave Leo the phone as he was trying to watch his movie.

Mary must have talked to Leo for 15 minutes just before bedtime. Leo kept saying, "No, I'm alright Mom." She was up to her old tricks using suggestive questions. "Are you alright, Leo? Are you sure, Leo? You'd tell mom if you weren't okay, wouldn't you?" Refusing to accept the answer. All the time implying that there must be something wrong, as Mary was so concerned about him. She wanted this to be the last thing on his mind before he went to sleep. Go to sleep, *Mommy's worried about you being with Dad and his family.*

Leo asked me at one point if I ever felt like my body got separated from my mind. I was a bit alarmed at this (I didn't show it). This to me suggested that the alienation was causing Leo to disassociate from his environment. Looking back, maybe this was what he had to do to survive his mother's abuse. To be there in body, but elsewhere in mind when she was trying to program him. Which was pretty much every chance she could get.

Unprompted, Leo also spoke to my Mom about the pink shirt episode. It had clearly bothered him, just as his mother and his sister had intended.

The next day, Leo and I went on a wonderful guided tour of some neat caves, and otherwise had a great father-son day. Mary made sure that would be the last one Leo would have for well over a year. With, of course, a little help from the less-than-sweet-and-innocent Kruël, Pasties CAS, judges, and the Government of Ontario.

But I'm getting ahead of myself.

6

Something Wicked
This Way Comes

If you wish to strengthen a lie, mix a little truth in with it.
—ZOHAR

In retrospect, Daphne did have one glaring 'fault' as a lawyer. She was and is a decent person. I don't think she was capable at the time of believing that Pasties CAS could be acting in such a purely malicious manner. Not that she was a fool; she wasn't. But the Pasties CAS bias and duplicity were so diabolical that it was difficult to believe such wickedness could exist. Perhaps other lawyers have been similarly deceived. Women would have to be utter scum to be so despicable as those from Pasties CAS. And we all know that little girls are made of sugar and spice, and everything nice.

Yeah, right.

It would have been some number of months before Daphne could have gotten us a date for divorce court. We could get before a judge in a child protection case much sooner. So Daphne thought CAS involvement might be good. There was logic to the way that Daphne was thinking. Unfortunately, it was based on the mistaken belief that Pasties CAS was acting in good faith. It was not.

It so very, very, very was not.

Part of high-conflict divorces is often to get an expert, court-appointed parenting capacity assessment. The person who does the assessment is the key to it all. In military language, it is a center of gravity. You and your adversary teeter about your centers of gravity. These are what truly must be attacked and defended, even if they are somewhat conceptual.

A big Toronto court case regarding alienation had recently made the headlines: *JKL v. NCS*. An alienating father had lost custody of his son in it. If you think that feminists were happy about this, think again. This case threatened their belief that only women can be victims, and hence there is no such thing as alienation.

There were two experts who testified in the case—American Dr. Richard Warshak, Ph.D. (real name), and Toronto expert psychiatrist and psychoanalyst Dr. Sol Goldstein (real name). I decided to try and get Dr. Goldstein to do our assessment, as he understood alienation and apparently had credibility with judges. Many therapists sadly lack this expertise.

On the 8th of July, Daphne and I had a telephone conference with Pasties CAS. On the Pasties CAS side of the telephone conference, it was Kruël, her supervisor, Wanda Whitless, and their lawyer, Biff Legalese Jr. I sensed Kruël's hostility from the start—it was rather evident in her ugly tone of voice. The essence of the CAS position was (from Kruël's actual case notes):

> *Advised that CAS was concerned for further emotional harm and the risk of the situation becoming physical.*

> *Advised that CAS initiating application to court for supervision order to move the domestic situation along. Advised that would consider withdrawing the application after this was remedied if the children are okay with the process.*

The situation being, of course, my not having surrendered full custody (and therefore child support) to Mary. And abandoning the kids to serious child abuse by leaving my own home. However, Pasties CAS would reconsider this if the situation 'resolved itself,' and the kids were happy with it.

There it was, then. Since the kids were alienated and rejecting me (except Leo, temporarily), for the kids to be 'happy' about it meant that I had to leave the home ASAP. Which Daphne said not to do until Mary signed an interim financial agreement. Which Mary refused to do, because she needed me to be a villain.

Kafkaesque would be a good way to describe the situation.

I was being threatened by the women of Pasties CAS. What I was *really* being told was this: get the hell out of the house and give up the kids, or we're going to take you to court and screw you like there's no tomorrow. Their lawyer was clueless as to what they were really up to. He was representing a pack of bullies and liars. In high heels, tights, and lipstick.

Daphne thought the telephone conference had gone well, and that Pasties CAS was going to support Dr. Goldstein's involvement. She thought that Pasties CAS cared about the kids. It wouldn't take too long for her to see what I was seeing. Pasties CAS was working exclusively for the best interests of Mary. Just like any good feminist coven would.

The next day, Mary informed me that I had to pay all her expenses as she hadn't worked in 20 years. This was a lie, as she had been working full time just two years previously. She told me that she didn't have to find a job. She told me that I had to maintain her in the lifestyle to which she was accustomed.

Pure narcissistic entitlement.

Mary refused to agree to use Dr. Goldstein, and insisted on a female doing the parenting capacity assessment. She obviously felt good about the Evil Sisterhood. Mary also mentioned the Pasties CAS supervision order court application. She smiled knowingly while mentioning this. It seemed her new best friend forever (BFF) Kruël had let Mary in on the plan to excommunicate me from the kids' lives. Wink, wink, nudge, nudge.

It was around this time that Mary also gloatingly informed me that kids' wishes are important, that courts will appoint a lawyer for kids, and that courts respects kids' wishes. She might as well have told me that the plan was that: a) she alienates the kids; b) Pasties CAS gets the Court of Injustice to have a lawyer appointed to parrot the kids' 'wishes;' and c) the court will give her the kids and excommunicate me as the kids 'wish.'

Mary and Kruël: alienation BFFs.

Mary also told me that since I hadn't left the home (because she refused to discuss support payments), she considered our informal joint custody agreement to be null and void. She said I could see the boys whenever I wanted—knowing full well that she had alienated them. I didn't accept this and continued to try to adhere to the agreement. She was trying to trick me into voiding our interim custody agreement.

I informed Mary that I was seeking a posting to Ottawa around late summer. This was what we had originally planned. My reasoning, which I didn't share with her, was simple. If I won custody of the kids, I would be a single parent until Mary got therapeutic help for her alienating. As a single parent, I would want the support of my family for the kids and me. If I didn't win custody, I would be powerless to stop Mary's alienation. In that case, I wanted to be near family for emotional support during a (more) brutal period in my life.

Mary, as usual, continued to be at her evil best in keeping me from Leo, the only one left who wanted his father in his life. I had given up a gift pair of field-level seats to a Jays-Yankees Major League Baseball game one Friday to take Leo to a cabin for a camping father-son experience. Mary arranged to have Leo go for a sleepover the night before at a friend's house. Mary asked me if this would be OK. Of course, she only ever spoke to me to either try to make me feel guilty, to try and provoke a fight, to gloat about her impending victory, or to alienate the kids.

I knew that if I said no, Mary would exploit this to alienate Leo. She'd find a way to let Leo know that I didn't love him, as I would rather force myself upon him than let him sleep over at a friend's house. So I said yes, wondering how she was setting me up. She was an expert at setting up lose-lose alienation scenarios: damned if you do, damned if you don't.

Mary merely arranged to have the friend's parent return Leo too late Friday night for us to make the drive to the cabin. I had waited hours after work for Leo to arrive, so we could go. I finally left the house that night after Leo returned. I later watched the last inning of the Jays game in a sports bar. Roy Halladay pitched a one-hit shutout for the Jays. As it turned out, Leo had already had a sleepover at the same friend's house two days before, which I didn't know about. He didn't need another one so soon. It was pure engineered alienation. Mary would do whatever it took to deprive me of Leo.

As if I needed a reminder of that.

What was even more interesting was Mary's response when I initially told her about my plan to take Leo to the cabin. She said he couldn't go, as Hillary was coming back the next day. Leo would rather go to that than be with me.

Somebody was up to something—something wicked this way comes indeed! Hillary was supposed to be spending the entire summer out of province. Yet with Mary losing control of Leo, she had to bring Hillary back as her proxy alienator, to keep Leo in the fold. Mary hadn't even asked Leo if he would rather greet Hillary at the airport than be with me. Mary just decided to say it, so it must be true. Hello Sigmund Freud and thaumaturgy. Only it wasn't true, as Leo later decided that he would rather be with me at a cabin. So Mary had to find a way to sabotage it, and thus she engineered the sleepover.

The Friday night at the cabin was supposed to start my two-week summer vacation with Leo. I planned to take him to Ottawa to be with my family. I had to go into work that Monday morning to finish off one minor affair, after which we'd leave.

Mary had developed a devious plan to ensure that wouldn't happen. Welcome back, Hillary, and hello again, Kruël!

I went to work Monday, 14 July 2008 to tidy up that loose end before leaving with Leo for Ottawa. Work took me a bit longer than planned, and I came home around noon. Mary was at work. Since I didn't see Hillary or Hugh, they must have been downstairs in Hillary's room. I found Leo on the computer, still in his pyjamas.

That wasn't a good sign.

Leo said that he felt sick, that his chest hurt, and that he wasn't up to going with me. The poor kid—how Hillary must have taken the red-hot tongs of guilt to his gentle conscience. Going with me was being disloyal to the Cult of Mary. Yet, to stay loyal, he had to lie to me about being too ill to go.

I used humour to relieve Leo's obvious discomfort. I wasn't going to put him in a guilt tug-of-war as the rope between Mary / Hillary and me. I told Leo with a big smile on my face that there was no way I was leaving without the only one of my kids who was still talking to me. I told Leo that if I had to call an ambulance and have him wrapped up like a mummy to get him to come, I would.

Leo smiled at the thought and said that he'd go with me. The relief on his face was obvious. Yet he had to report this to Overlord Hillary. So down the stairs Leo went. After a few minutes of being worked on, up he came to tell me that he really, really didn't feel well enough to go.

So I tried the humour again. I told Leo this time that even if he was so sick that he keeled over and died, I still wouldn't leave without him. I told him I'd put him in a coffin and hire a hearse to take us to Nanny and Poppa's place in Ottawa. He couldn't help but smile at that one, too. Again, he agreed to come with me, and down he went to report to Hillary.

Hillary couldn't take failure in her assigned mission any longer. She came storming up the stairs to confront me. Like her mother, Hillary spoke loudly enough to be heard throughout the house. She accused me of trying to take Leo against his will. Great, now Hillary was projecting. It was she who was trying to force Leo to do something against his will. I almost begged Hillary to stop what she was doing. I told her she was hurting Leo more than she could understand.

She wouldn't stop. She then went down to her room to call Kruël. In retrospect, it appears that this was part of the plan. Now, Leo genuinely didn't want to go, as he didn't want to be the cause of fighting in the family. Hillary was part of her mother's emotional terrorism cell—do what I want, or I'll hurt everyone. It was obvious why Mary had brought Hillary back—to prevent me from going on vacation with Leo. If Hillary couldn't complete her mission, Kruël would be on standby. Never fear.

While Hillary called Pasties CAS, I drove to their building to speak with Kruël. Only Kruël wasn't there, as she had already raced to my place after Hillary's call. It was almost as if she was on standby for the call. It was a well executed plan, if that's what it was. So back I went.

I came into my house to find Kruël and another towering Pasties CAS intellectual, Ms. Calliope Klewless, waiting for me in my living room. Klewless was to be the follow-on CAS worker after Kruël finished putting the boots to me. She was apparently named after Calliope Herringbone, a main character from the famous 1980's evening soap opera *The Successful Inter-Generational Fruit of His Loins*.

As they say, the apple doesn't fall far from the tree.

Klewless and Kruël, a terrifying pair of child protection geniuses if ever there was one, had entered my house without my permission. Kruël was an ugly sort of hostile towards me. When I told her what was going on, she refused to believe me. When I tried to show her a reference from Dr. Warshak's book *Divorce Poison*, she accusingly asked me if I had left it around for the kids to find (which I hadn't).

Kruël insisted that I leave without Leo. She was clearly using an implied threat of child apprehension. She had falsified my consent to Pasties CAS involvement. She had tried to deceive me into abandoning the kids, and then bullying me into abandoning them. When that failed, she illegally entered my own home to help Mary alienate them from me. Kruël was abusing her child protection authority to deprive me of Leo when I had legal custody of him.

Remember the 1987 case of *Tremblay v. Tremblay* with Madame Justice Trussler that I previously cited? Based on this, I have no problem saying that Kruël and Pasties CAS were not just aiding and abetting Mary's child abuse.

They were also co-perpetrating it.

So there's no mistake, I'll say it again. Pasties CAS willfully and maliciously perpetrated the abuse of my children as enshrined in Canadian case law.

There was nothing legal that I could do. If I refused, I would just be maligned. Kruël would probably have called the cops or something. That would have looked terrible once I got to court—Dad is violent, CAS had to call the cops! I didn't want Kruël to maliciously apprehend Leo and throw the boys into foster care, either.

I left for Ottawa, alone and broken-hearted.

After I came back from Ottawa, I had to check with Mary about her finances. She wasn't telling me anything. I knew she was trying to engineer a situation where she could make it seem that I had abandoned her and the kids financially. I had to continuously remain aware, so she didn't succeed—that would also have looked very bad in court. She was to later do a couple of rotten, dirty tricks to me to try and achieve success in this regard.

I contacted the folks at breakthroughparenting.com. I ordered their custody planning guide, and I later took their comprehensive parenting course. I was starting to get myself prepared for court. Life continued to be awful at home, as now even Leo didn't want to speak to me. They'd worked on him for the two weeks that I was away on "vacation," the poor little guy. He'd been 12 years old for less than a month.

I received my copy of documents that Pasties CAS submitted to the Ontario Court of Injustice. There was no doubt as to the malice and bad faith of Pasties CAS. I couldn't understand why these horrid women were being so evil, but there was no mistaking it.

For a child protection (child abuse) case, a CAS must fill out something called Form 8B. It tells the court why the CAS thinks that a child is in need of protection as defined in the *Child and Family Services Act* (*CFSA*). This can be due to physical harm, sexual abuse, not providing the necessities of life (e.g., starving the kids), emotional harm, etc. It can also be due to the risk of these types of harm happening.

The *only* thing that Pasties CAS told the court was wrong in terms of the *CFSA* was that Hugh and Leo were at *risk* of emotional harm under clause 37(2)(f.1). Thus, Pasties CAS effectively told the court that the boys hadn't been harmed yet. The grounds for this were set out in an affidavit dated 17 July 2008, which Kruël swore to the court was true.

So, a woman social worker whom I consider to be a manipulative liar and a child abuser, and who falsified her own case notes, swore she was telling the truth.

Jesus, give me a break.

Our *Charter of Rights and Freedoms* alleges that Canada is founded on principles that recognize the Rule of Law. Divorced dads know this is a cruel joke, but let's pretend that this is true for a bit. According to the *CFSA*, emotional harm is legally defined as occurring when a child demonstrates:

> (*i*) *anxiety,*
>
> (*ii*) *depression,*
>
> (*iii*) *withdrawal,*
>
> (*iv*) *self-destructive or aggressive behaviour, or*
>
> (*v*) *delayed development,*
>
> *and there are reasonable grounds to believe that the emotional harm suffered by the child results from the actions, failure to*

act or pattern of neglect on the part of the child's parent or the
person having charge of the child;

This, by the way, is almost the exact same language that Dr. Amy Baker used to later explain why parental alienation constituted emotional child abuse in her expert evidence. Justice Trussler clearly nailed it back in '87; Dr. Baker confirmed it in '09.

Pasties CAS offered absolutely no actual evidence—none—that the boys were at risk of displaying any of these symptoms. Right off the bat, their court application was garbage. I maintain that social workers are not competent to make such psychological assessments, no matter what they claim. Social work, in my experience, is an utterly bogus discipline. It has no rigorous, coherent, and testable underlying theory.

"It's always the man's fault" isn't exactly a rigorous theory.

What Pasties CAS asked the court for was an order of six months duration placing Hugh and Leo with Mary, subject to its supervision. (Technically, Hillary was not part of this, as she was over 16.) Only it proved to be 'supervision.' I was to have reasonable access, at the discretion of Pasties CAS *and consistent with the children's wishes*. Pasties CAS made certain to never define "reasonable." This way "reasonable" could mean "never." That is, in fact, what they really intended. That is, in fact, what happened.

There it was. Pasties CAS was helping Mary alienate the kids from me. It knew the kids had already rejected me, and therefore the boys' 'wishes' would be that I never had access. Pasties CAS was trying to drive me from the kids' lives, and they were lying through their teeth about it. They knew I would never have access under the conditions they sought.

They were right.

Kruël's affidavit was a subtle smear job, with innuendo and the like. Before I get into what she wrote, there are two little legal facts that I must mention.

The first is *CFSA* s. 15.(6) – Protection from personal liability. It reads:

> *No action shall be instituted against an officer or employee of a*
> *society for an act done in good faith in the execution or intended*
> *execution of the person's duty or for an alleged neglect or default*
> *in the execution in good faith of the person's duty.*

Good faith can be defined as "with honest and sincere purpose." This Good Samaritan clause is intended to protect child protection workers who unintentionally screw up. I can understand this. If CAS workers were getting sued all the time, they might be afraid to act for fear of being sued. A child who is genuinely in need of protection might not get the protection he or she requires if the CAS workers were afraid to act.

The danger with this is that now CAS workers are above the law, and they know it. There is no legal test for a CAS worker's good faith. (Following their own mandatory *Standards* might be a good start.) Thus, Kruël could do virtually whatever she pleased. She knew she had a get-out-of-jail-free card in the Good Samaritan clause in the *CFSA*.

The other legal point comes from the *Criminal Code of Canada*. Under the heading of "Misleading Justice" it states:

> *131. (1) Subject to subsection (3), every one commits perjury who, with intent to mislead, makes before a person who is authorized by law to permit it to be made before him a false statement under oath or solemn affirmation, by affidavit, solemn declaration or deposition or orally, knowing that the statement is false.*

According to s.132 of the *Criminal Code*, perjury can get you up to 14 years in jail. However, we divorced dads know that the Rule of Law is a sad joke. My experience is that not only is it OK to lie to the court if you are a woman, but that the court actually wants and rewards perjury. So long as it complies with feminist teachings. There is a reason why I wrote "Court of Injustice." It rewards women who lie that women are victims and men are villains.

In fact, the court more than rewards these women; it conspires with them.

So let's examine what Kruël wrote. I'll include the paragraph numbers of her affidavit, for reference (I'll substitute-in the false names where necessary):

> *8. As the investigation unfolded Mr. McConaughey's concerns about Ms McConaughey were elevated to include Munchausen Syndrome by Proxy, Narcissistic Personality Disorder and her being responsible for Parental Alienation Syndrome.*

This was her second paragraph under the heading "CURRENT CONCERNS," which formed the main body of her affidavit. When you read it, this carries with it a subliminal message: I was exploiting CAS, they didn't believe me, so I made even more outrageous claims against Mary.

> *10. I interviewed all of the children, each on two (2) separate occasions and each expressed a concern and fear of their father. Although they did not advise of any physical abuse or fear of physical harm, they expressed fear of his control and perceived authority in the home. Leo, at one point, was visibly shaky and verbalized his fear of meeting with me due to his belief that I could decide that he would have to live with his father.*

This paragraph alone shows why competent experts, and not social workers, are needed for cases of alienation. An expert would have recognized that, since the kids were all telling the same story, *they had been coached as to what to say to Kruël*. Further, with absolutely no physical violence, their fear of me was particularly suspect—it had been implanted or at least coached.

Leo's reaction was better explained by the terrible guilt he felt about having to lie about me. Lastly, an expert would have likely recognized that the kids' implanted fear of my "control and authority" was in fact the narcissistic projection of Mary's own self-shame onto me through our kids.

Mary was the only one who had control and authority over the kids. How could Kruël write that I had control and authority over a family that had completely rejected me? I had none. Absolutely zero.

> *11. Each child advised that they were very upset with Mr. McConaughey for the manner in which he announced the separation and the intrusive nature, which he sought, supports [sic], such as calling the police and the Society. Children have advised that Ms McConaughey has encouraged them to talk to and spend time with their father to work through their anger with him.*

First of all, note the terrible punctuation at where I added "[sic]." This basically means "I didn't make this mistake; I found it this way." This is actually important to note. Lawyers tend to be very competent in their working language. This and their knowledge of the law (except in Canada, where the law is irrelevant) are their bread and butter, so to speak. Daphne had asked to see my counter-affidavit with enough time in advance of the filing deadline so that she could review it for writing errors. She was pleasantly surprised to discover that my writing needed no correction.

The primary Pasties CAS lawyer for the case was Mr. Winston Whiffleby. There is no way that such a poorly written paragraph had seen the scrutiny of such a kind gentleman. I was to later learn that the Women of Pasties CAS had this scam down to a science. They knew the last moment that Mr. Whiffleby had before having to file documents with the court. They were getting their court documents to him at the last possible moment. This way, he wouldn't have time to review them before having to file them. They played him like a violin. A Stradivarius, in fact.

An expert reading Kruël's words in paragraph 11 would have noted something else. Not only were the kids again all saying the same thing, which further suggested that they had been coached as to what to say. An expert would have also recognized that Mary was implanting the suggestion that they were angry with me. She was deviously reinforcing the existing alienation she had already caused, while seeming to look like a saint. This was actually narcissistic mirroring: I didn't alienate the kids. Their father alienated them from himself, and super-Mom me is trying to help them overcome this.

> 14. The [boys'] school, based upon their involvement with the parents and children, do not believe that Ms McConaughey is exhibiting Munchausen traits, as the boys have no attendance issues..."

According to *CFSA* s. 15.(3).(a)., it is a function of a society to investigate allegations or evidence that a child under 16 is in need of protection. To investigate is to seek the truth in some matter. This is distinctly different than to refute. To refute is to disprove an argument or to undermine an individual's assertion or position on some matter.

Munchausen by proxy is a complex area of psychiatry. By using the opinion of a middle school principal—someone completely unqualified—instead of an expert psychiatrist or psychologist, Pasties CAS was not investigating my allegation. It was maliciously trying to refute it. There's a difference. Remember, Pasties CAS' Ms. Mindy Moorecock had already admitted to me that Munchausen by proxy required psychiatric expertise.

15. I have found these children to be extremely bright, intelligent and perceptive and all three of them have displayed the ability to communicate clearly, what they perceive to be the dynamics in the home. To our knowledge at this time, they do not present as being influence [sic] by either parent in their statements to me.

At least Kruël got something right. Unlike her, the kids were rather intelligent. Sadly, this didn't guarantee them immunity from alienation. Kruël was implying that the kids were not alienated, as they were too smart. So let's believe everything they say, without question. She did this after documenting clinical evidence that any competent expert would have recognized as the kids having been deeply influenced via alienation.

16. Ms. McConaughey presented as very open and honest with me when discussing her concerns for how the relationship was ending and the concerns presented to the Society with respect to her...

Kruël might as well have written, "Don't believe the man. Believe the woman. Feel sorry for her." While she was undermining my credibility through innuendo, she was simultaneously trying to portray Mary as the Patron Saint of Truth.

18. Ms. McConaughey has not expressed concerns with for [sic] the children in Mr. McConaughey's care, however has stated her concern for the children being forced to have access with Mr. McConaughey given their expressed fears...

In her paragraph 10, Kruël cites the kids as having all told her I had never hurt them. Then in her paragraph 18, Kruël cites Mary as having no concern about the children being with me. By Kruël's own affidavit, there is absolutely no reason to deny me access to my own children, which was my right (remember: in Canada, the Rule of Law is a joke).

20. ...Based upon the stressful nature of the home and the current difficulties that he has with his children, the Society does recognize that Mr. McConaughey will require assistance and support in developing a healthy relationship with all of his children.

Kruël was effectively implying that I was at fault for the kids' alienation, and that I had to have Pasties CAS oversight, or I'd never overcome my problems.

Also note how Kruël used "the Society." This is supposed to have been *her* affidavit. She may have been duly authorized to speak on behalf of Pasties CAS. However, I doubt it. It sounds more like character assassination by feminist committee, which went out under Kruël's signature.

> 21. *Although Mr. McConaughey, to our knowledge had not sought out supports for himself, he has played an active role in contacting various professionals who he feels would best address the issues he perceives to be the most problematic and concerning for his wife and children.*

Kruël swore as true the fact that I had not sought out supports for myself. This was despite knowing that I had seen the Chief of Canadian Forces Mental Health Services of my own accord. Having lied in a document she swore was true, Kruël then went on to say that I had contacted various professionals to help me deal with alienation and Munchausen by proxy. Professionals who, according to the Ontario Government's own definition, would constitute "supports."

When you fabricate a story, it's hard to keep your lies straight. Pasties CAS and Kruël certainly couldn't. Watch:

> 22. *At this time, the Society has verified the concerns about adult conflict in the home resulting in the children being emotionally impacted and is concerned with the risk of **further emotional harm.***

I added the bold. Kruël was stating that the children had already suffered emotional harm. But wait a minute! Back in Form 8B, the only thing Pasties CAS applied to protect the children from was the *risk* of emotional harm. That meant that Pasties CAS had already effectively said that no harm had yet occurred. There was a different box to check if the application was to protect children already being emotionally harmed. In which case it would have meant a psychiatrist or a clinical psychologist had made such a determination.

The Women of Pasties CAS were so busy crafting their evil fiction of me, that they couldn't keep their lies straight. There's more.

> 23. *The Society has further identified elements of **power and control**, most notably in regards to finances. Ms McConaughey is completely financially dependent upon Mr. McConaughey, giving her the perception that her choices in the separation are limited.*

There it was in a nutshell (I added the bold). When I first read this, I thought it was just a brainless feminist smear job. Surely no judge could be so stupid or biased so as not to recognize this.

Little did I know.

It turned out that this paragraph was a critical clue in unraveling a bigger mystery, but that comes later. What Kruël & Co. at Pasties CAS were doing in this paragraph was almost blatantly admitting that theirs was a purely malicious, utterly bogus child protection application.

All this had ever been about was getting Mary the child support payments. Anything else is a lie. Kruël and Pasties CAS were using feminist lingo to tell the women judges of the court that this was really about getting Mary the child support money.

Her child support money.

If you think I am being unfair, think again. Remember that incident nearly 13 years previously? When Mary was abusing Hugh by sleep depriving him, and she hit me? Here's how Kruël chose to portray it. Remember— Kruël swore that she was telling the truth:

> 25. *The Society worries that the stress of the separation will escalate, possibly creating a climate within the home, which has the potential for physical altercations. The Society has knowledge of one incident admitted to by both parents where Mr. McConaughey physically assaulted Ms McConaughey.*

Given the smear job, the implication was that this was a recent incident. Kruël conveniently neglected to mention that it had been Mary who struck me, thus provoking the relatively minor incident. Kruël also neglected to mention that Mary had been the subject of a child protection investigation in Nova Scotia around that same period.

Here's another important bit:

> 27. ...*The Society is in agreement with Mr. McConaughey that a parenting capacity assessment and psychological assessment of both parents, at their expense, would be useful in developing a permanent custody and access plan. Both parents have made suggestions for assessors and the Society at this time is in support of an assessment.*

If Kruël was to be believed (she wasn't), Pasties CAS supported a parenting capacity assessment. Only, they didn't seem to care who did it. It wouldn't take long for this lie to reveal itself as well. Psychiatric/psychological expertise was needed to investigate the types of child abuse that I reported, which Ms. Morecock had admitted to me. Pasties CAS was receiving tens of millions of dollars to perform its child protection functions. By saying "at their expense," Kruël effectively admitted that Pasties CAS was refusing to perform its investigative child protection function.

I guess $35 million a year or so didn't buy much child protection. Lots of child abuse, perhaps, but not much child protection.

> 31. *I make this affidavit for no improper purpose or motive.*

This was Kruël's last paragraph in her affidavit. It is my opinion that this, in and of itself, constitutes blatant perjury. Kruël's true purpose was to get an alleged child abuser *her* child support payments, deprive two boys of a loving father, and to screw me in divorce.

There's more. If a CAS is going to ask the Court of Injustice to abduct a father's children from him, there's another form the CAS has to fill out. We can't steal kids from their fathers without filling out the paperwork, can we?

It's Form 33B: Plan of Care for Child(ren) (Children's Aid Society). The CAS has to let the court know how it won't care for children that it and the court will abduct from the father. For the Pasties CAS Plan of 'Care,' I'll ignore much of the Orwellian conditions Pasties CAS was asking the court to impose upon me. There are a few gems worth mentioning, however.

> 6.2 *The Society is recognizes* [sic] *and is concerned that the parents conflict and inability to come to a form of resolution with respect to their living arrangements and custody of the*

*children is placing these children at risk of both **physical** and emotional harm.*

I added the bold. Well now, isn't that interesting? Pasties CAS said that the boys were at risk of *physical* harm, too. The problem was, it never bothered to apply to the court to protect the boys from physical harm. Even though they now were claiming that this risk existed.

A rather amazing oversight, wasn't it?

Pasties CAS was obsessed with maliciously excommunicating me from the kids' lives so that Mary could 'win' the kids and the child support. Kruël / Pasties CAS just couldn't keep the lies straight. They were such terrible liars, they even repeated the lie a second time!

> *7.1 This is the first involvement with this family. These parents each have their own representation and the Society is concerned that the process of the separation may be very time consuming resulting in the children being exposed to more conflict and in turn placing them at risk of both emotional and **physical** harm.*

It's not as if Pasties CAS can explain away this lie of a risk of physical harm (again, my bold) as having been a typo. Not given that they felt obliged to repeat it. Also, note that they claimed they were concerned that the boys were being exposed to conflict. This clearly implies that the conflict was exclusively between Mary and me, which later proved to be a HUGE legal point.

Except for the Rule of Law being a pathetic joke in Canada, of course.

What the Women from Pasties CAS were really saying was: read between the lines! Mother needs the money. We're maligning Dad as a bit of a wife beater. You have to kick Dad out and get Mother *her* child support money. Wink, wink, nudge, nudge. Monty Python style.

Then there was this little gem:

> *9. Children are to remain in the care of their mother, who had been their primary caregiver.*

This was another lie. Mary sure as hell hadn't been the "primary caregiver" during the last year of the marriage. Further, "primary caregiver" is a specific term for divorce proceedings. It's a means of discriminating against fathers in the matter of divorce custody, and belittling their traditional contribution to their families. The Women of Pasties CAS clearly thought they had better spell it out one more time. Just in case they got a really dumb judge: it's all about getting the woman *her* child support!

It should be blatantly obvious to even the most skeptical reader that Kruël and the Women of Pasties CAS were executing a purely malicious legal action. It was solely against me. It should be equally obvious, even to a village idiot, that the Pasties CAS case was so suspicious as to be utterly unbelievable. Surely, no judge could ever agree to what Pasties CAS was asking?

If you think that, think again. This is Ontario, Canada we're talking about. Not some place where the Rule of Law is actually respected.

In addition, Pasties CAS stated that "one of the parents" had to leave the home. Let's see. "Poor" Mary was supposedly completely financially dependent upon me. (Even though she had her own job by then, and I was supporting her and the kids like I always had.) Pasties CAS wanted the judge to give Mary the kids. Did Pasties CAS really not care if the judge then decided to throw Mary (and thus the kids) out of the house and onto the streets, instead of me?

Rubbish. Kruël had already let me know it was me that Pasties CAS wanted out. That putrid pack of CAS liars didn't have the honour to be truthful about what they were really up to.

Pasties CAS also asked that a lawyer be appointed for Hugh and Leo. In Ontario, part of the Attorney General's Office is the Office of the Children's Lawyer (OCL). It is an organization run by women, for women. While pretending to represent the best interests of children.

At least, this has been my experience.

The OCL would then parrot the alienated boys' 'wishes,' making it three against one (me). The OCL didn't let Kruël or Mary down. You can't let a little thing like serious child abuse interfere with a woman getting *her* child support money.

I wrote a strong counter-affidavit. Unlike Kruël's, mine contained only the truth. Not that truth is welcome in a Canadian court. I won't bother with the details, other than to say that I intended to implement Dr. Garnder's recommended protocol for countering severe parental alienation. Not to be confused with the Pasties CAS standing protocol for ensuring it.

I should disclose something. Before I entered the court, I used to believe that Canada was a just place. I used to believe that our judges were decent people. I used to believe our judges upheld the ideals of truth and justice. I used to believe our judges cherished the Rule of Law and the principles of fundamental justice. I used to believe our judges were worthy of our respect.

Now, I know better.

Judges can be a bit pompous at times. For example, a judge would never write something like, "The defendant was obviously biased." It isn't proper. The judge may appear biased in stating that the person who was obviously biased was in fact obviously biased. To be unbiased in judging other people who are obviously biased, judges have to have a test. No less an authority than the Supreme Court of Canada endorses and applies the test of the Honourable Justice de Grandpré in this regard.

Here's the simplified version of the de Grandpré test for bias: what would a reasonable person who was informed of all the facts think? I kid you not. Thank God we have judges to come up with these brilliant ideas.

Where would we be without them?

So, in dealing with bias, the judge imagines what a reasonable person with the same information would think. This imaginary person then finds that the obviously biased person is in fact biased. The judge can then find that the obviously biased person is in fact biased. Because the judge did not find that the obviously biased person is in fact biased. Because that would have been biased. The judge's imaginary friend did it for him or her, which makes it okay. Now the judge clearly isn't biased. Notwithstanding that the judge didn't really come to the conclusion of bias, even though he or she really did.

At least, this is my interpretation of the Supreme Court of Canada's *Baker v. Canada* [1999] 2 S.C.R. 817, paragraph 46. However, I am not a Professor Emeritus of Law. Thankfully.

For the record, I have applied the test of the Honourable Justice de Grandpré in all my assessments of judges. Because they were obviously biased. However, I can't say this, as I might appear biased in stating that the obviously biased judges were obviously biased. So I am not.

My imaginary friend is. I'm just reporting it. Sort of. Just like our unbiased biased judges.

As one who had been badly abused by obviously biased judges—I didn't say that—, at least I get the satisfaction of exposing their malice or incompetence (or both) for all to see. By using their own words against them, no less.

In the same *Baker v. Canada*, the Supreme Court cites Justice Iacobucci (paragraph 63):

> *An unreasonable decision is one that, in the main, is not supported by any reasons that can stand up to a somewhat probing examination. Accordingly, a court reviewing a conclusion on the reasonableness standard must look to see whether any reasons support it.*

I'm going to take this Supreme Court principle and expand it ever-so-slightly so that it covers both decisions *and* actions of judges. You can do this, too. Within your de Grandpré test of what the judge did and said, all you have to do is subject this to somewhat probing examination. Is what the judge did reasonable, especially given what she said in my case? Don't believe me, and especially don't believe the judge or anyone else.

Judge for yourself.

There is one little last bit from judges that can and will be used against them in the Court of Public Opinion. It comes from the Canadian Judicial Council's *Ethical Principles for Judges*. Page 19, paragraph 5. Here it is: *law is not just what it says; law is what it does.* So, in conducting your own de Grandpré test (with somewhat probing scrutiny) of judges, you must look past what they have said. You must scrutinize **what they have done**. Should you find a meaningful discrepancy or contradiction between what they have said and what they have done, you should suspect deceit.

I think the evidence is sufficient that I can reasonably voice my suspicion of collusion between Kruël and Mary. If it wasn't active and explicit, it was likely tacit but understood. Kruël and Pasties CAS were more than completely on Mary's side.

They were now leading her campaign to excommunicate me from my children's lives.

The court hearing happened on Wednesday, 20 August 2008. Pasties CAS didn't bother to send anyone other than its lawyer, Mr. Whiffleby. They didn't need to—the Evil Sisterhood had things well under control. The judge was Justice Gertrude Gavelbanger. She entered the courtroom and made initial pleasantries, after which she stated that she was concerned about the kids.

I knew it wasn't going to be good. Gavelbanger was going to stick it to me—she had already made up her mind before entering the courtroom. It was that obvious. There's a word for this: prejudice. In theory, it is supposedly a very bad thing for a judge to be prejudiced. I learned the hard way that women judges are *expected* to be prejudiced and biased. Against men.

And to lie like hell about it.

I didn't just write that. My imaginary friend did, but only after a somewhat probing examination.

Gavelbanger wasn't interested in anything Daphne had to say. Gavelbanger ignored my affidavit, especially my citing experts that kicking me out would be the absolute worst thing she could do in a case of alienation. Gavelbanger was going to kick me out of my own home with only one hour to pack my bags. Daphne had to fight to buy me until Friday to get my things out of the house. Gavelbanger wanted nothing to do with Dr. Goldstein. She was happy to bring in the OCL as Pasties CAS had asked.

Funny thing, though. Gavelbanger also said towards the end that I had raised serious concerns that had to be addressed, or something like that. How could she say something like that but want nothing to do with Dr. Goldstein? There was a logical contradiction between what she was saying and what she was doing. She was *saying* one thing. Yet what she was actually *doing* was the exact opposite of what a right-minded and reasonable person would expect.

Gavelbanger issued a 'temporary' order, against my will and without trial, that I move out of my own lawfully owned home and care of the kids be given to Mary. Under Pasties CAS supervision, of course. I was to have (no) access as duplicitously requested by Pasties CAS. Despite what Gavelbanger said— reasonable access—, what she effectively did was take my sons from me against my will, issue a no access order against me, and violate our rights and freedoms.

There are some interesting points here. First, by law a person in Ontario cannot advance to divorce proceedings while child protection action is ongoing. Pasties CAS had shut me out of divorce court, courtesy of Gavelbanger's order. Second, there is no authority under the *CFSA* for a judge to throw a parent out of his or her own home. If a child is genuinely in need of protection, the child has to be removed from the parent's care. If this was a genuine child protection hearing instead of malicious divorce interference, they should have taken the boys from our home.

There's a word for what Gavelbanger did: tyranny. In fact, one might almost be tempted to say that she displayed a sense of entitlement in ordering me from my own home without authority. That darn sense of entitlement again.

Third, I later went to ottawadivorce.com. There, I learned that the two biggest factors for child custody in Ontario divorces were status quo (i.e., the current status) and the title of "primary caregiver." There's that primary caregiver term again. By granting the Pasties CAS request, what Gavelbanger *did* was more or less give Mary insurmountable status quo and primary caregiver child custody advantages for the future divorce trial.

Pasties CAS certainly understood this. It's why they took me to court in the first place. What about Gavelbanger? Does anyone really believe that she was utterly ignorant of fundamental legal facts that I could easily find on the internet? To become a judge, she must have: had a university degree; graduated from law school; articled; been called to the Bar; and worked as a lawyer for at least 10 years. In fact, Gavelbanger had worked for the OCL and as a Crown Prosecutor.

Could such a person, then appointed to the bench as a judge, be so ignorant of the law or devoid of intellect as to not realize that she was prejudicing my divorce prospects? Especially given the blatantly fraudulent nature of the Pasties CAS' application?

Maybe Gavelbanger didn't just have a sense of entitlement. In retrospect, she was cunning, manipulative, and dishonest, too. It wouldn't take long for her to confirm this for me.

Consider the 1999 Ontario decision of Mr. Justice Henry Vogelsang in *Children's Aid Society of Hamilton-Wentworth v. S.(S.)*.

According to Justice Vogelsang, a court can indeed find that a child is in need of *CFSA* protection at a hearing without trial. This is to be only used in exceptional circumstances, with agreed-to facts, and when the outcome of a trial is a foregone conclusion. Exceptional circumstances might be something like a mother or a father who was previously convicted of killing a child.

Pasties CAS admitted that I had never hurt the children. The kids and Mary said the same thing. I adamantly disputed the alleged Pasties CAS 'facts.' (Indeed, I maintain that the Pasties CAS application and Kruël's affidavit constitute willful and malicious perjury.)

Not only did Gavelbanger have no authority to order me from my own home, she had no authority to limit my access by effectively declaring that the kids were in need of protection via an interim order. She had no lawful authority whatsoever to issue any order under the *CFSA*. Not even a 'temporary' one.

I'll say it with military candour. Gavelbanger was acting with pure malice and lying through her teeth about it. Either that, or she was far too stupid and ignorant of the law to ever be allowed to perform the duties of a judge. In fact, I'll later show that she would have to have been moron-stupid if she wasn't acting maliciously. It borders on inconceivable that a woman judge could be so stupid and ignorant of the law.

Gavelbanger wasn't that stupid. She couldn't have been.

I didn't write this, either. My impartial and reasonable imaginary friend did. As a result of a somewhat probing examination. After being in possession of all the facts.

For the record, he wears clean underwear, too.

7
Something Wicked This Place Stays

But, indeed, the dictum that truth always triumphs
over persecution, is one of those pleasant falsehoods
which men repeat after one another till they pass into
commonplaces, but which all experience refutes.

—JOHN STUART MILL

I did much of the moving myself. What I didn't take, I might never have seen again. I left virtually all of the jointly owned property. I didn't want the kids to suffer. The only major appliance I took, with the help of a friend, was a second deep freezer. I moved my stuff into the basement of another friend. He had generously given me the use of his house while he was away on training to deploy to Afghanistan.

I had less than two weeks before I had to report for duty in Ottawa. I was forbidden from going into my own home. I was forbidden from seeing my own children. All because I was a man who loved his kids and tried to protect them as the law said I must.

It is a crime to be a loving father in Ontario, Canada.

I wasn't ready to paint Klewless with the same brush as Kruël. Not yet. Before I left, I took Dr. Warshak's book *Divorce Poison* and extracted a few pages worth of the most relevant passages. I emailed these to Klewless. Dr. Warshak is a well-respected expert in the field of alienation. His book is easy to read, and an invaluable resource for a target parent. Any reasonably intelligent adult would have immediately suspected alienation in our case given those extracts.

Calliope Klewless did not suspect alienation in our case. However, in her defence, I can state that she had a nice hair perm and great nails. These are clearly the priorities for child protection workers.

I went to Ottawa as an outcast, a pariah from my own children. I found a place to stay, and I started my new job. Before I left, I had to get Daphne to tell me what fair support would be for Mary. Mary still refused to speak to me about money. Daphne gave me some numbers, I subtracted the mortgage and other expenses that I was paying on Mary's behalf, and I paid her the difference—$1,600 per month.

I literally had to force support payments on my estranged wife. Maybe that was the element of "power and control" with regards to finances that Kruël had spoken about. You know us evil men— always trying to dominate our ex-wives by giving them support dollars. Power and control at its very finest.

Ironically, I realized that it was I who was being dominated via power and control. By women. Please remember this—it becomes very important later on.

After I received the Pasties CAS court documents, it was obvious to me that feminism was the malignant influence behind what was happening. Sun Tzu advised in his classic *The Art of War* to understand both yourself and your enemy. Then you need not fear the outcome of a hundred battles. Despite it being too late, I resolved to understand my true enemy: feminism. And I'd analyze it from a military perspective. There were going to be no kid gloves in this.

I don't think such an analysis has ever been done before. Most senior military men would rather have their annual prostate exam than have to study feminism. This explains why these men have failed their country without ever having realized it. Why this is so comes later too.

All in good time.

I also continued to learn as much as I could about narcissism and alienation. I had to learn how to protect the kids from Mary. As it turned out, this also directly related to my analysis of the true nature of feminism. The two streams of inquiry converged. Mary wasn't going to be the last woman narcissist I'd have to deal with. Not by a long shot.

When I spoke to Daphne about the undefined nature of my "reasonable" access, she thought that every second weekend sounded reasonable. Not to me, but I'd take what I could get. I was writing each kid every week to try and keep a toehold in their lives. Having your kids alienated from you and then taken from you is like getting your heart ripped out. I hadn't heard a word from them when our next court date came on 5 September.

There was a different judge this time, Madam Justice Granimiah Everso Slough. She was an instant improvement over Gavelbanger. However, in and of itself, that isn't necessarily much of a compliment. Slough probably should have gone into baking cookies for grandchildren; law appeared to be outside her core strengths.

And not by a little.

Not being content with the evil they'd committed to date, Pasties CAS kept it going. It gave Mr. Whiffleby last minute instruction that they were against any parenting capacity assessment whatsoever. Having had me kicked out of my own house and excommunicated from my children's lives, the liars were now trying to shelter Mary from expert scrutiny. This, even though they had admitted to me that psychiatric expertise was needed in such cases! The Women of Pasties CAS left poor Mr. Whiffleby hanging in the wind; it was a completely ludicrous position.

And, of course, no one from Pasties CAS came to support their lawyer. It wasn't hard to see that Pasties CAS was hiding its personnel from the court. They wouldn't have lasted 30 seconds under any genuine form of scrutiny.

Slough appeared to be a nice lady. However, she seemed to take a let's-find-a-way-to-help-this-family-with-their-problems sort of approach. Our "problem" was that I couldn't find a judge who could even recognize the Rule of Law, let alone respect it and apply it. If Slough had genuinely respected the Rule of Law, she would have rescinded Gavelbanger's tyrannical order on the spot.

She did not.

To her credit, Slough politely shot Mr. Whiffleby down when he gave the CAS line about the kids doing better with me gone, that an assessment would be an unnecessary stress, blah-blah-blah, etc. Slough thought it unreasonable to say that things were so bad that an order of protection had to be made, and then say that no assessment was necessary.

However, Slough didn't appear to suspect anything. She wasn't part of the Evil Sisterhood. I think she failed her entrance test and was too naïve to comprehend that she had even taken it.

Mary's lawyer had taken the sweet and innocent we'll-do-whatever-Pasties-CAS-suggests position. Not a bad strategy when the Evil Sisterhood is on your side.

Slough seemed intrigued about our desire to employ Dr. Goldstein. Perhaps she'd heard about him via the *JKL v. NCS* case. The OCL hadn't bothered to appoint a lawyer yet—mother had the kids, and father was kicked out; what's the rush? The matter was adjourned until 8 October.

I will say this: although she appeared to me to have never read a law book in all her life, Justice Slough was not acting maliciously as a judge. Initially, that is. All good things must come to an end, as the saying goes.

And so they did. Eventually.

After hearing nothing from Pasties CAS, I emailed Klewless on 15 September. I wanted to warn her to make certain Mary kept Hugh going to Arrowsmith. I also asked about when I could see the boys—God, how I was missing them—, given that Gavelbanger had ordered that I have "reasonable" access. Beyond Arrowsmith, Klewless just replied that the kids didn't want to have access with me, so there was nothing Pasties CAS could do because of the court order.

That would be the court order which Pasties CAS had maliciously obtained.

The vile Women of Pasties CAS couldn't have cared less if the boys ever saw their father again. In fact, I believe they absolutely did not want me ever seeing the boys again. They wanted me completely out of the boys' lives.

As for Arrowsmith, Mary wouldn't have wanted Hugh to continue. This would have damaged her mirror. So she alienated Hugh against this too. The Women of Pasties CAS were too happy to have Hugh drop out of Arrowsmith, but they made certain to have the OCL join in before going ahead with this.

The Women of the OCL should be proud of themselves. It doesn't matter that a kid is deprived of essential help with a life-long learning dysfunction. So long as they feel good about it. To hell with Hugh or the $2,000 it cost for that year.

I wasn't taking no for an answer, so I kept up the emails regarding Pasties CAS exacerbating the alienation. Since I was such an ungrateful man—after all Pasties CAS had done for me and the kids—, Klewless' supervisor had to put me in my place.

This supervisor was Ms. Danica Dunsley. She was the sort who was always too busy being full of herself as a social worker to realize that she wasn't particularly bright. Here's part of what she said to me in her email of 1 October 2008:

> Calliope will forward a copy via mail of our agency complaint procedure.
>
> I have reviewed the interim order through the courts. The order speaks to you having reasonable access in the discretion of the CAS and according to the wishes of the children. Calliope has spoken to the children several times and they continue to tell her they do not want to speak or have access at this time. I understand a children's lawyer has been appointed and has been to speak with the children. The children's lawyer will update the court at next appearance.
>
> I understand at the next court appearance there will be discussions around a parenting capacity assessment. I understand the discussions about an assessment predated our involvement as well a family court application was before the courts before we initiated a protection application. The society supports your choice to do a parenting capacity assessment at your expense.
>
> You raise a concern that the Society is contributing to the abuse of your children. We have diverging opinions on this matter and we believe we are assisting your children during a difficult time. At times, the Society and parents will not agree on issues

and these are sometimes better addressed via the court process.
If Calliope can be of assistance in clarifying information in this
email or answering other questions/concerns, please do not hesi-
tate to contact her directly either through phone contact or email.

Sincerely,
Danica Dunsley

Well, well. Wasn't that ever-so-sweet of Ms. Dunsley to personally address my concerns? St. Danica the Social Worker. Pasties CAS wasn't aiding the abuse of the kids. It wasn't that Pasties CAS and Kruël had perjured themselves. It wasn't that Pasties CAS and Kruël were bearing false witness against me, in violation of the Ninth Commandment. No. It was just that we had a "divergence of opinion." See how silly a man I was being? See how reasonable the Women of Pasties CAS were being?

Since I was getting pretty good at reading between the lines, there are a couple of teenie, weenie little points about Dunsley's email that I noticed.

Like Klewless, Dunsley conveniently ignored the fact that Pasties CAS was solely responsible for getting the malicious court order. Along with its devious conditions to deprive me of all access. Also note how Dunsley mentions the divorce proceedings that Daphne had tried to start. Before Pasties CAS had them shut down via bogus child protection proceedings, that is. Dunsley was rubbing that in my face—you're not getting custody of the kids, and you can't do anything about it. Don't mess with the Women of Pasties CAS.

Also, look at that bit about it being better to address our differences "via the court process." What Dunsley was basically telling me was: "Bugger off. If you don't like it, take us to court. Don't forget what happened to you the last time we went there. The judges are women, too. Love, Danica. Oh, by the way, we're mailing you our complaint brochure. To add insult to injury. Don't worry—we'll ignore it if you fill it out."

Dunsley thought she was being soooooooo clever. She was, after all, a social work *supervisor*. That's better than Jesus and Albert Einstein all rolled into one, for goodness' sake. I mean, we all know that young, unwed, childless women social workers are better parents than any father who's ever lived.

Just ask them.

We'll get to see what a CAS worker speaking to kids "several times" means shortly.

The OCL ended up employing the young and newly married Ms. Didi Righteous-Butterkupps, somewhat fresh out of law school, to be their agent. Apparently, her sister-in-law, Ms. Beyoncé B. Butterkupps, was a lawyer, too, and an elegant one at that. Scuttlebutt amongst the local lawyers was that it really was a matter of preference as to which of the pair was the better of the two.

Regardless, as a lawyer for the kids' best interest, Didi proved to be more than a bit of a bust. Technically, the OCL lawyer doesn't work for the children. The lawyer executes the instructions given by the OCL. Which, in our case, was only ever in the best interests of Mary. Regardless, Didi was very firm in this, although she was also clearly restrained in her ability to openly reveal the truth.

Client-solicitor privilege, of course.

I ended up meeting with Ms. Righteous-Butterkupps the day before the next court date. It took me three and a half hours to go through what had gone on. Since Righteous-Butterkupps had recently started to practice law, it is probably safe to say that she wasn't far removed from the feminist finishing factory. Or, as it's more commonly known, law school.

I believe it diplomatic to say that Ms. Righteous-Butterkupps did not inspire confidence that she was capable of truly understanding the gravity of the situation. Maybe she had gone to the same Princess University (P.U.) Law School as had Justice Slough. I finally saw the lights go on when I explained why we needed to employ Dr. Goldstein and not the assessor that Mary wanted. I explained that cases of alienation needed specific expertise to identify it. Dr. Goldstein had it, but we didn't know whether or not this other person did.

If we used Mary's choice and that assessor said there was no alienation, we'd have a problem. We wouldn't know if her assessor was right, or if it was because her assessor couldn't identify alienation. However, since we knew Dr. Goldstein understood alienation, we could trust his opinion. If he said that there was no alienation, then there was no alienation.

I finally adopted this line of reasoning based on the arrogance that I had been encountering from the women who sought to ruin my life. I was angling for the OCL to root for Dr. Goldstein. In their arrogance, the OCL would think that Dr. Goldstein would come in, tell everyone that the stupid man was wrong, and that mother was a saint. I then wouldn't have a leg to stand on.

I wasn't in court the next day (8 October). Justice Slough, again to her credit, got everyone to agree to use Dr. Goldstein.

She would later regret it.

I think it went something like this—I still wanted Dr. Goldstein. Mary still wanted her expert. Pasties CAS, having looked stupid trying to protect Mary from scrutiny, went back to a position of having no position. So long as they didn't have to pay for someone to do their work for them. So when the OCL came out in favour of Dr. Goldstein (to prove me wrong), Pasties CAS didn't have a leg to stand on. They would have looked even more stupid arguing against Dr. Goldstein, when they were the ones who asked to bring in the OCL. It would then have looked very bad for Mary to not agree to use Dr. Goldstein, when her lawyer had said that Mary would do whatever CAS wanted.

It was an important victory against a crucial center of gravity.

Having lost the fight to keep Mary sheltered from competent scrutiny, Mary's lawyer Loveless-Hartt wrote a letter to Daphne the next day, offering a proposed interim financial settlement. It was a bit of a preposterous offer, and it was their first response to Daphne's letter of offer from back in June. It probably would have looked bad for Mary in the assessment if she had continued to refuse to discuss finances.

The next court date was 16 October. It would dispel any lingering doubts that I may have had about Gavelbanger's malice. Since everyone had agreed to use Dr. Goldstein at the last court date, we had to have another court date to agree on the wording of his retainer letter. None of this is free, of course. Family lawyers might otherwise starve to death.

Gavelbanger must have discovered to her horror that someone hadn't inducted Justice Slough into the Evil Sisterhood. Why, that clueless twit had gone and gotten Dr. Goldstein involved! That could screw everything up.

So Gavelbanger came in and openly wondered what the fuss was about. The kids were doing well now that father was out of the house—the Women of Pasties CAS said it was so, so it must be true! Gavelbanger suggested that we should just dismiss the case. The case had quickly gotten out of hand and was threatening to make her look very bad. She was trying to weasel out of it.

As usual, there were no Pasties CAS personnel in court. They had the young Biff Legalese Jr. lawyer standing in for Mr. Whiffleby. Biff didn't have a clue as to what had been happening in the case. Ms. Righteous-Butterkupps didn't have instructions from the OCL for what to do with such big curves. Daphne, to her credit, wasn't putting up with it. I believe the correct lawyer-speak would be to say that Daphne became "somewhat animated." I gather that this was rather exceptional.

I recall us taking a break, and, after we returned to court, Gavelbanger apologized. She claimed to have misread the court documents and wasn't aware that this session was to agree to the wording of the retainer letter for Dr. Goldstein. Sure. Millions wouldn't believe you, but I do.

Honest.

There was something not quite right about Gavelbanger's apology. It seemed just a bit grandiose and insincere. It was slightly false, just ever-so-slightly magnificent, and it triggered my sensitivity to narcissism. What it brought to mind was Hotchkiss' book *Why is it Always About You? The Seven Deadly Sins of Narcissism*. In particular, something from the chapter on envy came to mind.

When narcissists have an inadequacy exposed, they can shift their grandiosity to the moral realm. They then become a better person than you *in terms of their character*. They can be self-deprecating while superficially praising the person who exposed them to their inadequacy. Daphne's getting "animated" appeared to me to have triggered this sort of response from Gavelbanger.

After 19 years of living with narcissism, I was seeing it in Gavelbanger. I wasn't dreaming it. Her apology fit this moral grandiosity concept perfectly. Great. Just bloody fantastic. All hail Justice Gavelbanger, THE GREAT ARBITER OF JUSTICE AND PROTECTOR OF WOMEN. Abandon all hope, ye men who enter here.

A narcissistic dimension to Gavelbanger's personality would explain her (mis)conduct rather well. She used words like she used makeup: they were completely superficial, and they were spoken to disguise the ugly truth of what she was really doing.

After things got going again and the wording of the letter got sorted out (I think this was the order of things), Gavelbanger noted that I had submitted a Care of Child(ren) Plan, whereas Mary had not. Loveless-Hartt responded that, as previously mentioned in court, Mary was willing to do whatever Pasties CAS recommended. Ooooooh, my client is so sweet and innocent. She does whatever Pasties CAS says. She's in the Evil Sisterhood. Just like we are, Your Honour. Wink, wink, nudge, nudge.

Gavelbanger then said that she was concerned this would put Mary at a disadvantage in the parenting capacity assessment, so she was giving Mary two weeks to submit her plan.

My impression was quite clear: having failed to stop the assessment, Gavelbanger was actively abusing her authority to direct Mary's legal strategy. Yes, a narcissistic woman judge would do this. And yes, she would lie through her teeth about it. Loveless-Hartt wasn't stupid, and said that her client would do so.

You don't upset the woman judge who is actively working in the best interests of the woman. Not when that woman is your client. I still remember thinking that at least Gavelbanger had the decency to not break out pompoms and openly do a cheerleader routine to drum up support for Mary. Sis-Boom-Bah! Win-that-assessment-and-get-your-support-payments!

I later complained to the Ontario Judicial Council about this. They should have won a creative writing award for their excuse. A biased woman judge can cunningly abuse her authority to help a woman child abuser win custody by directing her legal strategy. This is not called judicial bias and misconduct. Maybe in Uzbekistan it might be, but not Ontario, Canada.

Here it is called "ensuring procedural fairness."

That's right. If a biased woman judge isn't abusing her authority to help a woman child abuser win custody of her children so she can further abuse them, then it's unfair to the woman child abuser. Canadian justice at its very finest, courtesy of THE GREAT Gavelbanger and your friendly neighbourhood Ontario Judicial Council.

Mary's Plan of Care was dated 31 October 2008. Now that she had some insight into how the Evil Sisterhood worked, what Mary wrote included:

> ... I would also ensure that the children receive the necessary counseling or community supports that may be recommended by Dr. Goldstein, ...

Throughout our marriage, there have been issues of control and power imbalance. The children have expressed fear of their father as a result of his behaviour directly towards them or myself and incidents that they have observed.

Calling all women! Calling all women! Mother in distress! Mary had obviously picked up on the feminist buzz words. Notwithstanding that this constituted perjury. The sort of perjury that a fundamentally biased Court of Injustice wanted to hear. From a woman. Keep in mind that Mary had now told the court that she would do what Dr. Goldstein recommended regarding the kids.

Lies, lies, and more narcissistic lies. And perjury.

I saw Dr. Goldstein three times in Toronto, that November. I gave him the whole story. I showed him copies of the family photos that proved that I had always been active in the kids' lives. (I had snuck the photos out of the house that summer and had them copied before Mary could think to hide them on me.) I told him that I didn't hate Mary, despite what she had done, and that I was sincere in wanting to implement Dr. Garder's protocol. If Mary successfully underwent therapy, we would have had a gradual return to joint custody. Dr. Goldstein interviewed my mother and sister Elizabeth separately from me.

Dr. Goldstein was an adult psychiatrist. He was a child psychiatrist. He was (or had been) an associate professor of psychiatry at the University of Toronto. He was a psychoanalyst. He had studied psychoanalysis under no less a narcissism authority than Otto Kernberg. Dr. Goldstein had four decades of experience in his field.

I don't think it took Dr. Goldstein very long to figure out what was really going on.

Mary also continued to remind me what a manipulative woman she was. I really didn't need to be reminded. I certainly didn't want to be reminded. On 19 November, I received a package from Daphne's office. In it was mail for me that had been mistakenly delivered to our house in Krakton.

It contained four bills (Mastercard, my military American Express, Bell Telephone, and Bell TV) that arrived to me overdue by a month. Mary, who used to do all our finances, would have recognized that these were likely bills that needed my attention. Instead of forwarding them to me directly, she waited until she could be certain that I would get them past due. Then, to make it worse, she sent them via her lawyer, which then had to go through Daphne, before coming to me.

Mary continued to build her mirror. In it, I was so inferior that I couldn't even pay bills on time.

There was one slight problem with Dr. Goldstein's ongoing parenting capacity assessment. He wasn't allowed to see me with the boys, because of Gavelbanger's malicious order. They could only be with me if they wished it. Which they didn't, due to the alienation. Mary sure as hell didn't wish it, so neither did the boys.

Dr. Goldstein couldn't complete his court-appointed parenting capacity assessment, due to the court order which effectively prohibited him from completing his court-appointed parenting capacity assessment. This probably wouldn't have happened under Sudan's justice system. Not even North Korea's. But this is Ontario, Canada we're talking about.

I emailed Klewless and Dunsley on 1 December, to relay that Dr. Goldstein wanted to see me with the boys but couldn't. Let's see—what would even a village idiot come up with for a solution to this incredible legal conundrum? Maybe ask the court to modify Gavelbanger's order so that the boys had to be with me for the hour that Dr. Goldstein's assessment would require?

If you think this, you underestimate the Evil Sisterhood. Dr. Goldstein could not be allowed to see me with the boys. If he did, it would then be difficult to ignore his report when he identified the alienation. "How can he say there's alienation when he hasn't even seen father with the boys?" Once again, conveniently ignoring the fact that the court had maliciously engineered this to be true. Words used like makeup. Cunning, manipulative liars.

Feminist women liars.

If you find this a bit harsh, consider this. Daphne's legal assistant was Ms. Sunny Smyle, who was an absolute sweetheart. Later, on 16 January 2009, when the issue of Dr. Goldstein seeing me with the boys had still not been resolved, Sunny submitted an affidavit to the Court of Injustice. In it, she wrote:

> 6. I ask that Justice Gavelbanger's order which gives the boys discretion to refuse to see their father, be temporarily suspended

and that the children be compelled to attend the sessions with Mr. McConaughey in order for Dr. Goldstein to complete his assessment.

Never happened. There was no good faith on the part of Gavelbanger. There never was. Just like Pasties CAS. It was always and only about getting Mary *her* child support payments. The Evil Sisterhood hard at work.

· · · · · · · ·

As we go forward for the next half year or so, the story splits into four unequal threads. This is a result of my multiple-front counter-offensive against the abuse of the kids. I'm going to try to keep them somewhat segregated. However, in doing so, there will be a little back-and-forth time wise. I don't think it will be too difficult to follow if you keep the following four story threads in mind:

1. The ongoing malicious, fraudulent, and utterly illegal child protection court action;

2. My hearing against Pasties CAS with the bogus Child and Family Services Review Board;

3. My forensic analysis of Pasties CAS annual reports, the results of which I communicated to the Auditor General of Ontario; and

4. My realization that what Kruël, Pasties CAS, and Gertrude Gavelbanger maliciously did constituted the offences of abduction as per sections 280.1 and 281 of the *Criminal Code*.

I had not heard a peep from the kids since being excommunicated, despite writing them weekly (Dr. Warshak said to "plant seeds"—always keep trying, no matter how bad it seems). I wasn't taking this lying down. I'd been combing through mandatory CAS documents to see what I could find. Always high on one's casual reading list: *Child Protection Standards in Ontario*, and the associated *Ontario Child Protection Tools Manual*. These are mandatory for a CAS to adhere to. The *CFSA* is explicit about this, and these documents say so themselves. For example, the absolute first thing the *Standards* specifically states is:

*The purpose of the **Child Protection Standards in Ontario** (dated February 2007) is to promote consistently high quality*

> *service delivery to children, youth and their families receiving*
> *child protection services from Children's Aid Societies across the*
> *province. The new standards are the **mandatory** framework*
> *within which these services will be delivered. They establish a*
> *minimum level of performance for child protection workers,*
> *supervisors and Children's Aid Societies, and create a norm that*
> *reflects a desired level of achievement. The standards will provide*
> *the baseline for demonstrating the level of performance within*
> *the ministry's overall accountability framework for child welfare.*

My bold. This is actually propaganda from the Ontario Government. CAS social workers are above the law, and they know it. Plus, they're members of the Evil Sisterhood. The *real* purpose of the *Standards* is to lie to the people of Ontario. They covertly contain feminist instructions to the Evil Sisterhood. Sadly, this isn't conspiracy theory, as I'll later demonstrate.

Accountability framework?! That's a laugh.

I was working blind in what appeared to be a very corrupt system. The best plan that I could come up with was to pursue multiple complaints within that corrupt system, but to carbon copy as many important individuals as possible. I thought that additional scrutiny might stop a cover-up from taking place. Was I ever wrong. The Ontario child and family 'justice' system is rotten to its absolute core.

I wrote a letter to the Honourable—it pains me to say—Matilda Rype-Blumers dated 3 December 2008. She was then the Minister of Children Abuse Services. I informed her of what was going on. I informed her that I was going to make a serious complaint against Pasties CAS. I copied the Executive Director of Pasties CAS, Mr. Percival Pryck, and the Ombudsman of Ontario.

Rype-Blumers' office wrote me back and suggested that I try either the Society's complaint process or the Child & Family Services Review Board.

This is part of what I wrote to Pryck when I sent him his copy of my letter to Rype-Blumers:

> *It is my firm resolve that every person at Pasties CAS who either*
> *failed to protect Hugh and Leo from abuse, contributed to*
> *their abuse, or actively participated in their abuse will be held*
> *accountable for their actions or inaction through due process. I*

*shall likewise insist that the Society itself be held accountable for
its reprehensible conduct.*

Due process failed. Perhaps it will be different in the Court of Public
Opinion. It's the only place left in Ontario, Canada with any semblance of
real family justice left. I'd have been better off under Rwanda's justice system
than Ontario's.

Pryck had obviously received his copy of my letter to Minister Rype-
Blumers. His Director of Services, Monsieur Maurice leDouche, wrote me
back, offering to discuss things. As if. They did *nothing* to help poor Hugh
and Leo. Even if Pryck and leDouche weren't in on it, they'd probably
have tried to cover up what their wretched Society had done. I'd seen from
Danica Dunsley's email just how 'sincere' Pasties CAS was about complaints.

I was tired of being lied to by that social work Special Olympics of child
abuse known as Pasties CAS. So I chose the toothless tiger of the Child &
Family Services Review Board. My complaint went to Ms. Siobhan Ball-
Gowan. She was the Board's Stoolperson, and was perhaps a tad too formal
for her farcical position.

When you read the *CFSA*, it doesn't take a rocket scientist to figure out
something. The Review Board is the fraud perpetrated on the people of
Ontario that a CAS can be held accountable. They are not accountable. Just
like their workers, Ontario's Children's Aid Societies are above the law. And
this isn't by accident—it's by design.

Ontario is the only province that shields its child protection agencies
from its Ombudsman. And any other legitimate form of scrutiny. The
Ombudsman publicly said as much in his 20 June 2011, "Who oversees children's aid societies?" thestar.com (*Toronto Star*) article.

Christmas 2008 was approaching. Christmas 2007 had been a near fiasco.
For Christmas 2006, I had spent pretty much an entire night in a line with
other parents outside a Toys-R-Us store. We were all hoping to get one of
the 20 or so new Nintendo Wii game consoles that were rumoured to have
come in. The rumour had been true. I got something like the 19th one, and
the kids had a blast with it.

For '08, I'd taken great care in selecting the kids' gifts. Especially after
what Mary had done to me the previous Christmas. I needed the kids' gifts
to be special. The one gift that I really remember was Hugh's. Hugh loved

water. He loved swimming. He loved kids' fact books about marine animals. I gave him a home-made gift certificate for scuba lessons that I had done up on a computer. I had an uncle deliver my gifts for the kids to them, which he did when he took them out for supper one evening. My uncle usually took us out when he visited us in Krakton.

According to my uncle, Hugh was a very happy kid when he opened his early Christmas gift and saw what it was. I'd hit a big home run. Yet, when Elizabeth visited the boys a few months later, Hugh was indifferent to doing scuba. When I eventually mentioned his liking the gift to him nearly two years afterward, Hugh looked at me as if I had three eyes. He not only didn't remember, he *couldn't* remember. Mary had worked on him. Either directly, indirectly through Hillary, or both. Mary couldn't have me giving a Christmas gift to Hugh that was better than any she had ever given him.

That wasn't part of her mirror.

She had to alienate Hugh against his dream gift. Yes, Mary was that cruel. Were you to ask her about it today, she'd look you in the eye and lie straight to your face. Daphne heard the same thing regarding Hugh's gift from the boys' lawyer, Didi Righteous-Butterkupps. Here's what Daphne actually wrote to me on the subject:

> Didi told me you were spot on for Hugh and Leo was also pleased with his gift. Apparently Hugh is very interested in scuba.

My complaint to Ball-Gowan was substantial. It identified over 40 violations of the mandatory *Standards* (and *Tools*) by Pasties CAS. According to the Rule of Law, there should have been no violations—not even one. These were mandatory under the *CFSA*. The *Standards* are a cruel joke because the Rule of Law is a cruel joke.

Daphne had started advancing the divorce, in anticipation of when the fraudulent and malicious child protection action would be over. Mary and I had to disclose to the Superior Court of Injustice our financial information. Mary swore to the court via her Form 13.1: Financial Statement (18 December 2008) that she was paying the mortgage and other expenses, and was in a monthly cash flow deficit of $974.60. Only she was perjuring herself. I was paying the mortgage, and she knew it. By her own numbers, she had a monthly surplus of about $275. I had the financial records to prove it, not that it mattered.

Thank God I was surrounded by people who loved me and cared for me. Christmas 2008 would have been emotionally gruesome otherwise. It was the first Christmas in 18 years that I had been without the kids. God, I missed them so. There was an emptiness in my life without them.

January came, and I wasn't being especially understanding when it came to Pasties CAS. I was blatantly accusing them of malicious and fraudulent interference in divorce. I couldn't really have Daphne say this in court, as Gavelbanger was in on it. "Excuse me, Your Honour, but my client says you're a cunning, manipulative, dishonourable, lying feminist judge. No, that's not a compliment. Please stop maliciously persecuting him, and spare the kids from their mother's abuse. For a change."

Yeah. As if that would have worked.

Mary remained at the top of her narcissistic form. In early January, Daphne's law clerk, Sunny, contacted me to ask if I was expecting anything from Mary. Daphne had received a package for me from Loveless-Hartt. I had Sunny forward it to me in Ottawa, and it arrived around 8 January 2009

It was the mortgage transfer documents related to that line of credit. They were dated 25 November 2008. Mary would have recognized what they were when the envelope arrived at the house. Like the overdue credit card bills, she delayed them getting to me by routing them via the lawyers. The documents left Loveless-Hartt's office with a cover letter dated 23 December 2008, a month later. Who knows when it actually went in the mail? Regardless, there was no way that the documents would have reached Daphne before Christmas break.

I only had a few days to sort this out. This was complicated by the fact that the house was jointly owned between us, so all the documents had to be jointly signed. Just another dirty trick by Mary to try to make me fail as a provider and financial manager. The Court of Injustice didn't give a tinker's damn about it. Nor did the Superior Court of Injustice. It's okay for women to abuse men in Ontario, Canada.

We had our first divorce case conference with the Superior Court of Injustice on 13 January. A case conference is where the issues in the case are identified. This is where I learned that Mary's perjury in falsely claiming she was paying the mortgage was okay with the Superior Court of Injustice. The court was also indifferent to Mary's trick with the mortgage documents.

Loveless-Hartt told the judge that I was paying Mary $1,600 per month plus I was also paying for "sundry other things."

I guess paying the $900 / month mortgage on a house that I was maliciously driven from was a sundry thing.

The judge was Krakton's venerable Justice Stilton Pugh. Contrary to what you might think, I immediately became fond of the old guy. He was a sharp character. He actually read what the law said, something no self-respecting feminist judge would ever do. He then tried to tell me in an indirect and obtuse way about the odious feminist court bias. But without seeming to do so. He would have appeared biased, otherwise, by having directly told me of the obvious feminist court bias. So he did not; this way, he was unbiased.

Sort of.

Or, in other words, Justice Stilton Pugh was telling it like it was by not telling it like it was. I respected his mature and tasteful approach to the matter, all things considered.

Meanwhile, that bunch of Mensa geniuses known as Pasties CAS was trying to figure out how to get on with the assessment. The assessment that couldn't be completed because of the malicious order that they had been successful in obtaining. My complaint to the Review Board might have been causing the normally arrogant Women of Pasties CAS to become just a little less certain of themselves.

Little did the Evil Sisterhood know how badly they'd upset this snake. They were clearly used to turning fathers-in-divorce into child protection roadkill. They didn't know what to do with one who refused to die.

Sorry—not in this father's job description.

After nearly five months of my relentlessly asking to see the kids, Klewless sent me (after being prompted) this two-sentence email on 14 January 2009:

> *I have spoken to the children and they all received the [Christmas] gifts and have enjoyed them. I believe that they appreciate them as they were excited to tell me what the gifts were.*

Let's see. The boys were consistently saying that they wanted nothing to do with me. Yet they were excited with my Christmas gifts, and appreciated them. What's wrong with this picture?

Nothing that a CAS social worker would see. Any typical parent, however,...

Other than telling me the kids wanted nothing to do with me, this was the first time Klewless had really told me anything about the kids. Two crummy sentences. I guess protecting her nails from the keyboard was far more important than letting a father know how his abused kids were faring.

I had to shame Klewless to get more information out of her. Nearly a month later (11 February), she sent me only the second email in which Pasties CAS told me something meaningful about the kids they had abducted from me:

> ...Thirdly, **I am glad to you asked** [sic] about the children. I would be more than happy to update you **every month** about how the children are doing, **if you wish**. I can tell you that Leo[sic]

> He is doing very well in school and spending time with his friends. Hugh has signed up with the travel club and is fundraising for a trip to Italy.

> Hugh is looking forward to this adventure in 2010. Hugh has completed his first semester of High School and passed with excellent marks.

> Should you have any further questions or concerns please feel free to contact me.

My bold. Note Klewless' sanctimonious "I'm glad you asked" bit. It's pretty clear that the Women of Pasties CAS were starting to feel the heat. Calliope Klewless was laying down an email trail to protect herself. She was trying to disguise the fact that she had been part of a plot to utterly deprive me of my children. The implication is clear enough. *We didn't think he was interested in the kids—he abandoned them, after all, to go to Ottawa. All he had to do was ask—just like we said in the email.*

I believe this is what is cynically known in my world as C.Y.A.: Cover Your Ass.

With the kids still wanting nothing to do with me, it was starting to look bad for Pasties CAS and Mary. Small wonder that Klewlesss had written an affidavit about a week earlier. These feminist women of Pasties CAS were still operating under the premise that if they wrote it, that made it true. Here are the important parts of Klewless' 4 February 2009 affidavit:

> 7. I have interviewed Leo and Hugh on the following dates:

> a. July 14, 2008 [when she and Kruël maliciously ruined my summer vacation with Leo]
> b. August 25, 2008
> c. September 5, 2008
> d. September 23, 2008
> e. November 21, 2008
> f. December 10, 2008

When I checked the calendar, this averaged out to one visit a month. There was even a two-month gap between visits. This apparently is what Pasties CAS considers 'supervision' of kids in need of protection. "Hi guys. Want to see your Dad? No? Okay. See you next month. Maybe. Bye." No wonder kids have died while under CAS 'supervision.' We also see what "several" actually meant from Dunsley's October email—three.

> 10. The children have stated at every visit that they do not wish to see or speak to their father at this time. Leo and Hugh's reasoning include the following:

> a. The tension in the home has decreased since Mr. McConaughey has left the residence.

Not surprising. Mary's victim-mirror was stabilized by Pasties CAS and Injustice Gavelbanger. She would have stopped having narcissistic hissy-fits.

> b. Their belief that Mr. McConaughey's behaviour has changed over time and they are confused as to why this has occurred. They state that Mr. McConaughey has "no emotion" and they view this as "weird". Further, they have stated that Mr. McConaughey is "angry: [sic] and has detached himself from the family. They

also have stated that their father is "militant" when playing with
the children, which they do not enjoy.

Social workers would have us believe that social work is a profession. I'll get to this joke later. If Klewless and Dunsley had actually been professionals, they would have bothered to read *Divorce Poison*. Perhaps they didn't because Dr. Warshak didn't produce a social worker's Dr. Seuss version that rhymed and had kids' illustrations in it. It's about the only way he could have made his book any easier to read.

If they had, Klewless and Dunsley would have read a chapter entitled "THE CORRUPTION OF REALITY." In it, Dr. Warshak describes specific strategies and techniques "... to warp the child's mind against a loved one."

One such strategy is what Dr. Warshak calls "The Total Change Theory." Remember: Klewless quoted the boys as saying that I had changed. Dr. Warshak specifically describes this phenomenon. Here's what he has to say about "The Total Change Theory" (2nd ed.):

> *Sometimes a child's past relationship was so positive, so filled*
> *with gratification and memorable moments, that any attempt to*
> *obliterate the good memories would be futile. In that case, what*
> *is revised is not the past assessment but the current one.*

Once again, I was faced with a worker from Pasties CAS documenting evidence of alienation that any competent expert would have recognized. She was documenting proof of the strong, loving relationships that I had enjoyed with the kids. Before Mary's campaign to destroy them.

Thank God that I don't believe in eugenics. Otherwise, I might be tempted to suggest that the feminist women of Pasties CAS should not be permitted to reproduce. Unless we run out of loser penguins to push off the ice to check for hidden killer whales.

One has to be pragmatic about such things.

The "no emotion" part was something that Hillary said to me before I was maliciously thrown out of my house by Gavelbanger. It was back when she and Mary were trying unsuccessfully to start fights with me as part of their mirroring. They'd get even angrier that I wasn't getting angry. So they had to again corrupt the truth to preserve their mirror. They corrupted their anger and my calmness as their being normal and my being "emotionless" (and hence uncaring). The truth was that I wasn't getting angry.

Yet again, any competent expert in alienation would have understood this.

To give you an idea of what continually banging your head against a brick wall feels like, consider this: Klewless, in the same paragraph, quotes the boys as saying that I was emotionless *and* angry. These are the types of young women whom we entrust child protection to. Ones who cannot realize that it was impossible for me to have been both emotionless AND angry, given that anger is an emotion.

Children in elementary school can easily figure this out. Child protection social workers, apparently, cannot.

The militant bit was from Leo's paintball birthday party that I held for him that past summer. The boys had a great time there with their friends. Yet, half a year later, the truth had been corrupted in their minds to them having not enjoyed it due to my having been "militant." Mary couldn't permit the boys to have fond memories of the best birthday party they'd ever had, as she hadn't organized it. I had.

I'll extract one last piece from Calliope Klewless' affidavit:

> e. *They* [Leo and Hugh] *have stated that they want to see Mr. McConaughey again in the future, however they are not ready to see him at this time.*

This reveals just how cunning and manipulative Mary could be. Knowing how bad it was starting to look, Mary found a way out. She got the boys to tell Klewless this line, which was Mary adjusting her mirror. See?—there's no alienation. The boys just don't want to see their father *at the present.* While the assessment is going on. Everything will be all right a little later. Right after Dr. Goldstein leaves. Trust me. Would I lie?

Bloody right she would.

Yet Calliope Klewlesss and Danica Dunsley apparently didn't think that the timing of this change—the boys wanting to be with me "in the future, but not just yet" (during Dr. Goldstein's assessment)—was suspicious. Maybe Klewless and Dunsley were in on it. I have trouble believing that any human beings could be that stupid.

Even social workers.

Not long afterward, I received a telephone call at work from a lady named Ms. Mariah Alyiawaiz deMansfalt. This came from out of the blue—I'd never even heard of her before. deMansfalt was a social work therapist, if there really is such a thing, who had been seeing Hillary for depression. Only it was 'depression'. deMansfalt was excited to report that she had made great gains with Hillary. Hillary was very close to wanting to see me again "in the future."

Sigh. This was very early 2009. Five years later, I still have heard absolutely nothing from my daughter. This hasn't been from lack of trying on my part.

That patterning brain of mine saw that Mary was again manipulating the kids to make it seem as if nothing was wrong. Look, there's no alienation. Now Hillary, too, wants to see her father again. Just not at the moment, but *in the future*. After Dr. Goldstein's assessment. Honest. There's no alienation—see! Just like with Klewless' affidavit. deMansfalt was a necessary addition to Mary's mirror—if a counselor believed what Hillary said, then it must be 'true.'

I had to tell poor Ms. deMansfalt that she wasn't dealing with depression. I told her that she was dealing with covert narcissism. She was being used to create the perception that there was no alienation. She was a facet of Mary's ever-twisting mirror. Ms. deMansfalt's tone of voice changed from pleased to displeased. She clearly wasn't expecting to be told that she had been duped. I told her that I'd love to see Hillary again, but that I doubted that it was going to happen.

History has proven me right.

Unlike the Women of Pasties CAS that I dealt with, Ms. deMansfalt was a fundamentally decent person. She was acting in good faith. She genuinely cared about people. Sadly, having a master's degree in social work in no way qualified her to deal with either covert narcissism or parental alienation. (Nor basic addition or subtraction, for that matter.)

My records are imperfect here, but I believe it was on or about 20 February 2009 when we had another Court of Injustice child protection hearing. Justice Slough presided. It was to figure out a way ahead, given the impasse of the boys refusing to be with me for Dr. Goldstein's assessment.

I recall Justice Slough asking where Calliope Klewlesss was. Mr. Whiffleby answered that Klewless was on vacation. Hiding from the court was more like it. Then Slough gushed that Klewless certainly deserved her vacation time. It was mildly disgusting. Slough clearly doted on Klewless— sorry, but that's bias. Gotta love great hair and great nails—child protection at its very finest. I had neither seen nor heard from my own children for nearly six months by this point. Not that anyone in court other than Daphne really gave a damn.

We can't deprive a woman of *her* children, can we? Father? Meh.

Well, what to do about the court-ordered parenting capacity assessment? The one that couldn't be done, due to the court order that effectively prohibited it from being done. Slough ignored Sunny Smyle's common sense suggestion that Gavelbanger's order be suspended long enough to let Dr. Goldstein finish his work.

Sweet Jesus, we can't do that! Makes far too much sense—this is a Court of Injustice, after all. Instead, Slough came up with this brilliant legal solution: have Dr. Goldstein drive from Toronto to Krakton to try and convince the boys to wish to be with me for the assessment.

Sigh.

Top Toronto experts in Dr. Goldstein's field bill at around $350 per hour. Toronto is not a cheap place to live and work. It is around a 2.5 hour drive from Dr. Goldstein's place in Toronto to Krakton, especially with gas and washroom breaks considered. Let's say that Dr. Goldstein took at least an hour to convince the boys to wish to be with me, and then spent only an hour with me and the boys. The hours are 2.5 + 2.5 +1 + 1 = 7 hours.

Thanks there, Justice Slough. For the extra $2,450 bill. Let's see—who had to pay that? Oh, that would be me.

Someone in the court—probably Daphne—then asked Slough what would happen if Dr. Goldstein couldn't convince the boys to wish to be with me. Slough had an interesting response. She said the court (of Injustice) would "draw a negative inference" from this.

I was watching Loveless-Hartt, as she normally watched the judge like a hawk. Sailor Loveless-Hartt read the winds of court and tacked accordingly. Maybe she was a Feminist Sailor Scout. Sailor Uranus, most likely. Loveless-Hartt's face puckered when Slough said this. I interpreted Slough's statement as: the boys had better 'wish' to be with their father for Dr. Goldstein's assessment. Or else it will be rather obvious that we're dealing with alienation. I gathered that Loveless-Hartt had gathered the same thing that I had gathered.

It was quite a gathering, all things considered.

Just wait until the Evil Sisterhood hears about this negative inference thing! Little did Slough know what she was dealing with. We'll see later just what "negative inference" the Court of Injustice drew under Slough's gavel.

I won't get into too much of Dr. Goldstein's visit to Krakton. The Women of Pasties CAS were trying to tell me that it would be okay for me to go into my own home if the boys "wished it." They seemed to forget about Gavelbanger's malicious order, which I understood barred me from my own home. I didn't know if ignorance, arrogance, or entrapment (me being in contempt) was motivating Pasties CAS. Eventually, I had it arranged that if Dr. Goldstein could convince the boys, he would bring them to the same friend's house (by then gone to Afghanistan) to be with me. It was in the same small subdivision.

Dr. Goldstein came. He even brought his old English Bulldog, Winston, to help put the boys at ease. Even with 40 years of experience and Winston, the boys were too alienated by this point. Thanks to the Pasties Child Abuse Society, the Ontario Court of Injustice, and the Office of the Mothers' Lawyer, Dr. Goldstein could not get Hugh and Leo to wish to be with me. Dr. Goldstein came and told me the news before he left. He clearly felt sorry for me, as he mentioned that he wouldn't charge me for his trip back to Toronto. He was a very decent gentleman. Unlike Pasties CAS, the OCL, the Court of Injustice, and the Ontario Government, Sol Goldstein genuinely cared about kids.

Dr. Goldstein was no fool. He was so experienced that he stopped counting his high conflict divorce custody cases after 500. He almost certainly knew I was getting screwed by The Evil Sisterhood. He probably knew better than I did. Yet he was far too professional a gentleman to say anything.

Somewhere around this time, the Women of Pasties CAS began a new inquiry. I was still writing the kids every week, but never hearing back. I was trying to put what I'd learned from Dr. Warshak's *Divorce Poison* to good use in the letters. I was trying to provoke the kids' critical thinking in a non-threatening way. Mary couldn't have that. So she claimed the letters were threatening or inappropriate or some such thing. Of course that dynamic duo of child 'protection' known as Dunsley and Klewless had to check this out.

I think the best line from my response was something to the effect that when I told one of my kids, "I love you," what I really meant was, "I love you." That's Pasties CAS for you. They absolutely refused to investigate repeated allegations of a woman seriously abusing the kids. Instead, they investigated the father for trying to protect the kids from the same serious child abuse.

The work leading up to my hearing against Pasties CAS continued. Pasties CAS tried to argue that the Review Board didn't have the authority to hold a hearing in this case. It didn't work. No worries, though. The Review Board is a fraud perpetrated on the people of Ontario. It wanted to hear the case. So it could cover it up. I don't think Pasties CAS necessarily understood this.

Not wanting to leave any stone unturned in my effort to expose Pasties CAS, I decided to peruse its annual reports. They were available for all the world to see on its website. I knew to dig past the surface lies about it caring for children, just to see what I could find underneath. Well, well. Didn't I find some interesting things about good old Pasties CAS?

I critically analyzed its 1999 to 2008 annual reports. I used the Bank of Canada online inflation calculator to adjust every financial figure to fiscal year (FY) 2007/2008 dollars—I compared apples to apples, so to speak. It seems that back in FY 1999/2000, there was a change to the way Pasties CAS was funded. The new funding mechanism was based upon the volume of services provided.

I wondered if Pasties CAS then started to conduct fraudulent child protection to ratchet up its funding. Maybe as part of working at Pasties CAS, Kruël had to generate a certain volume of child 'protection,' or her job would be in jeopardy.

In examining the FY 98/99 to FY 07/08 decade, what I found (with Pasties CAS' own numbers) was:

- Pasties CAS' expenditures, which drove its funding, increased from $6.3 million to $33.0 million (all FY 07/08 dollars). It grew to slightly over 500 percent of its original size in inflation-adjusted terms.

- The Bank of Canada's online calculator stated that average inflation over that period was 2 percent.

- The number of full time workers went from 79 to 183.

- There was a large corresponding increase in office space.

I found another gem. In its FY 99/00 annual report, Pasties CAS stated that their lawyers made 3,572 court applications. That's a surprisingly large number given the population. But wait—out of those 3,572 court applications, 1,329 did not result in court orders. Over one-third of its court applications were useless! And this was before Pasties CAS went on its big growth spree. This was the only time I saw court case figures mentioned. I think Pasties CAS realized how bad that looked in an annual report, so they never mentioned it again.

I thought this was clear evidence that Pasties CAS may have been abusing the courts— malicious child 'protection' or the threat thereof—for its own financial benefit, even as far back as FY 99/00. If this were true, then it would have gotten progressively worse as Pasties CAS continued to fatten itself at the taxpayers' funding trough. If a CAS is mostly about child protection, they probably had adequate funding as far back as FY 98/99. I estimated that Pasties CAS may have wasted in excess of $100 million over the decade I analyzed.

Each time I mentioned these facts to the guys at work, I invariably got the same response: that's empire building! And guess who the Executive Director was the entire time? The same Percival Pryck. When I inquired as to what his annual salary was over these years, I was told only that the information was "in the public domain," but not where. I couldn't find the numbers. I wondered if Percival's salary only grew at the 2 percent inflation rate, or if he was at the trough along with his beloved Pasties CAS.

(I later found an internet source that alleged it went from $102,000 to $152,000 over the decade. A couple of years later it was up to $163,000. Oink, oink there, Percy Pryck.)

I thought that the Auditor General of Ontario might be interested, so I wrote him (5 March 2009) with the results of my analysis. He sent me a polite letter back dated 9 March. Under the provisions of the *Auditor General Act*, he didn't have jurisdiction to comment on matters brought to his attention by members of the public. Nor could he intervene on their behalf (sorry—can't help you). He did say, however, that he could take concerns and information from the public into account when planning future audit activities.

The Patron Saint of ~~Pasties~~ Child Protection wasn't looking quite as holy as he once did.

If you find all this hard to believe, consider another CAS four years later. *Toronto Star* reporter Katie Daubs wrote a 14 March 2013 article entitled, "In leaked memo, Peel CAS staff asked to keep cases open to retain funding."

Need I say more?

Being one seriously unhappy snake, I was looking for other places to inject a little venom. Or a lot. Never underestimate what an unhappy and motivated wood snake with a little military training, education, and operational experience can come up with.

Never.

Since it felt like my kids had been kidnapped from me, I decided to look at something called the *Criminal Code*. Just a little bedtime reading for a curious snake.

We are the most subtle of God's creatures, after all.

Kidnapping turned out to be a bust. Abduction, however, did not. My, my. Whatever had the Evil Sisterhood gone and done? Here are some important quotes from the *Criminal Code*:

> *19. Ignorance of the law by a person who commits an offence is not an excuse for committing that offence.*

Well, I guess certain child 'protection' workers and judge couldn't hide behind ignorance, whether real or feigned, if they were acting criminally.

> *280. (1) Every one who, without lawful authority, takes or causes to be taken an unmarried person under the age of sixteen years out of the possession of and against the will of the parent or guardian of that person or of any other person who has the lawful care or charge of that person is guilty of an indictable offence and liable to imprisonment for a term not exceeding five years.*

Isn't that interesting? As it turns out, when Gavelbanger made her malicious order, Hugh was 14 years old, and thus under 16. He was also unmarried. He was taken out of my possession against my will, even though I had lawful care of him (as did Mary). Gavelbanger took Hugh out of my possession. Kruël and Pasties CAS and Mary caused Hugh to be taken out of my possession.

All criteria but one are clearly met. If Hugh was taken out of my possession *unlawfully*, then he was criminally abducted from me. Then, everyone at Pasties CAS who participated in this was party to the crime. Gavelbanger and Mary, too. Five years' worth of harmonica practice and making license plates. At an all-expenses-paid gated community that boasts excellent security for its occupants.

What else might an innocent wood snake learn from this delightful bedtime story book?:

> *281. Every one who, not being the parent, guardian or person having the lawful care or charge of a person under the age of fourteen years, unlawfully takes, entices away, conceals, detains, receives or harbours that person with intent to deprive a parent or guardian, or any other person who has the lawful care or charge of that person, of the possession of that person is guilty of an indictable offence and liable to imprisonment for a term not exceeding ten years.*

Isn't that interesting again? When Gavelbanger made her malicious order, Leo was 12 years old, and thus was under 14. Neither Gavelbanger nor anyone from Pasties CAS were Leo's parent, guardian, or person having lawful care of Leo. They took him away from me with the intent of depriving me, his parent having lawful care, of the possession of his person.

The Criminal Code doesn't say that the child has to be *physically* taken away. If it had been the intent of Parliament that the criminal offence of abduction be so narrowly defined, they would have said so. They did not. Thus, taken away by fraudulent (and malicious) child protection application and a judge's malicious order still applies.

Again, all criteria but one are clearly met. If Leo was taken out of my possession *unlawfully*, everyone at Pasties CAS who participated was party to this criminal offence. Same for Gavelbanger. Up to ten years' worth.

Oh. As well as being at least an accessory to taking Leo away from me, Mary was also harbouring him. However, she was also a parent with lawful care. Thus, in accordance with the Rule of Law, Mary could not have committed this crime. Even if the CAS action and Gavelbanger's order were *unlawful.* (However, there's another offence of abduction at play that I'll discuss in *Book Two.*)

Let's see? What does five years in jail plus ten years in jail equal? Exactly what feminist women like Kruël and Gavelbanger deserve. If they took the boys away from me *unlawfully.* And Canada is a just nation which respects the Rule of Law.

As it turns out, the former is true, and the latter isn't.

Sometimes, being a wood snake is just plain wonderful. For those who don't like where this is going, don't blame me. I didn't write the bloody *Criminal Code.* I just read the damn thing. Unlike feminist CAS social workers, feminist lawyers, and feminist judges, my mother taught me to read and think.

And to wear clean underwear.

To see that both my sons were *unlawfully* taken from me, let's start with what unlawful means. It's rather simple—it is being without basis in law. So, if there was no basis in law for depriving me of my sons, they were criminally abducted from me.

It really is that simple.

We already know that the *Child and Family Services Act (CFSA)* says that Children's Aid Societies must adhere to the *Child Protection Standards in Ontario.* At the time (and of this writing), these were the 2007 *Standards.* The *Standards* are part of regulatory law—they have meaning.

Lo and behold, if we examine page 10 of the *Standards,* doesn't it say?:

Domestic Violence

*All referrals are universally screened for the presence of domestic violence. A referral in which the only allegation is exposure to domestic violence **does not in itself meet the definition of a child in need of protection under the Child and Family Services Act.***

I added the bold. Although the wording isn't perfect, it's rather clear that this passage is exclusively talking about domestic violence *between parents.* Remember that form which Pasties CAS filled out to tell the Court of Injustice why the boys were in need of protection? It was exclusively due

to the supposed risk of emotional harm caused by exposure to 'divorce conflict'—*between Mary and me.*

Even if Mary and I had been whacking each other with baseball bats
(we weren't), in accordance with the Rule of Law, our children **were not in
need of protection.** This is more than just being without basis in law—this
is directly disobeying the law! This was not just unlawful; it was manifestly
unlawful. It was illegal. It was well beyond any possible dispute.

We've already seen that ordering me from my own lawfully-owned home
was also unlawful. There was no authority whatsoever under the *CFSA* for
Gavelbanger to have done this. It was completely without basis in law. It was
again unlawful.

I want to be very clear here. I'm not suggesting that anyone committed
criminal offences of abduction. Nor am I alleging it, nor implying it, nor
insinuating it.

I'm stating it as a matter of fact in law.

I've been writing that my sons were abducted from me for only one
reason: it's true. In legal language, we're into something known as *prima facie.*
On first examination of the facts, it is self-evident that Gavelbanger is guilty
of two serious criminal offences. So, too, is Malyssa Kruël and anyone at
Pasties CAS who was in any way involved in this. Mary certainly isn't innocent, either.

I'll come back to this little *Standards* passage a bit later. It turns out that
this 'screening' is a cunning violation of men's right to be free of unreasonable search under the *Charter of Rights and Freedoms* s.8. That's right. Every
child 'protection' allegation comes with its own unconstitutional secret
search. Free of charge. Your man-hating, feminazi CAS Gestapo. Hard at
work, thanks to your tax dollars.

And mine.

Ignorance of the law is indeed no excuse for criminal acts. However, there
is another sacred legal principle that needs to be considered. It's called mens
rea, which is Latin for "guilty mind." In theory, to be guilty, one must have
or should have at least known or suspected that the criminal act was at least
bad or wrong. There must be both a guilty act AND a guilty mind.

Let's see what the Court of Public Opinion thinks. The Women of Pasties
CAS made a fraudulent and malicious child protection application. This
application was in direct and blatant contravention to their own mandatory

Standards. It was made for the exclusive purpose of helping an alleged child abuser win sole custody of her children. They worked to deprive two boys of a loving and devoted father. They falsified case notes. They implied threats. They almost certainly committed perjury. They illegally entered my home to deprive me of my vacation with Leo. They coerced the kids to call CAS if I failed to abandon them. They tried to shelter an alleged child abuser from any expert scrutiny whatsoever.

Do you think a reasonable person, making a somewhat probing examination of all the facts, would think that the Women of Pasties CAS maybe, just maybe, knew they were doing something a little bit wrong?

Or what about Gavelbanger? We've seen how it was inconceivable that she didn't know what the score was. She had to have known that she was really being asked to screw me in divorce. Do you really believe that she made her 'temporary' order in total innocence?

Didn't think so either.

Gavelbanger was so arrogant in trying to screw me that it didn't even occur to her that she was committing the criminal offences of abduction of a child under 16 and a child under 14. And she was a former Crown Prosecutor, no less! Now that's embarrassing. That's Maxwell Smart embarrassing— "Sorry about that, Chief (Justice)."

With regard to Gavelbanger, there is an additional issue to consider. Technically, she belongs to the judiciary, which is a branch of the government. The other branches are the *Executive Branch*, which runs the government, and the *Legislative Branch*, which makes the laws.

Supposedly, we have to have an independent judiciary to protect us plebes from the other branches of government. Because the other branches are evil. Judges are the sacred protectors of justice. Just ask them, and they'll tell you. Judges thus have to be protected from the evil other branches by being completely independent. If they weren't, the evil other branches would persecute the innocent and noble judges whenever the judges protected us plebes.

Or so the theory goes.

To be independent and hence protected, our judges enjoy what is known as immunity from civil and criminal proceedings. Just like CAS workers, our judges are above the law, only more so. And they know it, too. I cannot sue

Gavelbanger for what she did to the kids and me. Nor could the police arrest her.

Let's see what one judge wrote on this subject. I get the sense that this Honourable Judge was being sincere—I'm not a total cynic—, so try not to laugh:

> *Thus, protection of salaries and benefits, security of tenure, lifetime annuities upon retirement, and* **immunity from civil and criminal process** *are all important bricks in the wall intended to protect judges from extortion, attempted bribery, improper influence, intimidation or harassment.*

> Mr. Justice Jamie W. S. Saunders
> Nova Scotia Court of Appeal
> Halifax, NS
> May 23, 2003
> (http://www.courts.ns.ca/bench/independence.htm,
> accessed 26 Nov 2012)

I added the bold. I regret that I should use this Honourable Judge's words against his own kind. However, justice demands it.

Law isn't just what it does; law is what it says.

Here' a bit more from Justice Saunders:

> *The community must have confidence in its system of justice and be comfortable in the knowledge that fairness, openness and immunity from improper influence are characteristics of its judiciary. In that way the community will believe that all of its citizens can expect the same treatment according to the Rule of law.*

And

> *Canadians ought to know that justice isn't fickle. It does not depend on the judge's whim or preference. It does not bend to the mob, or to political winds, or to the agenda of special interest groups. It isn't dispensed as a flavour of the month. Rather, justice's only loyalty is to the Rule of law.*

Right. I doubt any divorced dad actually believes this. Empty theory that has nothing to do with our reality. Mere meaningless words; nothing more.

Just because judges enjoy immunity from prosecution doesn't mean that they can't commit crimes while on the bench. It only means that they can get away with it. That's why Canada has its judicial councils. To help feminist judges like Gavelbanger get away with crimes that would put ordinary people like you and me behind bars for years.

There's one other little interesting tidbit from Justice Saunders. A *really* interesting tidbit. According to his Honour, the independence of the judiciary (and hence immunity from criminal prosecution) is enshrined in the *Constitution Act*'s sections 96, 99, and 100. According to s.99, a judge holds his or her office during "good behaviour." Gavelbanger's behaviour was anything but good. According to the Rule of Law—not that this matters to judges, His Honour's words nothwithstanding—, Gavelbanger does not enjoy immunity from prosecution for her serious criminal offences.

The *Constitution* says so.

Of course, judges won't admit to this. They love being above the law that they get to 'interpret.' If they respected the Rule of Law and admitted to what Gavelbanger did, many, if not most, feminist judges would likely be in jail for their abuses of power.

They should be.

Anyhow, after a little inquiry, I learned that I had to contact the Royal Krakton Constabulary to initiate a claim of criminal activity. This didn't make much sense to me, as it was not a police issue. I knew where the kids were. It was purely a legal issue. Regardless, I faxed my allegation regarding Pasties CAS to the police on 9 February 2009. I received a call about this the very next day from Staff Sergeant (S/Sgt.) Shamus O'Flaherty. He sounded like a decent guy and said he'd look into it.

I also wrote the Attorney General of Ontario, the Honourable Guy Smiley. He should not be confused with the Guy Smiley Muppet from *Sesame Street*. Any resemblance is merely a coincidence.

I had left no stone unturned in my attempt to fight off the wicked feminist women perpetrating the malicious child protection fraud against me. I'd contacted Minister Rype-Blumers and Attorney General Smiley directly. I'd tried the Ombudsman, but in Ontario that was useless. I exposed the real Pasties CAS to the Auditor General. I'd told Percival Pryck in no uncertain

terms what his wretched society was up to. I had one of the most experienced clinicians in the field of alienation conducting a parenting capacity
assessment. I had a hearing against Pasties CAS with the Child and Family
Services Review Board coming up. I'd uncovered a province-wide criminal
abduction program run by feminists, and had tipped off the cops.

Things were coming to a head.

8
Vive la Revolution!

*In a time of universal deceit, telling
the truth is a revolutionary act.*

— ATTRIBUTED TO GEORGE ORWELL

As per good old Sun Tzu, I'd been learning about the public enemy called feminism. One crucial academic paper that I came across was co-written by Professor Don Dutton (University of British Columbia) and Associate Professor Kenneth Corvo (Syracuse University). These are their real names.

Their peer-reviewed, published paper is entitled "Transforming a flawed policy: A call to revive psychology and science in domestic violence research and practice." It appeared in *Aggression and Violent Behaviour* 11 (2006) 457-483.

Dutton and Corvo are academically critical of the status quo regarding domestic violence. They start out by identifying that the public policy response to the problem of domestic violence has been defined by feminist activists for the past 30 years (as of 2006). These feminists insist that **patriarchy** is the sole cause of domestic violence. Feminists' views have underpinned policy, legal responses, and regulations in both Canada and the US.

Patriarchy is like the Lord's Prayer to feminists: According to feminists, men (all of us) dominate women (all of you) via *power and control* as a socialized norm. "As a socialized norm" sort of means "because society makes them do it." This is the excuse feminists use to pervert our society in complete contempt of democratic ideals, true justice, and the Rule of Law.

You'll recall that Kruël used these same words in her affidavit to malign my character: *power and control*. This wasn't a coincidence. *Power and control* is a feminist mantra.

With my background, it wasn't hard for me to discern that the Dutton and Corvo paper was very rigorous. Here are just some of the research-based truths about domestic violence that these two dedicated academics highlight:

- Women are as domestically violent as are men, both in terms of frequency and severity of injuries inflicted.

- Women are at least as likely to instigate domestic violence as are men.

- Women are significantly more likely to hit back than are men.

- The stereotypical "wife beater" relationship is actually the least common form of domestically violent relationship.

- Lesbian couples have higher levels of domestic violence than do heterosexual couples.

- Women are more likely to use severe violence against non-violent men than the reverse.

- A huge Government of Canada survey of 135,573 child abuse investigations found that mothers were more likely than fathers "to be perpetrators for physical abuse, emotional maltreatment and neglect" of their children.

It should be rather obvious that there are no men, by definition, in lesbian relationships. The simple fact that lesbian couples have higher rates of domestic violence exposes feminist 'theory' on domestic violence as complete rubbish.

Feminists insist upon what are known as "psycho-educational" models as a basis to intervene in situations of domestic violence. Yet psycho-educational models have been shown to be effectively useless. So why would feminists insist upon them?

As it turns out, there is a reason, and a very sinister one.

Another aspect to the feminist approach to domestic violence is also disturbing. They either completely ignore female-perpetrated domestic violence, or else they state that it can only ever be in self-defence. This explicitly contradicts the known facts from the rigorous research that the paper highlights.

When I looked at Dutton's and Corvo's paper, I had another one of those beautiful insights. I immediately recognized that feminists had a pathological aversion to the truth. In my experience, that's a big, big flag for narcissism. (In every work critical of feminism that I read after Dutton and Corvo's paper, I repeatedly encountered this and other blatant flags for narcissism. I also saw these flags in the behaviour of the feminists whom I dealt with in my case.) I assess that feminists are narcissists, but of a specific subtype. I could only find one insightful American psychoanalyst who has recognized this. I'll have more to say on this in *Book Two*—it's why feminists are truly feminazis.

Perhaps the most widespread variant of these feminist approaches to domestic violence is known as the Duluth Model, developed in Duluth, Minnesota. As Dutton and Corvo put it:

> *The primary goal of this model is to get male clients to acknowledge "male privilege" and how they have used "power and control" to dominate their wives.*

If we work from the perspective of feminists actually being narcissistic women, we can read Dutton and Corvo and make perfect sense of the otherwise absurd feminist beliefs. Narcissistic feminists have a deeply pathological need for men dominating women via power and control to be 'true.' Women must be victims of men (due to society). It is their mirror, and one they all share. Why this is so will have to wait.

Understanding narcissism, however, makes it easy to see that this is indeed the reality of feminists. This is why feminists want men to admit to "power and control" as part of their Duluth 'intervention.' By forcing men to admit to this, it becomes 'true' in the eyes of feminists. This is narcissistic mirroring on a social scale.

This is also why feminists act to expressly forbid other models that are effective in reducing genuine domestic violence. If these were allowed to happen, then women being perpetual victims of men wouldn't be 'true.' That's also why Duluth and similar models don't work. That is actually what feminists need and want, even though they probably aren't capable of understanding or accepting this.

Feminists actually unconsciously want women to be victims of domestic violence—either real or fraudulent. They deeply need women being victims of men and society to be 'true.' Being narcissists, feminists can be absolute pathological liars. They would have us believe that they are tirelessly fighting to protect women from abuse. However, when analyzed from the perspective of narcissism, the opposite is true. As narcissists, feminists lack empathy – they genuinely do not care, and indeed cannot care, about the harm they are actually causing women. And men and society. Feminists do this to ensure the stability of their shared narcissistic mirror. There is no length to which they won't go to make this appear 'true.' They are cunning, controlling, and manipulative.

Another big clue that the feminist influences behind the Duluth model are narcissistic again comes from Dutton and Corvo. Citing previous work by Dutton (2003), the

> Duluth models had two major flaws that were contraindicative
> of effective treatment; they attempted to **shame** clients and, in
> taking a strong adversarial stance to clients (based on a view
> of male sex role conditioning as a major issue in domestic
> violence),...

Well, well. There's our old narcissistic friend, shame. This should probably give experts pause for thought. The projection of shame is normally something that is thought to occur in individual narcissistic behaviour. Yet, what Dutton and Corvo appear to have exposed without realizing it is that narcissistic feminists have embedded the projection of their own narcissistic shame of being women into the very fabric of the Duluth Model's intervention. Through Duluth, this narcissistic feminist shame is then projected onto all their male "clients."

Dutton and Corvo cite the actual manual for the Duluth Domestic Abuse Intervention Program:

> *According to the manual, the basis for these beliefs came from a sample of 5 battered women and 4 men who had completed the Duluth program. This then became the empirical foundation of domestic violence practice: a sample of nine clients recently completing an ideologically infused intervention. The authors (and those who support this model) apparently do not realize the obvious problems with the samples' small size or lack of representativeness.*

I've read the manual, which is entitled *Education Groups For Men Who Batter—The Duluth Model* by Ellen Pence (who was a graduate student at the Ontario Institute of Education) and Michael Paymar (who was a licensed social worker), (1993). Contributors to the manual were: Tineke Ritmeester, "a Dutch feminist, scholar, and activist," who held a Ph.D. in German Literature; and Associate Professor of Social Work Melanie Shepard, Ph.D. While I'll go into more detail in *Book Two*, the feminist influence in the manual is blatant.

In terms of the five women and four men, technically this applies to "... which beliefs frequently articulated by batterers would be most important to discuss in groups,..." Thus, it may seem that Dutton and Corvo are being unfairly critical here in saying that the entire intervention was based on two flawed samples. In fairness to Dutton and Corvo though, the Duluth manual does have this in Chapter One "Theoretical Framework." So, it would be fair to infer that this does exert an influence throughout the entire manual. Regardless, Dutton and Corvo are absolutely correct that there is an undeniable problem with these numbers of the Duluth Model intervention.

When I was a student on the Aerospace Systems Course, I was taught the basics of statistics. (Sometimes companies try to present data or statistics in a way to make things appear better than they really are.) I was taught that when dealing with new areas of research, often the population's standard deviation is not known, and we have a small sample size. For example, we might only have a couple of prototypes for a new radar system.

In such situations, we get into something called Student's t-distribution. As a very general rule, in these cases we'd like a sample size of at least 31 before we are sufficiently confident in the results. Also, the sample must be representative of the population from which it is drawn.

As a common sense example, we don't pick two centers from the boys' varsity basketball team from which to estimate the average height of all high school students, male and female. These are probably two of the tallest students in an entire school. This is just common sense.

Also, the expression "ideologically infused" is quite concerning. My read is that Dutton and Corvo are suggesting that the intervention was fundamentally biased by feminism. My experience in real life says that this is indeed the case. After independently reading the Duluth manual, this remains my resolute opinion, too. Though I say it is actually narcissism instead of ideology. Thus, my opinion is that Duluth was engineered to make patriarchy appear to be 'true.' I am not impugning the authors of the manual; yet the whole thing just screams narcissistic feminism to me.

Besides the narcissistic or ideological influences, the sample sizes (five women, four men) are far too small for us to be confident in the results. Also, the samples are definitely not representative of the broader populations. You can't take the results from abused women (even if there were enough of them) and project those results onto all women. I'm not suggesting that the authors have done this, but feminists certainly seem to.

Not all women are abused. Unless you're a feminist, of course. Then the opposite is 'true.'

Let me apply similar research 'methods' to a fictional example, and watch what results. Suppose that I was bitter and twisted like feminists, but in a masculine way. So I set out to engineer research to make women look bad and men seem like good, innocent victims. I go to brothels and find four female prostitutes who had drugged their clients and stole their wallets. I then find five of their male victims (johns). I give them all an "ideologically-infused" intervention.

What do I get? The New Duluth Model of sexual exploitation: women indirectly dominate men via sexual power and control for financial gain as a socialized norm. In other words, Matriarchy! New Duluth would then say (or at least imply) that all women are exploitative whores, because I found four women prostitutes in a brothel. All men would then be victims of sexual exploitation, because I found five johns who'd had their wallets stolen.

I could have great academic conferences about this New Duluth. I could indoctrinate university students in New Duluth. I could pervert judges via 'educational' seminars and 'skills' training. I could go before legislative standing committees and swear that this was all God's honest truth, and lots of other stuff. Why, I could advance my New Duluth Model to argue that marriage is really state-sanctioned prostitution. Wives are really prostitutes, husbands are really financially exploited johns, and society is really the pimp.

I could even create a Wheel of Sexual Power and Control. Hot damn! I could have things in there like: telling him you're pregnant when you're not; lie and tell him that it's his baby; getting sugar daddy to change his will before you poison him; saying that you have a headache to deny him sex; making him feel guilty just for practice; divorcing him to take all his money and kids away; and hiring a hit man to kill him for his insurance money.

Can you imagine the outrage that would arise were I to try and publish such an offensive intellectual fraud? Yet, my New Duluth is no more offensive than the existing one, in my view.

When a feminist speaks of "woman abuse," she is speaking of this Duluth patriarchy stuff. Most people would mistakenly believe that the feminist is speaking of genuine domestic violence against women. Nothing could be further from the truth. Narcissism must corrupt the truth. This is fundamental to narcissism's very essence. "Woman abuse" does not mean genuine domestic violence. As with a Munchausen by proxy perpetrator, the feminist will rarely be capable of admitting to this.

There are not hordes and hordes and hordes of abused women. Unless you're a narcissistic feminist. Then all women must be 'abused.' By definition. Only this is not reality. Yet the manual would have us believe that the ratio of battered women to battered men is on the order of a thousand to one! (In reality, it is about an even 50-50 split.) If you're finding it difficult to believe that this highly influential yet completely absurd Duluth thing even exists, consider this feminist gem that our two academics expose:

> Women often kick, scratch, and bite the men who beat them, but that does not constitute mutual battering.

Dutton and Corvo also state:

> *The Duluth model's negligible success in reducing or eliminating violence among perpetrators in tandem with the iron-grip of prohibition of other approaches is perhaps its most damaging feature.*

This absolutely screams of narcissistic mirroring, especially the "iron-grip prohibition" part. An essential aspect of the feminist mirror is that society is responsible for everything they hate. They need this as their excuse to covertly execute the terrible social engineering required to maintain their narcissistic mirror. This is an example of the narcissistic trait of being controlling, which manifests on a social scale.

Another major clue that we're dealing with narcissistic mirroring comes from "Coordinated Community Response" or CCR. As Dutton and Corvo write:

> *The CCR seeks to bring the ideological assumptions underlying the Duluth model to law enforcement, criminal justice, human services, and other sectors of the community.*

This has been going on for decades. This likely explains why the Krakton Constabulary came to my home and tried to convince me to leave, even though I was the one that called 911. They may not have known them by the terms Duluth or CCR. However, you can bet that the policies of the Royal Krakton Constabulary came from deranged narcissistic feminists. CCR is feminist narcissistic mirroring—feminists have engineered much of society into their mirror of women being victims of men's "power and control."

See? Patriarchy must be true—even the police now follow our policies!

Dutton and Corvo identify feminism as an ideology. They aren't the only academics to have done so. Technically, it is a fundamentalist ideology. As I'll argue in *Book Two*, all such fundamentalist ideologies—the bad "isms" such as feminism and Communism and National Socialism (Nazi)—likely are or were, in fact, narcissistic social phenomena.

Dutton and Corvo's lucid paper seems to have had no actual impact on government practices and policies. This is due to the fact that they are dealing with narcissistic feminism, which has a natural aversion to certain truths. It has intrinsic, built-in defences against these truths—this is fundamental to its nature. Feminists will ignore, deny, suppress, or attack the truth as necessary to protect their women-victims mirror. They are heartless, cruel, and consider themselves above the law. However, they tend to work indirectly. Were feminists to permit their mirror to be shattered, they would psychologically self-destruct, just like Narcissus.

I'm not being disrespectful to Dutton and Corvo here. Quite the contrary—they are some of the few academics with the courage and integrity to challenge feminist disinformation and propaganda. Theirs was a hugely important academic paper. It's that the problem of feminism cannot be solved by purely academic means. It requires a non-traditional, comprehensive solution. Feminism as it now exists must be purged from society. As I'll demonstrate in *Book Two*, this is a much easier thing to do than anyone realizes.

If you understand your enemy, as per Sun Tzu.

Feminism is absolutely not about equal rights, no matter what feminists say. It is absolutely not about equality for women. It is absolutely not about protecting women. It is absolutely not about "social justice" or righting "historical injustice." It is only about making women the victims of male "power and control" be 'true' as much as possible. Or, even worse, actually true. It is about a specific corruption of truth. It is about building and maintaining a specific narcissistic mirror.

There is one other aspect to Duluth that needs exposing. According to feminists, even the most trivial of "woman abusers" must be treated as villains. Feminists need to believe that men (due to society) will always become progressively more abusive unless a Duluth-type 'intervention' is used. According to feminist 'theory,' all men are to be treated the same: as complete villains, as they either are or will be.

This explains why I was gleefully persecuted with a vehemence approaching that which a serial rapist might expect. This despite the fact that I was only ever a loving and caring father obeying the law.

This one sentence from Dutton and Corvo's "Conclusion" section of their paper speaks volumes:

> What was intended to be a progressive force for safety and liberation has become a rationale for narrow-minded social control.

Narrow-minded social control is, in fact, narcissistic mirror preservation. What is interesting here is that Dutton and Corvo imply noble motives to the originators of this domestic violence paradigm. There was nothing noble about the feminist influence upon Duluth.

Nothing.

Now let's reconsider InJustice Gavelbanger. The Attorney General's office issued a press release about the creaky old bat on November 32, 1929. (**1929 was an ultra-leap year, apparently.**) I've had to doctor the press release so that the actual judge can't be identified by it. It announced Gavelbanger's and Slough's appointments as judges. Guess what it said about Gavelbanger?

> *Madam Justice Gavelbanger was called to the Bar in 1929 and since 1962 has been an **assistant Crown Attorney** in Bountiful County. For 33.3 years she was in private practice in Krakton, primarily in family and children's law but her practice also included criminal law. In 1937 she was appointed by the **Office of the Children's Lawyer** to represent mothers involved in custody disputes and child welfare matters. She has been **co-lead of the provincial domestic violence court program** in Krakton and Bangdalot, and a family law mediator. Madam Justice Gavelbanger has been a board member of the **The Sacred Ovaries Foundation for Abused or Wayward & Wanton Women** and an advisory member of the Bartholomew Jones Foundation's Guilty Buggers Working Group to identify court support programs needed for people in conflict with the law.*

(My bold. Apparently, Krakton has a lot of drug problems, whereas Bangdalot has a problem with teen pregnancies.)

Gavelbanger was clearly steeped in the feminist concepts of "woman abuse," having worked in this field as a lawyer. She absolutely knew what Kruël meant by "elements of power and control." She knew she was being asked by the Women of Pasties CAS to participate in a fraudulent, malicious, and thus illegal child protection action. She knew she was being asked to completely screw me in terms of divorce custody.

So she did.

Dutton and Corvo are also very critical (academically) of Ontario's Professor Peter Jaffe. Jaffe is cited in the *Child Protection Standards in Ontario* as a reference. His influence is clearly significant. As I understand things, Jaffe is a hero to feminists, especially Ontario feminists.

Simplifying Dutton and Corvo, what Jaffe has done is basically gone into "non-representative samples" (e.g., women's shelters) and extrapolated to women in general. If this is the case, Jaffe's research methodology is of such poor quality that the results cannot be trusted. These are not trivial academic criticisms—they are very significant.

In other words, the quality of Jaffe's work appears to be highly suspect, according to the criticisms of Dutton and Corvo.

I've no doubt that I'll be vilified for my thoughts and beliefs regarding Jaffe's work, but again, so be it. Dutton and Corvo inform us that Jaffe's work blinds assessors into believing that men are perpetrators, and that perpetrators lie, so expect the man to deny his abuse. This advice rigs things so that the woman being abused and the man being guilty can only ever be 'true' as often as possible. In other words, feminist CAS child protection workers are virtually guaranteed to find that a mother is abused and the father is the abuser. By definition.

According to Dutton and Corve, Jaffe has alleged that there exists a high degree of coincidence (i.e., they tend to happen together) between "woman abuse" and child abuse. Yet, we've seen that the "woman abuse" concept is itself junk. Thus, so is Jaffe's claim of a "woman abuse"-child abuse link. Remember the *Child Protection Standards in Ontario*, which cites Jaffe as a reference? Speaking from personal experience, here is what is really happening:

1. Every child protection referral is unconstitutionally 'screened' for domestic violence (between parents).

2. The 'screening' is actually a secret, unconstitutional feminist search for "woman abuse," which is in the *Standards*.

3. By feminist definition, every woman is a victim of "woman abuse," and every man is guilty of it. Thus, feminist CAS workers are guaranteed to 'find' it. Especially if the man denies it, thanks to Jaffe.

4. Thanks again to Jaffe's behind-the-scenes influence, since there is "woman abuse," there's likely to be child abuse (but not really).

5. If this occurs in divorce, mother not getting *her* kids and *her* child support is "woman abuse," which means child abuse (but not really).

6. Therefore, drive father from the home to ensure mother gets insurmount-

able status quo and "primary caregiver" advantages in divorce via bogus child protection allegations. If necessary, commit perjury and falsely allege that father is domestically violent. By feminist definition, every man is domestically violent. So perjury is okay, sort of. It's even a feminist's duty.

By virtue of parallel 'logic,' feminists and their supporters also need to believe that mothers can only ever be violent (if it's even admitted that they are) towards their children as a result of being subjected to "women abuse." If mother is a child abuser, the feminist CAS social worker then figures that father must be a "woman abuser." (Remember, rudimentary intelligence is not a job requirement for social work.) So, her solution is to drive father from the home. This way, mother won't be subjected to "woman abuse," and then she won't harm her children.

Only, it's all a deranged feminist fantasy. What these CAS social workers are really doing is trapping kids with their abusers and depriving kids of their loving fathers. The extent to which Jaffe's research, influence, and activism contributes to this in Ontario or other jurisdictions is a question that must be asked.

Who knows just how influential he and his work really are?

Jaffe is the Academic Director of The University of Western Ontario's Centre for Research and Education on Violence Against Women & Children. Clearly, Jaffe isn't too concerned with violence against men. This doesn't get you feminist accolades. Or, as Dr. Goldstein testified at my later divorce trial, "He [Jaffe] has never seen a male who is hurt."

In 2010, Jaffe was invested as an Officer of the Order of Canada for his work. I'll have more to say on this in *Book Two*. The Order of Canada is now how feminist saints are canonized in the Holy Canadian Matriarchal Empire.

I'm not suggesting that Jaffe hasn't helped some women or children in genuine need. He almost certainly has. However, my experience suggested to me that his indirect influence was very harmful to my children.

If you're a judge, consider this: based on Dutton and Corvo, Jaffe's work would fail either the Canadian *Mohan* or American *Daubert* legal tests for scientific expertise, if fairly applied. (Feminist 'experts' in the Duluth patriarchy stuff wouldn't pass muster either.) According to the Centre for Research and Education on Violence against Women and Children's website:

Peter Jaffe assumed the role of Academic Director of the Centre for Research & Education on Violence against Women &

Children and Professor in the Faculty of Education at Western University in 2005. He is the Director Emeritus for the Centre for Children and Families in the Justice System (London Family Court Clinic). He also holds an appointment as Professor (Part time) for the Department of Psychiatry.

... He has presented workshops across the United States and Canada, as well as Australia, New Zealand, Costa Rica and Europe to various groups including judges, lawyers, mental health professionals and educators. Since 1997, Peter has been a faculty member for the US National Council of Juvenile and Family Court Judges' program on "enhancing judicial skills in domestic violence cases".

(http://www.crvawc.ca/section-about_us/p_faculty_peter_jaffe.htm, visited 3 January 2012)

Jaffe sounds very impressive on paper. Yet any judge who believes Jaffe's work without question is fundamentally biased. In legal *Mohan* terms, these judges have failed in their "gate-keeping" duty. They're supposed to keep questionable or suspect academic work out of courts. Yet, it gets in via the insidious back doors of regulations, judicial 'education,' and judicial 'skills.'

I've been diplomatic regarding Professor Jaffe's research, activism, and influence. However, what if (hypothetically speaking) Jaffe decided to sue me for libel, for expressing my rational thoughts, beliefs, and opinions about his work? This would go before a judge. However, in having Jaffe contribute to judicial 'education', and 'skills,' judges have displayed bias in favour of Jaffe.

If a judge then said Jaffe failed the *Mohan* or *Daubert* tests for expertise, the judiciary would look like a pack of idiots for having listened to him in the first place. If a judge found that I hadn't libeled Jaffe (I haven't), the judiciary would again look like a pack of idiots for having listened to him.

Thus, there would clearly be an incentive for any judge to find in favour of Jaffe in this hypothetical case. In contempt of fundamental justice and the Rule of Law, no less.

The Canadian Judicial Council's *Ethical Principles for Judges* specifically states:

Judges should strive to ensure that their conduct, both in and out of court, maintains and enhances confidence in their impartiality and that of the judiciary.

No judge could ever hear such a hypothetical case, rule in favour of Jaffe, and still appear impartial. At least not in theory. In reality, Canadian courts are so blatantly biased by feminism that judges could not care less about what people think.

As far as I know, no one forced Professor Jaffe to help judges with their feminist "skills." In this, he exercised his legal right to liberty. That is, he acted of his own free will, and must accept responsibility for the consequences of his actions. One consequence, in my opinion, is that he has effectively waived any and all rights to legal action against someone who criticizes his work in this regard.

Not that disrespecting the Rule of Law or being blatantly biased is a problem for Canada's judges. Not so long as they lie about it, which they are very good at doing.

In considering the *Charter of Rights and Freedoms*, the *Child Protection Standards'* 'screening' / secret feminist witch hunt is a clear violation of the *Charter of Rights and Freedoms* Section 8 (also written as "s.8"):

8. *Everyone has the right to be secure against unreasonable search or seizure.*

Try not to laugh, but this supposedly is a legal right in Canada. The *Child and Family Services Act* has absolutely nothing to do with spousal violence. The *Standards* even say that when the only allegation is spousal violence, the children are not in need of protection under the *CFSA*. There is absolutely no legal justification whatsoever to violate fathers' s.8 right to be free from the unreasonable search for "woman abuse." For those into law, this violation blatantly fails something called the *Oakes* Test.

If the secret feminist CAS witch hunt search for the bogus "woman abuse," which every man is guaranteed to be guilty of by fraudulent definition, isn't unreasonable, I don't know what is.

According to Dutton and Corvo, Jaffe is big into the Duluth Model's "Wheel of Power and Control." As a symbol, feminists revere the Wheel even more than Americans revere the bald eagle. Even more than Canadians

revere the Tim Horton's paper coffee cup. The Duluth manual states, "...,
more than 200 battered women in Duluth who participated in 30 educational sessions sponsored by the shelter designed the Power and Control
Wheel, which depicts the primary abusive behaviors experienced by women
living with men who batter."

From a research perspective, the Wheel of Power and Control is garbage.
It is junk. Feminists at the shelter biased 200 women with feminist poison.
The 200 women then regurgitate their experiences through the biased femi-
nist perspective they've been given. Feminists—not surprisingly —engi-
neer it so that they hear what they want, and then—bingo!—they create the
Wheel of Power and Control.

It's not that there aren't elements of truth in it. But, taken as a whole, the
Wheel—this sacred Holy Grail thing to feminists—is garbage. It's copyright,
so I can't show the image. It's all over the internet if you want to see it. The
Wheel is basically a wagon-wheel with eight sections. Each section is a major
area of male "power and control." Inside each section are specific examples.

Here are the actual eight (pie-shaped) section descriptors, along with
one Duluth example relevant to my case. Remember—as demanded by law
(*CFSA*), I absolutely had to contact Pasties CAS to report Mary's actual
child abuse. The only therapeutic remedy for serious alienation required
getting the kids away from her. This was happening in marriage breakdown.

USING IMTIMIDATION: *Making her afraid by using looks, actions, gestures*
(I called 911)

USING EMOTIONAL ABUSE: *Making her think she's crazy* (Saying that
Mary was narcissistic, suspecting Munchausen by proxy)

USING ISOLATION: *Controlling what she does, who she sees and talks
to* (Trying to stop Mary from alienating the kids, countering her lies to
counselors)

MINIMINZING, DENYING AND BLAMING: *Shifting responsibility for
abusive behaviour, saying she caused it* (truthfully saying that it was Mary who
was alienating the kids)

USING CHILDREN: *Making her feel guilty about the children, threatening
to take the children away* (Mary was abusing the kids, which she certainly

should have felt guilty about. The only protocol for serious alienation is separating the kids from the alienator. Trying to move to Ottawa as was in the best interests of the children.)

USING MALE PRIVILEGE: *Making all the big decisions* (Since Mary was a child abuser, I had to try and make decisions in the best interests of the children.)

USING ECONOMIC ABUSE: *Giving her an allowance* (My trying to come to a support arrangement with Mary, which she repeatedly refused to discuss.)

USING COERCION AND THREATS: *Threatening to leave her, to report her to welfare* (My divorcing Mary and calling Pasties CAS)

This feminist rubbish—this "woman abuse"—is what supposedly all of us men do to all women. This is what has replaced genuine domestic violence as far as our social organs are concerned.

I don't want to sound as if I don't care about women who are genuinely abused. I do. Being in a genuinely abusive relationship is terrible, and I should know. There certainly are genuinely abused women, just as there are genuinely abused men. These women AND men need our help. However, feminists don't really want abused women (and especially men) to be genuinely helped. Men must always be villains to feminists; and women must always be victims. Either fraudulently or for real.

Also, it's not that these Duluth descriptors can't be forms of genuinely abusive behaviour. They can be. It's that feminists insist that all men do this (or will, without feminist intervention), and that all women are victims of it. Feminists will twist any behaviour or event to fit this utterly perverse construct and then lie through their teeth about it.

When you analyze the *Standards* and its associated Jaffe-Duluth influences, the mandatory *CFSA* act of reporting your estranged wife's child abuse (especially alienation) actually constitutes "woman abuse!" But woman abuse equals child abuse to some extent, thanks to Jaffe's dubious claim.

So, **the mandatory act of reporting that your estranged wife is abusing your children is itself 'child abuse' according to the Ontario Government's covert feminist instructions.** Feminism has so utterly corrupted Ontario child protection that the mandatory act of reporting that your estranged or ex-wife is abusing your kids *guarantees they'll be subjected to it.*

By following the law to protect the kids, I was guilty on all counts of "woman abuse," and thus child abuse. This is the outrageous but inescapable conclusion that one comes to when actually subjecting this to somewhat probing scrutiny. There was no other rational explanation for what was going on and what was done to Hillary, Hugh, and Leo. According to feminist theory, Mary could only be a threat to the kids if she was a victim of "woman abuse." So, drive me from the home, and everything would be fine.

Right.

If you have trouble believing this, consider the true case of Elaine Campione (real names here). Her murder trial made major headlines in 2010. The CAS of the County of Simcoe had interfered in her earlier divorce to help ensure that Elaine had the exclusive care of her two young daughters. As Christie Blatchford wrote in the *Globe and Mail* article "Mother who drowned children was not without social support":

> *This CAS, as a letter to Ms. Campione dated June 16, 2005, shows, had conducted a protection investigation when the couple split up, pronounced that Serena and Sophia had suffered as a result of their parents' battling and that they were "likely to suffer further harm," and deemed Ms. Campione as the safe parent.*

> (cited at http://www.oacas.org/news/10/sept/28drown. pdf, accessed 16 August 2013)

Sound familiar?

In the same article, Ms. Blatchford also wrote:

> *"She* [Elaine] *was doing her best to use available services...there was a lot of involvement of the CAS [the Children's Aid Society of the County of Simcoe], she was getting counselling, taking programs to help with life skills."*

Sound familiar, again? Sounds like a covert narcissist 'victim' mother playing a CAS to be part of her mirror. Have sympathy for me, I need so much help. Admire how hard I am working at your self improvement programs. Look how wonderful I am, unlike my brute ex-husband.

The father, Leo Campione, had what were almost certainly false accusations of domestic violence made against him by his ex-wife. He was afterward on the verge of getting a court to open and consider her medical (psychiatric-ish) records. This may have cost Elaine custody of her daughters—she was a crackpot. So, Elaine drowned her daughters and made a very sick video about it.

She was under CAS 'supervision' at the time. Ontario feminist social worker child protection at its very finest.

The jury at the murder trial found Elaine Campione guilty. After the verdict, Mr. Justice Alfred Stong went on a rant about 'poor' Elaine. He strongly seemed to imply Mr. Campione was at fault for everything.

As Rosie DiManno so eloquently wrote (thestar.com, 16 November 2010):

> *Yet shockingly, inexplicably, against all the rules of jurisprudence, Stong levelled his stinging indictment not at the accused and now convicted defendant, a woman who has never denied her crime, but — there's no other way for me to interpret this — at the husband ....*

> *Disregarding all of that, Stong extended to this vengefully embittered woman moral cover that all but made a mockery of the jury's verdict, at the same time veering off into a completely inappropriate polemic, a non sequitur, on perceived social ills as contributing factors in Campione's lethal behaviour — essentially putting the stamp of approval on a defence exculpation that the jury had just rejected.*

No journalist could figure it out. I can. Our judges have been fundamentally biased by this narcissistic feminist Duluth-CCR propaganda. It is my opinion that Stong had clearly bought into this feminist filth. The question of whether or not Professor Jaffe's influence may have been an additional factor is disconcerting.

Poor Mr. Campione had his daughters taken away from him only to have them ruthlessly murdered by his ex-wife. Thanks in large part to the child 'protection' of the CAS of the County of Simcoe. Elaine may well have been a covert narcissist—a self made victim if ever there was one. Apparently in the video she declares: *I was a perfect wife . . . I was a great mother.*

If that isn't narcissistic grandiosity in a woman, I don't know what is.

With a self-made woman victim, the feminist Matriarchy of Ontario, a CAS and its workers being above the law, Professor Jaffe's suspect influence, and rather blatant judicial bias, what did we get? Two innocent girls murdered. And Mr. Campione unjustly and cruelly vilified by implication, for all the world to see.

According to feminist 'theory,' Elaine Campione could only ever have hurt her kids if she herself had been the victim of "woman abuse." I believe it was this sort of malignant feminist bias that prompted Stong to cruelly imply that it was Mr Campione's fault. Appeasing feminists appears to trump upholding the ideals of truth and justice. Plus, it's better for the judicial career.

Fundamental feminist bias—that's what being a judge is all about these days, isn't it?

For those judges who aren't fundamentally biased—all two of you—, know this. If a social worker ever tries to testify that a man is abusive, either directly or via implication, the odds are better than even that the social worker is deceiving the court with this Duluth crap. She may even be blatantly perjuring herself.

Back to my story. Given that the entire social apparatus of Ontario—government, courts, police, social work, child protection, and everything else—had been fundamentally perverted by narcissistic feminists, it was a bit of a miracle that I achieved what I did.

I attended the Canadian Symposium for Parental Alienation Syndrome in Toronto, which I recall being during the weekend of 28-29 March 2009. Even having worked with some smart defence scientists in my time, I was still highly impressed by the experts at the Symposium. It was probably the single finest collection of intellects that I have ever been privy to. Dr. Amy Baker was one of the speakers.

There were other heartbroken target parents in attendance, too. From them, I heard other stories of a CAS coercing mothers in divorce to drive fathers from the home and the children's lives. This they did via implied threats of child apprehension if the mother didn't do as they demanded. Just as appears to have happened in my case.

I actually met Mariah Alyiawaiz deMansfalt there. I recognized her from her website's photo. She cared enough to attend the Symposium, so she could learn more about what I had alleged was going on. When she says that she cares, deMansfalt is telling the truth. She is a genuinely decent and nice person, and you'll never hear me say anything to the contrary. Sadly, decent and nice people are easy marks for narcissists, and Mary was a devious one.

All the speakers at the Symposium were excellent. Besides Amy Baker, there were three that I'd like to mention.

First was Toronto Lawyer Brian Ludmer (real name), who had been a target parent himself. Mr. Ludmer presented and quoted from Sun Tzu in his legal approach to addressing alienation. He was a lawyer and a father after my own heart.

Second was Dr. Jayne Major, Ph.D. (real name). She was the expert behind the *Breakthough Parenting* program and resources that I was using. Dr. Major made one statement that really caught my attention. She said that people didn't realize how dangerous narcissists were. No kidding!

The last and most disturbing for me was Montreal's Dr. Abraham Worenklein, Ph.D. (real name). To give you an idea of the caliber of speakers at the Symposium, here is part of Dr. Worenklein's bio:

> *Abe Worenklein, M.Sc., Ph.D., is a clinical and forensic psychologist in private practice in Montreal, a professor at Dawson College, and a lecturer at Concordia University. In addition to his practice in clinical and forensic evaluation and psychotherapy, he is certified as a family mediator. Dr. Worenklein has been declared an expert witness in Superior Court and in Youth Court several hundred times, primarily in Canada, but also in the United States and the Caribbean, and he has presented on this topic at numerous professional conferences in Canada, the United States, and Europe. He has been quoted in significant judgments dealing with parental alienation and high-conflict divorces.*

What Dr. Worenklein said that was so sobering—I'm going from memory here, but this is the sort of thing that you tend not to forget—was that he and other experts considered parental alienation to be even *more harmful to kids than sexual abuse.*

Wasn't that just bloody wonderful? I knew from having read Dr. Darnall's book that the kids had likely already suffered permanent psychological damage. Now I had a perspective of just how bad it really was.

My kids would have been better off in the care of a pedophile than having been in Mary's care. Way to go Kruël and Whitless—nice job protecting children. Good supervision there, Klewless and Dunsley. What a champion of rights and freedoms that Gertrude Gavelbanger was. It clearly is every child's God-given right to experience something worse than forced sodomy, obviously. What a caring CAS leader was Percival Pryck and his sidekick, Maurice leDouche.

Thanks to you lot, my kids would have been better off with a pedophile than with what was done to them. Absolutely outrageous. Absolutely unbelievable.

Perhaps they all deserve the Order of Canada. Why is Professor Jaffe so special?

The Monday after the conference, I was back in Krakton for my bogus Child and Family Services Review Board Hearing against Pasties CAS. Dr. Goldstein's report hadn't made it in time. I represented myself to save money. This fraudulent child protection racket was burning my funds at an alarming rate.

I'd listed Kruël and Klewless as witnesses. I knew they wouldn't have lasted 30 seconds under genuine scrutiny. I saw them seated in the hallway outside of the small hotel conference room being used for the hearing. They looked very glum and dejected. They clearly thought they were in trouble.

Mr. P. Phineas Portmanteau was the presiding member. He seemed to have two parts to him. The first was very much a gentleman in explaining procedural matters to me, given that I wasn't a lawyer. Yet, with the second, I also recall him asking me around three times before we started the hearing if I had any recording devices on me. He seemed very concerned about this possibility. He alleged that they were forbidden by regulations, but he never specified which regulations.

I later learned at canadacourtwatch.com that it was my right to have recorded the hearing's proceedings. In retrospect, doing the de Grandpré and Iacobucci things, it is clear that the fix was in from the start. P. Phineas

Portmanteau's pathetic panel had to make certain that there would be no evidence to expose the cover-up. They had to make certain I wasn't recording the proceedings. They could then write whatever they wanted in their decision.

This second part of Mr. Portmanteau wasn't pleasant like the first. Quite the opposite, in fact.

The two other Board members were Ms. Harriett Honda-Carr and Ms. Tabitha Tabbou. Neither of them said much, if anything. I got the impression that Honda-Carr was generally reliable. However, something told me to stay clear of Tabbou.

The hearing went very badly for Pasties CAS. Mr. Portmanteau kindly informed me that if I called Kruël and Klewless as witnesses, then the panel would have to accept what they said as true, due to procedural rules. Knowing Kruël at least would likely lie to the point of perjury, I decided against calling them.

What was interesting was that Mr. Whiffleby didn't call them, either. He could have. This meant he was afraid of my cross-examining them. In cross-examination, the panel didn't have to automatically believe what they said was true (not that it really mattered). This looked bad, but Mr. Whiffleby needn't have worried.

Mr. Whiffleby tried to get me to agree that I had been "heard" by the Society, as they had sent me a complaint brochure. My response was that being "heard" doesn't mean that a CAS just ignores you when you speak. I said that I wasn't heard. If I had been heard by Pasties CAS, then they would have obtained Dr. Goldstein's services, instead of trying to prevent his involvement.

Interestingly, Mr Portmanteau seemed to be very interested in the Dutton-Corvo paper. I had included it into evidence. Mr. Portmanteau was quite specific in querying me about whether or not I believed that the paper accurately explained the basis for what CAS had done.

I replied that I was certain of it.

I felt good after the hearing, but I hadn't clued into the fix having been in from the start. The military is generally an honest outfit. I just couldn't fathom that I lived in such a dishonest society.

Dr. Goldstein's long-awaited report came out a few days after the hearing. The Child and Family Services Review Board refused to consider it even though I sent them a copy. We couldn't have the truth interfering in an Ontario Government cover-up of criminal wrongdoing!

Here are the highlight items from Dr. Goldstein's report dated 23 February 2009:

> - *Later on mother did acknowledge that she was not open to the children having contact with father's family because if the children would see his mother, she would try to turn them against her. She went on to reiterate that the children had been told, after all, by the police that they did not have to talk to any of their parents should they not wish to do so and they were now exercising that option with regards to their father.*

> - *The interactions between mother and children seemed to be somewhat strained and restricted with a seeming lack of spontaneity and warmth between them.*

> - *It was of particular interest to observe Hillary's interaction with her mother, the question of whether she should join in the meeting with all of us during which we would discuss whether or not to visit father. At that time mother asked Hillary whether she "felt up to it" and whether she was "feeling well enough to do so." At the same time Hillary was glancing furtively at mother seemingly searching for a clue as to whether to be involved or not – searching for either permission or encouragement…. All of them had virtually the same messages to deliver.*

> - *It was clear when I met with all of the children together that the boys are quiet while Hillary is the spokesperson for the group.*

> - *Mother also spoke about "Mr. McConaughey's legal team" having taken the stance that this is a case of Parental Alienation Syndrome. She then went on, in the presence of the children, to recount the story of how and why they had broken up and to list all of the accusations which he has leveled against her.*

- *With regards to the gift of the diving course, Hugh pointed out that his father had given him a sheet of paper about a course taking place in Ottawa and included the price tag for this. It seemed to him that his father was spending money on things in which he no longer had any interest.*

- *With regards to his attendance at Arrowsmith...When his mother took over she realized that his work load was too heavy and after that they decided that he did not have to go.*

- *When referring to the Christmas card from father, Leo suddenly seemed to hesitate, interrupted his former diatribe, paused and then, obviously embarrassed, said "I can't remember what is wrong with that one."*

- *Hillary also spoke about the fact that each time she is ready to talk to father "something else happens which makes me decide not to do so."*

- *Hugh spoke of Leo's decision not to go with his father around the time of his birthday this past mid July saying "Hillary and I told Leo that he did not have to go if he did not want to go. The people from Children's Aid told all of us that we did not need to go if we did not want to."*

- *I would indicate here that neither parent shows evidence of any major psychiatric disorder. Having said that, however, I am concerned about the narcissistic traits displayed by the mother.*

- *During the latter part of this couple's marriage she did involve herself in the internet to the detriment of her family in general and her children in particular. She **projects** her own difficulties onto her husband,... [my bold]*

- It is clear that she involves the children and has rallied them around her to protect her as the victim of their father, the villain.

- In addition to this, the Society seems to have become involved with mother to the point that they appear to have given up their questioning or more accurately evaluating her contribution to, and responsibility for, the current impasse between the children and their father.

- With regards to mother's relationship with Hillary and the question of whether this is a relationship of Munchausen's by Proxy is something which I cannot substantiate from this assessment as far as it went. I can, however, say that I am concerned about how Hillary is very much controlled by her mother, glances at her in order to obtain the cues as to how to act, while mother is overly solicitous of any perceived or actual physical problems of Hillary.

- Although I cannot substantiate the diagnosis of Munchausen by Proxy there is definitely an over involvement between mother and daughter, of living the life of someone who is over zealous in the pursuit of dealing with physical ailments. It is interesting that mother's first career was that of a nurse – a career which she has given up but continues through her involvement as an overly concerned parent.

- Father has thoroughly investigated and has a rather sophisticated knowledge of psychiatric syndromes with which he suspects his wife to be afflicted. He has no difficulty presenting his findings to all who are concerned with dealing with his family. It is this assessor's opinion that he is genuine in his beliefs and is seriously concerned for his children. There is no doubt that he is being marginalized from his family to the point where he feels, quite accurately so, that **he is the subject of a process of alienation from them which is being perpetrated by his wife.** [my bold]

- Major McConaughey has, unfortunately, fallen prey to this and has approached his marginalization from his children by declaring war upon anyone who contributes to this. One may question this, or alternatively, one may view this as behaviour arising from a parent who is not ready to accept passively his children being endangered by someone who holds them captive – witness the parent who will physically attack a wild animal which holds their child captive.

- It was clear to the assessor that mother was invoking comments made by the Court, by the Society, by the police to justify lack of contact between the children and their father and in this way totally denying any contribution of hers towards the process.

- Many of the children's complaints about father and his letters are presented with adult based ideas, atypical of the usual perception of children this age. They are in fact almost carbon copies of mother's complaints.

- Hillary has long been aligned with mother with father being seen as the enemy. She is very much mother's assistant and lieutenant in dealing with her younger brothers – enabling them and encouraging them in their accusations, perceptions and actions.

- It is my opinion that one of the most, if not the most important questions to be answered in Section 24 of the Children's Law Reform Act is "the recognition of first the need and importance for the children to have a relationship with both of their parents and a clear demonstration of commitment to that belief." The second quality to be determined is "a parent's ability and willingness to put the needs of the children before their own." In my opinion **the children's mother fails to pass the test on either of these most important issues.**" [my bold]

*- ... I would address, at this time, my alarm at the seeming lack of sensitivity to, and dealing with, the process of the separation of these children from their father which, in the impression of this assessor, **has been perpetrated** by not only the mother but also supported through the involvement, through a seeming lack of understanding of or ability to deal with this process, **by the Children's Aid Society**.* [my bold]

- The children have thus been enabled by the seeming lack of proper understanding and intervention by the Society.

*- I am well aware of and concerned about the harm which such a process – termed by others as Parental Alienation Syndrome – to the psychological make up and future emotional development of children who are victimized by this. **Clinical intervention is mandatory**. This can only be effective if ordered by the Court. The Order must be firm, clear cut, unambiguous and definitive in order to have a chance at success.* [my bold]

I suspect that Dr. Goldstein completely understood what had transpired. I suspect that Dr. Goldstein understood that Gavelbanger was in on the entire scam. Dr. Goldstein worded the final portion of his report so that the court could have blamed everything on Pasties CAS. Dr. Goldstein offered the court an honourable way out, not that it deserved it.

He recommended that Mary be given three months, either on her own or with an expert's help, to have the boys make regular and meaningful visits with me. Failing that, I should get custody, and there should be a no-access order against Mary. As with the *JKL v. NCS* case.

I suspect that Dr. Goldstein knew that Mary could not stop alienating and undo what she had done. By giving her three months to fail, the court could have said it had given Mary every chance. This was child protection and not divorce court, but there still could have been an interim order to this effect that would cease upon the completion of the divorce trial.

However, the Court of Injustice was honourable in name only. It wanted nothing to do with an honourable way out. It wanted Mary to 'win' custody and get *her* child support.

The Child and Family Services Review Board decision came out as something else, but I'll call it *M.M.M. v. Pasties CAS*. The last time I checked the real decision was still in the online canlii.ca database. It wouldn't surprise me if it now gets suppressed. Regardless, it was a masterpiece of fraud and deception. Pasties CAS didn't seek to have me excommunicated and the kids handed to Mary. No, Pasties CAS had only been seeking a "supervision order." And according to this official decision of an agency of the Ontario Government, I hadn't been ordered from my home. No, of course not. The decision states that *I had moved out of my home prior to the hearing*.

The audacity of this lie is simply breathtaking. It is written in a fashion so as to imply that it refers to the hearing at which Gavelbanger ordered me from my own home and out of my kids' lives. Yet I still have copies of Gavelbanger's malicious order. I suppose that, if queried, the Board could then have claimed that it was referring to the Board hearing against Pasties CAS. Yet even this is blatant misrepresentation, as it implies that I left my home of my own free will. I left under duress; I was forced out against my will.

It was a brilliant fraud.

The decision materially misrepresents other elements of what went on. Despite knowing the truth—it by then had Dr. Goldstein's report -, the Board did throw me a very thin bone in its decision. It found that Pasties CAS had not given me reasons for the manner in which Pasties CAS implemented the court order. Nor had it given me reasons for not giving me information regarding the boys. So the Board ordered Pasties CAS to provide me with written reasons for the manner of its supervision and the manner for the frequency of its communication regarding the children.

But was this a bone? Were the press to have then queried Minister Matilda Rype-Blumers, she could have simply said something like: "The Board held an independent hearing and found that it was merely a matter of Pasties CAS having not sufficiently explained its actions. The Board directed that Pasties CAS remedy this. I can't really comment beyond this, as the matter is still before the courts."

That way, I wasn't an outraged and grossly abused victim of a CAS. No, I was just an ill-informed man. He's ignorant, so we're having the CAS explain it a little better, that's all. You know how thick men can be sometimes. No story here. You can leave now, reporters. Be off with you.

I wrote to Rype-Blumers after the hearing. I urged her to exercise her powers as Minister under the *Child and Family Service Act* to revoke the status of Pryck's empire as a Children's Aid Society. Here's what she wrote back on 19 May 2009:

> *Thank you for your letter regarding your concerns with the Pasties Children's Aid Society. I appreciate being made aware of your personal situation and recognize that you're in a difficult position.*
>
> *I understand that you've gone to the Child and Family Services Review Board and are awaiting their decision. As your case is before the courts, it would be inappropriate for me to comment on your complaint.*
>
> *Should you require further information, please contact Ms. Kitty Klaus, Program Dominatrix in my ministry's South East Regional Office, at 613-123-4567.*
>
> *Thank you again for sharing your concerns.*
>
> *Sincerely,*
>
> *[signed]*
>
> *Matilda Rype-Blumers*
>
> *Minister*

How nice that Minister Rype-Blumers took the time from her busy schedule to write me such a polite please-get-lost letter. (I made some minor edits to protect Kitty's true identity.) Let me share my concerns about the Minister, while I'm on the topic.

First of all, I am 'concerned' about how this appears for Minister Rype-Blumers. Try as I might, I can only think that there are two possible ways to interpret things. The first is that the Minister was the influence behind the fraudulent hearing. The second was that she wasn't in any way behind the fraudulent hearing. In this case, she wasn't in control of her own ministry, and clearly failed to discharge her public duties.

Choose your poison. However, if there is another logical alternative that I've missed, somebody please tell me. I'll be happy to apologize to Rype-Blumers, however odious I might find it. I'll apologize for being such a meanie regarding how her Ministry covered up the malfeasance of a CAS under her authority.

And unless I've really missed something, that malfeasance would be of the criminal variety.

I am also concerned about a minister who appeared to be indifferent to the malicious abuse of authority of a CAS under her jurisdiction. I am concerned about a minister who appeared to be indifferent to children being subjected to something that is more harmful than sexual abuse. I am concerned about a minister who appeared to be sufficiently ignorant or incompetent (or both) that she permitted the *Standards* to condemn children to be abused at their mother's hands.

Very disturbingly, there exists a compelling argument that what Matilda Rype-Blumers allowed my sons to be subjected to is the same form of abuse that turned Russ Williams (real name) into the deranged rapist-woman killer that he became (more on this in *Book Two*).

Danica Dunsley and Calliope Klewless ended up jointly sending me a short letter. This was the pathetic response of Pasties CAS to being ordered by the Child and Family Services Review Board to explain itself. The letter basically said that they didn't agree with my position that there was parental alienation. They felt that they had been helping Hugh and Leo through a difficult time.

Liars, right to the bitter end. By the time they wrote their letter, Pasties CAS had already received Dr. Goldstein's report. Parental alienation wasn't "my position."

It was expert-confirmed fact.

. . . .

I didn't know what to expect from Staff Sergeant (S/Sgt.) O'Flaherty of the Royal Krakton Constabulary. He seemed like a decent guy when I spoke to him on the phone. Military guys and cops tend to have mutual respect for one another. Both groups are protectors in our society.

I obtained a copy of O'Flaherty's General Occurrence Report dated 20 February 2009. What I didn't know back then was how badly feminist propaganda and policies had penetrated society. The Duluth CCR stuff, even if it's not known by that name. The Royal Krakton Constabulary was clearly a victim of this insidious feminist campaign of disinformation. I know this now.

The feminist narcissistic mirror insists that all women must be victims of men and society. Alienation is most prevalent in divorce. The current research isn't definitive, but it appears to indicate that the majority of perpetrators are women. Parental alienation is thus a huge threat to the feminist mirror. Accordingly, feminists have worked relentlessly to suppress, deny, and corrupt the truth about parental alienation.

It's what narcissists do best—corrupt the truth.

Let's consider the sexual abuse of children for a moment. According to the Canadian Children's Rights Council (www.canadiancrc.ca, 16 January 2013), 75% of perpetrators are men and 25% are women. (This website is a real eye-opener about women who sexually abuse minors. Highly recommended.) The actual numbers aren't important here; it's the principle: the majority of sexual abuse perpetrators are men. Can you imagine if I was a man with issues, and claimed there was no such thing as sexual abuse? Can you imagine if I alleged that feminists had just made up sexual abuse to oppress men?

It would be an outrage, and rightfully so. Yet this pretty much illustrates what feminists have done with parental alienation. Yes, more research is needed to better understand alienation. But the facts of its existence, its fundamental nature, and the permanent and serious harm that it does children are now well beyond dispute.

As a reasonably well-adjusted man, I can look at the gender numbers of sexual abuse and accept them as they are. We can't solve problems that we don't understand. Likewise with parental alienation. Based on my earlier chapter on narcissism and female bullying, it makes perfect sense that women perpetrate parental alienation more often than men. There is an inherent truth to this, so let's get on with addressing it. Just as with sexual abuse.

But the insidious and pervasive influence of feminism will fight any progress whatsoever. By its fundamental nature, it will resist accepting the truth about alienation by whatever means necessary. You can't reason with Narcissus looking at his reflection in the water. You can't reason with terrorists. Likewise, narcissistic feminists cannot be reasoned with.

Never. Don't even bother trying.

Bearing in mind how CCR had probably perverted the Royal Krakton Constabulary's policies and assumptions, let's see what S/Sgt. O'Flaherty wrote:

> Mr. McConaughey is of the opinion that the actions of the CAS and his estranged wife are unlawful and as such believes these circumstances would support a criminal code charge of abduction in regard to his two sons: Leo age 12 and Hugh age 14.

> Parental Alienation Syndrome (PAS). This unsophisticated pseudoscientific theory explains a child's estrangement from one parent or allegations of abuse at the hands of one parent by blaming the other. The theory, developed by the late Richard A. Gardner, M.D., portrays the preferred parent (usually the mother under PAS) as an evil "alienator" who is virtually solely responsible for turning a vulnerable child against their estranged parent (usually the father under PAS.)

> Parental Alienation Syndrome is not recognized as a valid psychiatric or medical disorder. Parental alienation syndrome has been extensively criticized by scientists and jurists, who describe it as inadmissible in child custody hearings based upon both science and law. They assert that though presented as a reliable concept the syndrome lacks scientific validity and thus reliability. The self-published nature of the theory and lack of peer-reviewed publication corroborating Gardner's theory has been critiqued. Many articles supportive of the syndrome are anecdotal case reports, and research by other professionals has not substantiated some tenets of the theory.

I don't know where S/Sgt. O'Flaherty got the feminist propaganda that he based his report on. It may have been forced upon him by way of policy. The concept of parental alienation has not been "extensively criticized." It has been pathologically attacked by feminists.

If S/Sgt. O'Flaherty had visited the Fathers Are Capable Too website (http://www.fact.on.ca/), he would have found this quote from Dr. Richard Gardner:

> I am pleased to report that on Wednesday, November 22, 2000, a family court in Tampa, Florida, ruled that the PAS had gained enough acceptance in the scientific community to satisfy Frye Test criteria for admissibility. Richard Warshak and I both testified at the Frye hearing, which lasted two days. H. Michael Bone was also involved in the case and provided valuable assistance. I believe that my website list (www.rgardner.com/refs) -- which includes approximately 100 articles on the PAS in peer-review journals and 38 courts of law that have recognized PAS -- played an important role in the court's decision. The citation for use in future cases: Kilgore v. Boyd, 13th Circuit Court, Hillsborough County, Fl., Case No, 94-7573, November 22, 2000.

Even back in 2000, it would have been preposterous to state that parental alienation theory was "self-published" in nature. Also, with (at least) 38 courts of law having accepted alienation back in 2000, it was preposterous in 2008 to claim that alienation had been extensively criticized by jurists.

It gets even worse for S/Sgt. O'Flaherty. In a professional article published in *Family Court Review*, 39(3), July 2001, (less than a year later) Dr. Gardner wrote:

> ... the 19 articles I have written that have been published in peer-review journals...

> Furthermore, on my website are citations from 74 courts of law in the United States (21 states), Canada (7 provinces), Australia, Germany, Great Britain, and Israel that have recognized the PAS [Parental Alienation Syndrome]

I'll emphasize just two more court cases beyond those that I've already explicitly cited. The first is the European Court of Human Rights in the 2000 case of *Elsholz v. Germany*. That court is pretty much the supreme court of all of Europe. In *Elsholz*, the court stated that expert psychological evidence was needed in cases of alienation. If you didn't have it, you did not have a "fair and public hearing ... by an independent and impartial tribunal established by law."

That is a blatant violation of essential rights and freedoms. In such cases, courts fail to meet the most basic requirement of fundamental justice. That may not sound too dramatic to the average person. To any decent and honest judge, it's like getting socked in the jaw by the heavyweight justice champion of the world. Failing to meet this requirement would be a failure of great shame for any judge.

The Supreme Court of Canada has said that Canadian judges must consider international human rights law when interpreting Canadian law (*Baker v. Canada*). In light of this, Justice Slough's deliberately ignoring Dr. Goldstein's report of serious alienation was a reprehensible miscarriage of justice. From the perspective of the Rule of Law, she *deliberately deprived Hugh and Leo of fundamental justice*. So did Gavelbanger, via her malicious order.

Those two women should be absolutely ashamed of themselves, as judges and as women, for what they did. Especially Gavelbanger. What they did was utterly despicable. Their actions were a disgrace.

The other court case is an American one. It's from the Supreme Court of New Hampshire in *Miller v. Todd*, 2011. In that decision, the Supreme Court of New Hampshire cites the 1998 Vermont case of *Renaud v. Renaud*:

> *"across the country, the great weight of authority holds that conduct by a parent that tends to alienate the child's affections from the other is so inimical to the child's welfare as to be grounds for a denial of custody to, or a change of custody from, the parent guilty of such conduct."*

This would appear to have been the opinion of the courts of these two and many other US states for at least a decade. There are other US and Canadian decisions acknowledging alienation. Any lawyer who understands alienation will know of them. Yet our judiciaries and law societies, which have become fundamentally perverted by feminism, actively resist the truth.

The only judges who deny alienation are feminists, fools, careerists, cowards, and feminist sycophants (suck-ups). It's that simple. Not one of them is fit for the bench. Not one.

Now let's consider S/Sgt. O'Flaherty's allegation that alienation has been "extensively criticized" by scientists. And this even though alienation had already formally passed the *Frye* Test. I bought a $200 used copy of the 2006 post graduate-level textbook entitled *The International Handbook of Parental Alienation Syndrome—Conceptual, Clinical and Legal Considerations*. Look at contributors' credentials (real names):

1. *Walter Andritzky, Dr. Phil. Dipl.-Psychologist, Dipl.-Sociologist*
2. *Richard B. Austin Jr., Ph.D.*
3. *Eduard Bakalar, Ph.D.*
4. *R. Christopher Barden, Ph.D., J.D., LP*
5. *William Bernet, M.D.*
6. *Sandra S. Berns, Ph.D.*
7. *Barry Bricklin, Ph.D.*
8. *Barry Brodin, Ph.D.*
9. *Janelle Burrill, Ph.D., J.D., B.C.D.*
10. *Glenn F. Cartwright, Ph.D.*
11. *Gail Elliot, Ph.D.*
12. *Craig A. Everett, Ph.D.*
13. *Richard A. Gardner, M.D.*
14. *Daniel J. Gottlieb, Psy.D.*
15. *Tony Hobbs, J.P., L.L.M.*
16. *Ursula Kodjoe, M.A.*
17. *Leona M. Kopetski, M.S.S.W.*
18. *Annelie Kunneth, M.A.*
19. *Werner Leitner, Ph.D.*
20. *Jeffery M. Leving, J.D.*
21. *David L. Levy, J.D.*
22. *Demosthenes Lorandos, Ph.D., J.D.*
23. *Ludwig F. Lowenstein, M.A., Ph.D.*

24. *Jayne A. Major, Ph.D.*
25. *Deidre Rand, Ph.D.*
26. *Randy Rand, Ed.D.*
27. *S. Richard Sauber, Ph.D.*
28. *Lena Hellblom Sjogren, Ph.D.*
29. *Barbara Sobal, J.D.*
30. *Wilfried von Boch-Galhau, M.D.*
31. *Richard A. Warshak, Ph.D.*

The text was edited by Ralph Slovenko, B.E., LL.B., M.A., Ph.D. Professor of Law and Psychiatry at Wayne State University Law School in Detroit, Michigan.

These learned individuals would seem to very much disagree with S/Sgt. O'Flaherty. Add to this list Canadians Dr. Sol Goldstein, Dr. Abraham Worenklein, Ph.D., and Dr. Barbara-Jo Fidler, Ph.D. Oh, let's not forget American Dr. Doug Darnall, Ph.D., either. Or other Ph.D.s or lawyers, some of whom spoke at the Canadian Symposium for Parental Alienation in 2009. I won't get into the reasonably many peer-reviewed, professionally published papers in the field.

Only eight months after S/Sgt. O'Flaherty's report, Dr. Amy Baker, Ph.D., testified at my divorce trial. She informed the court that she was on the committee to have parental alienation included in the next edition of the Diagnostics and Statistics Manual (DSM).

Quite simply, S/Sgt. O'Flaherty's claims regarding parental alienation couldn't have been any more wrong. It would be so easy for me to trash his investigation and report. I could write something like the only thing "pseudo" was his pseudo-investigation. Or I could have listed all those experts and then written "v. S/Sgt. O'Flaherty," to try and belittle him

However, were I to do that, I would be doing O'Flaherty an injustice. My impression of him is the same as for the Krakton Constabulary who attended my 911 call. Small city police with big city dedication and professionalism. There's nothing wrong with O'Flaherty and the guys; the Krakton Boys in Blue are okay by me. Whereas Pasties CAS acted with malice and willful negligence, the Royal Krakton Constabulary acted in good faith.

Yet how could S/Sgt. O'Flaherty have gotten it so, so wrong?

While police and the military have similarities, there are differences, too. I have an advantage over the Krakton Constabulary in this matter. I have been exposed to the military doctrine of information operations (i.e., information warfare). I'll explain this more in *Book Two*. Simply, feminism naturally behaves as an "info op." It operates to profoundly change beliefs and behaviour through disinformation and "psyops." It influences, and in a malignant way. Narcissism is the natural enemy to truth and reason.

This is why I believe that the Canadian military, including me, has until now failed its country. We were the only ones who had the doctrine and theory to understand feminism and sound the warning. In this duty, we failed.

By being forced to incorporate feminist policies and beliefs, the Royal Krakton Constabulary has been badly influenced, to use info ops language. It may be so bad that some Force members might actually believe the feminist rubbish (like patriarchy and "woman abuse") that has been foisted on them.

Just like our courts, the Royal Krakton Constabulary has, to a certain extent, been corrupted by feminism. Ontario appears to be the most feminist jurisdiction in Canada, if not all of North America. Perhaps many, if not most, Ontario police departments are similarly influenced. Indeed, feminism may have penetrated so deeply by now that you have to be a "true believer" to be a police chief in Ontario.

Thus, in some cases, Ontario police are not officers of the law. They are Officers of Feminist Ideology. It is not disrespectful to tell them the truth. It would be an insult to do otherwise.

S/Sgt. O'Flaherty's report suggests he believed what he was told by Pasties CAS. That was a mistake. He also wrote:

> Given the above information S/Sgt O'Flaherty can see no basis
> for pursuing Mr. McConaughey's request to investigate a charge
> of abduction under the Criminal Code.

The Crown Attorney's response to S/Sgt. O'Flaherty's report was written by Mr. Vladislav Gettemov. He replied:

> I have reviewed the report you provided regarding the allegations of Michael McConaughey. I agree with your assessment of

the situation. There is no evidence to support criminal charges which would have a prospect of conviction at this time. The matter is before the family court where it should be. It is clear that the family court is receiving a full account of the dispute on an ongoing basis and that the Honourable Court is taking steps to ensure that appropriate third party professionals are involved. The Ontario Court of Justice is the appropriate forum for the resolution of this family law dispute.

Yours truly,
Vladislav Gettemov, ACA

The 'honourable' court was in on it in from the start! The question of criminal offences in this case is not a police question. It is purely a legal question. I can hardly complain about S/Sgt. O'Flaherty's work outside of his own field of expertise. Not when he's been force-fed feminist propaganda regarding alienation. Especially not when the Ontario Crown Attorney's office can't even recognize blatant, serious, and likely irrefutable offences against the Criminal Code.

At no point in S/Sgt. O'Flaherty's words or those of Mr. Gettemov is there any mention of what the law actually says. None. Yet again, the Rule of Law is exposed as a joke. Nor is there any analysis whatsoever of the facts of the matter versus the law. None. The evidence was a matter of court record (except for Kruël's case notes and logs). These are the application documents of Pasties CAS and the 20 August 2008 order of Gavelbanger. I have copies of all the evidence. The evidence cannot be contested.

The Rule of Law means absolutely nothing in the Matriarchy of Ontario, Canada. It is the supreme joke of our age. Canada is NOT founded upon principles that recognize the Rule of Law. It simply isn't.

If it was, Gavelbanger, Kruël, Mary, and others would be behind bars.

I afterward received a letter from someone at the Attorney General's office. No alienation, good bye, and have a nice day. Thanks there, Honourable Mr. Guy Smiley & Co. Nice to know what good hands justice was in.

Or wasn't.

Who knows? Maybe someday I'll get to have a beer with O'Flaherty and the guys. For purely medicinal purposes, of course. I think I'd like that.

· · · · · · ·

One of the many pathetic jokes that I have had to endure is that social work is a profession. I gather that at one point there was a large volume of complaints about these reprehensible CAS social workers. In response, the Ontario Government created the Ontario College of Social Workers and Social Service Workers (OCSWSSW). Maybe they should have tried to find a longer name for it. In my opinion (and experience), the College was the fraud that social work is a profession and that social workers are accountable. Just like, again in my opinion and experience, that the Child and Family Services Review Board is the fraud that Children's Aid Societies are accountable.

The College was ostensibly created to hold CAS social workers account-able—keep that in mind. Also keep in mind that the College has done nothing, as far as I can tell, to get rid of the Duluth-patriarchy feminist pro-paganda that its members were being indoctrinated in.

When I complained to the College about Kruël, I outlined everything that she did. I showed how this constituted flagrant violations of the College's Code of Ethics. By definition, this would have constituted 'profes-sional' (try not to laugh) misconduct.

All Kruël had to do was write a letter and say that she wasn't allowed to really say anything, but that she had been a good little social worker. Then it was "not guilty." So we have a College that was created to discipline CAS social workers for misconduct. Only it doesn't discipline Kruël for her mis-conduct, as Kruël alleged that she wasn't permitted to talk about her mis-conduct. By her CAS, which paid her for her misconduct. With money that it got, in part, from my tax dollars.

So why do we have the College again? Oh, yes. So we can pretend that social work is a profession, and that its members are accountable.

Here's all Kruël had to write (31 July 2009) to the College to get off free as a bird:

> *At this time I am employed as an Intake Child Protection Worker*
> *with the Pasties Children's Aid Society. As such, I am bound by*

*the confidentiality standards required for my position in addi-
tion to those as a member of the College. Although I would be
happy to provide you with information in response to this complaint, I am unable to present or provide anything to the college
for consideration. Consent from each family member over the age
of 12 has not been provided and all of the information obtained
within my position as a child protection worker is the property
of the Pasties Children's Aid Society. In order for me to be able
to provide any detail into the concerns that have been presented
it would require all parties consent, including the Society's to
discuss or release information relating to this complaint.*

*I have always been diligent in upholding the confidentiality of
the families that I have worked with and have always remained
ethical in my practice. As such, I plan to continue this throughout
this investigation, without compromise. I am aware of the extent
of my qualifications and limitations for assessments. I understand, and I am held to mandatory standards that are required
throughout any investigation and recognize the impact that my
work has on each member of the family. I am proud of the work
that I have done in my career and will continue to be a strong
advocate for the safety and well being of children, while respecting and providing support to the family unit.*

*To my knowledge, I have never been investigated for any criminal
offence, nor have I been accused of a criminal offence prior to the
documentation received in this complaint.*

Let the entire world know that Kruël was proud to have ensured two
boys were subjected to something possibly worse than sexual abuse. That
she was proud to have subtly vilified me to the point of perjury. That she
was proud to have literally met the legal definitions of the criminal abduction of a child under the age of 16 and another under the age of 14. That she
was proud to have not only aided and abetted serious child abuse, but to
have co-perpetrated it as well. That she was proud of having denied me my
children. That she was proud of having denied children their loving father.

That she was proud to have falsified her own case notes. That she was proud to have repeatedly violated the mandatory *Child Protection Standards*.

Also, let it be known that the College—the OCSWSSW—feels that this constitutes ethical and professional social work conduct. Here's a brief excerpt from their 18-page **DECISION AND REASONS** dated March 17, 2010:

> **Decision**
>
> *It is the Committee's determination that there is no basis for a decision to take any further action in response to this complaint.*

Yep. Ignoring the mandatory *Child Protection Standards in Ontario*. Ignoring the *Child and Family Services Act*. Falsifying her case notes. Trying to deceive me into agreeing to CAS involvement in the divorce. Trying to bully me into abandoning the kids to child abuse. Depriving me of my vacation with my own son, when I had agreed-to custody/care of him. Threatening me with fraudulent child protection action unless I abandoned my kids to a child abuser. Making a purely malicious child protection application to assist a suspected child abuser have exclusive care of her kids. Perjuring herself in a sworn affidavit to the Court of Injustice. Aiding and abetting serious child abuse. And, last but not least, acting as a, or even the, primary malefactor for two criminal offences of abduction for the purpose of child abuse.

All of which, if you're in the "profession" of social work in the Matriarchy of Ontario, is no basis for disciplinary action whatsoever. The six panel members included two registered social workers and two registered social service workers. For some reason, this brings to mind that Ontario also registers its sex offenders.

All things being equal, I might prefer that a registered sex offender live in my neighbourhood than a registered social worker. I'd have to think about it some more; it's a tough choice.

Although prostitutes clearly have the stronger claim to constituting a profession, I have found someone with a social work background worth listening to. He's Edward Kruk, M.S.W., Ph.D., of the University of British Columbia. Here are words that he wrote only a few short years ago in a major paper entitled "Child custody, access and parental responsibility:"

> *Sole maternal custody often leads to parental alienation and father absence, and father absence is associated with negative child outcomes. Eighty-five per cent of youth in prison are father-less; 71 per cent of high school dropouts are fatherless; 90 per cent of runaway children are fatherless; and fatherless youth exhibit higher levels of depression and suicide, delinquency, promiscuity and teen pregnancy, behavioural problems and illicit and licit substance abuse. These studies also found that fatherless youth are more likely to be victims of exploitation and abuse, as father absence through divorce is strongly associated with diminished self-concepts in children.* [references omitted]

Kruk's words rather damn Kruël and the College, don't they? Maybe we should start the Ontario College of Registered Sex Offenders. So they can be a profession too. And find no reason to proceed with disciplinary action against any of their clearly upright members. We could even buy them white lab coats to wear. That would make them Clinical Registered Sex Offenders. Then we could give them master's degrees, as well.

I realize that there are intelligent individuals who enter social work with good intentions. However, social work has no coherent, rigorous, and unique body of knowledge that it: a) employs to the benefit of society; and b) maintains on behalf of society with that society's blessing. For those social workers of good faith who haven't swallowed feminist poison, social work is a *calling*. It is not, nor has it ever been, a profession.

If you think that I am being unfair to social workers, consider this. The U.K.'s *The Telegraph* newspaper had an interesting online article dated 12 April 2010. The title was, "Social workers 'enthusiastic removers of children.'" Citing two senior judges from the Court of Appeal—Lord Justice Wall and Lord Justice Aikens—, social workers were said to be working as if they were in "Stalin's Russia or Mao's China."

My Dear Most Honourable Lord Justices Aikens and Wall: Your social workers aren't the only ones! Ontario child protection social workers can be said to be working as if they are in femiNazi Germany.

It appears as if the OCSWSWW clearly needs things explained in the simplest possible way. So let me try a different approach for the OCSWSSW, and see if they can figure this out.

Here is a list of people for them to consider: **Ms.** McConaughey; **Ms.** Kruël; **her** supervisor, **Ms.** Whitless; **Ms.** Klewlesss; **her** supervisor, **Ms.** Dunsley; **Her** Honour, Justice Gavelbanger; and **Madame** Minister Matilda Rype-Blumers.

Oh, and **Mr.** McConaughey. Mustn't forget **HIM**.

Now let's think about a little song that I used to love to hear when I watched *Sesame Street* on the television as a child:

> *One of these things*
> *Is not like the others*
> *One of these things*
> *Doesn't belong*
> *Can you tell which thing*
> *Is not like the others*
> *By the time we finish our song?*

· · · · · · ·

The big moment in court finally arrived. 22 April 2009. I had been maliciously and criminally deprived of my two sons for over eight months. I had exposed the Pasties CAS / Gavelbanger child 'protection' scam, and everyone knew it. Minister Rype-Blumers knew it. Attorney General Smiley knew it. The Ombudsman knew it. The Auditor General knew it. The Child and Family Services Review Board knew it. Pasties CAS knew it. Gavelbanger knew it.

As it turned out, so did Justice Slough. Or rather Injustice Slough. She had been given a feminist promotion.

My position going into the hearing was that we implement Dr. Goldstein's recommendations. Unless Mary could have undone her alienation to Dr. Goldstein's satisfaction by 22 July, the court should order that I have sole care of the kids. I also wanted the court to order that the family undergo expert reunification therapy. This was specifically created for cases of parental alienation.

I had Dr. Amy Baker's fantastic affidavit by this time, and I had submitted it to the court for the final showdown. It speaks for itself:

4. *The premise of this affidavit is that **parental alienation is a form of emotional child abuse**. Thus, when allegations of parental alienation are made, they should be treated as seriously as any other abuse allegation and should be investigated with vigor and competence. However, because parental alienation is a specific subset of emotional abuse, it requires specific training in its identification. It is unlikely that an investigator without training in parental alienation dynamics would be able to ascertain whether a child's estrangement from a parent is due to legitimate causes such as deficiencies in the rejected parent or due to parental alienation, which is the concerted use of alienation strategies in order to effectuate the child's rejection of a competent and capable parent. This differential diagnosis requires familiarity with a specialized body of knowledge. **It is highly unlikely that a child protection worker in North America would have such a familiarity and the necessary competence to apply it correctly**.*

5. *Further, should an investigation occur, it is essential that the investigator be objective in the exercise of sound clinical judgment regarding all possible causes of the child's estrangement from the rejected parent. Should an investigator have a preexisting assumption or bias regarding the likely cause of the family dysfunction and the child's alignment with one parent against the other (such as adopting the **Duluth Model** in which it is assumed that the father was a batterer or deserves to be rejected because of his abuse of "power and control"), it is unlikely that a fair and honest conclusion can be drawn.*

6. *A further complicating factor is that alienating parents may have a type 2 dramatic personality disorder (**narcissism**, histrionic, or borderline) that **makes them appear to have been victimized** by the parent whom the child is rejecting. This victim stance can appear to corroborate the investigator's assumption of male abuse of control and power and legitimize the child's rejection of that parent. Again, special training and knowledge is*

*required to allow an investigator to accurately ascertain the true nature of the family dynamics. In the absence of such training and in combination with **a bias against fathers**, it is likely that parental alienation will be ignored, overlooked, and unidentified, due to a failure to employ the necessary forensic techniques.*

*9. **Alienating parents sometimes pay lip service** to the importance of the relationship of the child and the target parent **once they have successfully programmed a child** to reject the target parent, but **they will make statements to the effect that they must respect the child's "wishes,"** that they are powerless to change the child's attitudes as these attitudes are the target parent's fault, or that **they are concerned about the child being forced against his/her wishes to be with the target parent.** **Child protection activity** which ostensibly respects a child's wishes to reject (i.e. not want access with) a parent in cases where suspicions of alienation exist **may well serve to assist in the abuse of the child,** as it would reinforce the programming that it was the child's choice and decision to reject the target parent. **Hence, such child protection action is strongly contraindicated in cases with allegations of alienation that have not yet received competent expert forensic evaluation. Doing so via a successful child protection application to a court may be even more harmful to the child, as it would likely appear to the child that the potent and impartial authority figure of the judge was agreeing with the alienating parent's programming content. This independent and powerful validation of the programming may worsen its severity, causing greater emotional harm and increasing the difficulty of achieving effective therapeutic intervention.***

I added the bold. I trust my disgust at the conduct of Kruël, Klewless, Pasties CAS, Pryck, leDouche, Gavelbanger, Slough, the Ontario Judicial Council, The Ontario College of Social Workers & Social Service Workers, the Child and Family Services Review Board, the Office of the Mothers'

Lawyer, Minister Rype-Blumers, and Attorney General Smiley is by now far, far beyond question.

I'm not exactly cheering for Professor Peter Jaffe to win the Nobel Prize, either.

I am not exaggerating to even the most minute degree when I state that Ontario's family 'justice' system is rotten to its absolute core. The stench of Ontario's matriarchal and oppressive family 'justice' is unbearable. From the Attorney General and the Minister on down to the stupidest child protection worker imaginable, the entire system is foul and odious beyond comprehension.

This is the filth that we divorced fathers are forced to wallow through in our hopeless quests to protect our children.

Pasties CAS had its tail between its legs. It had been a bad dog and knew it. It had been badly embarrassed and was trying to drop the case like a hot potato. Here's part of what those utterly craven individuals submitted to the court:

> 3. The Society would like to withdraw its involvement with this family. The children are safe in the care of their mother. Access for the father needs to be arranged and agreed upon.

More lies from your friendly neighbourhood CAS. Perjury, in fact. The boys were not safe with Mary, and Pasties CAS knew it. It had ignored the very expert whom it had agreed to employ in the case. Pasties CAS knowingly asked a court to leave children with an expert-confirmed child abuser. Better that children be abused and psychologically maimed for life than the malice and willful negligence of Pasties CAS be admitted to.

The position of the Office of the Mothers' Lawyer—the OCL—was that it didn't have a position. That's right. Despite knowing that its clients, Hugh and Leo, were being subjected to serious expert-confirmed child abuse, the OCL had no position. Can't be too hasty with something potentially worse than enforced child sodomy, can we? The OCL, too, is paid for by our tax dollars. To ensure that the kids' best interests are represented in legal proceedings.

Only it's the mother's best financial interests that are represented. Not the kids'.

Mary's position was that the boys should remain in her care. And that I have access that was "progressive, in accordance with the children's wishes and best interests." Which, from a narcissistic alienator—a pathological liar—, meant "never."

Well, into the courtroom came Slough. Remember, this was the judge who had said that the court would draw a "negative inference" if Dr. Goldstein couldn't get the boys to wish to be with me. He couldn't.

Pretty much the first words out of Slough's mouth were to the effect of, "We can't use Dr. Goldstein's report, so what are we to do?" Slough had clearly been inducted into the Evil Sisterhood. I half suspect that Gavelbanger had to use sock puppets to explain things:

> *Right Sock Puppet*: "Oh, no Your Honour! The Women of Pasties CAS are NOT interfering in divorce. NOT us. Wouldn't dream of it. NEVER. We are concerned about the risk of 'emotional harm' due to 'divorce conflict.' That's why you have to excommunicate father. We mean, that's why you have to issue an unlawful and criminal order. Oops again. We mean, it's why you have to 'protect' the children. It's just his bad luck that this will screw him in divorce."

> *Left Sock Puppet*: "Why, Women of Pasties CAS, what a coincidence! I, the GREAT Gavelbanger, too, am concerned about the children. That is why I will make an unlawful and criminal order to utterly screw father in divorce. Ahem. I mean an order to ensure I protect the kids from the risk of emotional harm. Or was that further emotional harm? Or the risk of physical harm? Whatever. It's not like the law matters. Yet I, Gavelbanger THE MAGNIFICENT, will magnanimously condescend in my greatness to let father have 'reasonable' access. To his own sons. Whom he's never abused or harmed in any way. And always loved. I would say that "never" is reasonable. Wouldn't you agree, Women of Pasties CAS?"

Right Sock Puppet: "Absolutely, Your Honour. Thank you so much for being the GREAT DEFENDER of the Rule of Law. And for being such a GREAT CHAMPION of the IDEALS of TRUTH and JUSTICE. It is every woman's duty to prevent 'woman abuse.'"

Left Sock Puppet: "Indeed it is. Yet there is no need to applaud me, Women of Pasties CAS. Nor should you throw rose petals beneath my feet. Neither is kneeling before me necessary. Duty is reward enough for someone as GREAT as I, burden though that may be."

Slough made some lame excuses as to why we couldn't use Dr. Goldstein's report. I recall her saying that Dr. Goldstein had only spoken to the CAS on the phone, and not in person.

Let's see. The Court of Injustice was in the not-quite-mega metropolis of Krakton. We had a top alienation expert in Toronto. I cared enough about the kids that I made the four-hour drive from Ottawa to Toronto three times to meet with Dr. Goldstein. Pasties CAS couldn't be bothered to make the two-hour Krakton to Toronto drive even once?

And, because of this, we couldn't use Dr. Goldstein's report?

Slough also said something about the fact that Dr. Goldstein had not spoken to the boys' teachers. How can one of Canada's foremost experts say there's alienation? He's a man, and he hasn't spoken to the women teachers and principal. They would have told him that there's no alienation.

Silly man.

What? Did Slough expect me to shell out a few more thousands of dollars for another waste of Dr. Goldstein's valuable time?

The real reason that Slough had to ignore Dr. Goldstein's report was self-preservation. That report was humiliating for the Court of Injustice and the two judges (especially with Dr. Baker's affidavit). It was particularly bad for Gavelbanger. I know it's absurd, but let's pretend that the Rule of Law was actually respected by the Court of Injustice. Here's what would (and should) have happened.

We would have gone to trial. Pasties CAS would have applied to find that the boys were in need of *CFSA* protection. Protection from: their mother;

their older sister; Pasties CAS itself; and Injustice Gavelbanger. Gavelbanger would had to have found that the boys were in need of protection. Protection from: their mother; their older sister; Pasties CAS; and herself.

So, Slough chose to knowingly abandon two boys to serious, expert-confirmed child abuse. Just like Pasties CAS; her skin and Gavelbanger's were more important than kids or justice.

As Slough struggled to find a way out of the mess, 'sweet' Lisa Loveless-Hartt chimed in. She suggested that we use Mariah Alyawaiz deMansfalt to help the family out. I have to hand it to Loveless-Hartt. It was a sharp legal maneuver. She had read the winds of court accurately—Sailor Slough was rudderless and adrift. By getting deMansfalt involved, Loveless-Hartt was trying to bring in someone incompetent in alienation to undermine Dr. Goldstein's expert opinion.

Well, didn't Slough just think that was a wonderful idea! I wouldn't be surprised if she sent Loveless-Hartt a thank-you card afterwards. Yes, let's get someone with a master's degree in social work to help the family out. By golly, that'll solve everything!

If there is a hell, it involves being 'helped' by people with master's degrees in social work. For the rest of eternity.

We took a break so the parties and their lawyers could talk. The only way the Court of Injustice was going to drop the malicious case and rescind its order was if I 'agreed' to employ deMansfalt. Who, sadly, had no actual competence with either narcissism or alienation. I could not get to a divorce trial until the malicious child protection case was dropped.

I had to get to divorce trial to have any hope of saving the boys from alienation. The Court of Injustice, Pasties CAS, and the Office of the Mothers' Lawyer all favoured expert-confirmed child abuse. They weren't going to help. I was effectively forced by Slough into 'agreeing.' As I later learned, Ontario judges bullying men into 'agreeing' is a common tactic.

I had to agree, but did so only on the condition that deMansfalt's work was to be non-admissible at the divorce trial. As it turns out, non-admissible evidence from women social workers incompetent in alienation IS admissible in divorce court. Via the backdoor of innuendo. When it benefits the mother, of course. And a feminist judge presides.

But I'm getting ahead of myself.

The question of whether Dr. Goldstein's report was admissible in divorce proceedings was left to the divorce court to decide.

The court rescinded Gavelbanger's malicious order around 8 May 2009. After, of course, having secured for itself a lie as its excuse to drop the malicious case. My children had been abducted from me for more than eight months. So they could be subjected the entire time to something potentially worse than buggery.

Because, in Ontario, Canada that's okay, so long as mother gets the child support payments. That's called 'justice' here. Maybe not in North Korea. But here?—yes.

At no point during the entire period did any Pasties CAS worker or supervisor ever set foot in a court room. Not once. All the Women of Pasties CAS had to do was fill out the paperwork for their lawyer to submit. Having done this, a feminist judge of the Court of Injustice did the rest.

It is not sexist to tell the truth.

Mary did not have to utter a single word in court the entire time. Not one. The kids were just handed to her on a silver platter, as was the child support.

That's because kids in divorce have no rights. They're not people, thanks to our judges. They are nothing more than mother's property. They are her little magic piggy banks. They spew out money for her every month. That's all kids are to Ontario courts, nothing more.

This is what law does. What the law says is all lies.

I went to the home which I still jointly owned (and for which I was paying 100 percent of the mortgage) as soon as I could after Gavelbanger's malicious order was rescinded. When the kids realized who was at the door, they ran and hid from sight. Mary came to answer, and she wasn't happy. When I asked to see the kids, she bellowed in an ugly voice to inquire if they wanted to talk to me.

Needless to say, the kids wanted nothing to do with me. Just as Mary had wanted and had worked so hard to achieve. Just as Pasties CAS had wanted and worked so hard to achieve.

Hillary failed Grade 12 for the second year in a row under Mary's exclusive 'care.' This was exactly what Mary wanted. Far too much non-attendance due to bogus medical reasons. Which in Mary's mirror was Hillary's 'depression' due to my having 'abandoned' the family. Just as Pasties CAS had requested. Just as Gavelbanger had ordered.

What did Pasties CAS, the Ontario Court of Injustice, the Office of the Mothers' Lawyer, or the Ontario Government care? They'd done their true jobs. Make certain to ensure mother gets HER child support payments, whatever it takes.

And lie through their teeth the whole time about what they were doing.

. . . .

Despite the cover-up, it appears as if my hearing against Pasties CAS had been more effective than I had realized. Daphne suspected that my efforts to expose Pasties CAS had provoked the Ontario Government into creating The Commission for the Promotion of Sustainable Child Welfare. For those who don't understand government deceit, "sustainable" means funding cutbacks. As in, we can no longer afford this; we're reining you in.

However, the *Child Protection Standards in Ontario* are still the same. Every CAS referral still has its secret feminist witch-hunt for "woman abuse" built-in.

Nothing has really changed. Nothing.

. . . .

I waited until after my divorce trial before I registered a formal complaint against Gavelbanger. I didn't want the divorce judge to stick it to me for having exposed another judge. In retrospect, that might have been a mistake. I probably should have let it be known that I would not hesitate to expose an ideologically corrupt feminist judge. Regardless, since Gavelbanger was a provincially-appointed judge, my complaint went to the Ontario Judicial Council (OJC).

I'd read the few OJC decisions that were online. They claimed to balance the need for a judge to operate free of fear of persecution for screwing up versus the need for public confidence in our judges. Judicial independence v. judicial accountability.

Sounds good in theory. What it really means—remember, judges are above the law, and they know it—is that unless it gets in the press, judges will cover up for other judges. I had little faith in the complaint process, but I left no stone unturned in my quest for justice. No matter how many judges I had to fight to get it.

My complaint was dated 27 November 2009. Included in my specific complaints were:

> 1. *Gender bias and prejudice demonstrated against me in court*
> 2. *Issuing an order which was in direct contravention to the law under which it was made*
> 3. *Tyranny*
> 4. *Abuse of judicial power to effect child abuse*
> 5. *Abuse of judicial power to effect emotional abuse against an innocent man*
> 6. *Gross abuse of judicial power on 20 August 2008 to effect the criminal act of abduction of two minors for the purpose of child abuse as can reasonably be held under the Criminal Code of Canada*
> 7. *Gender bias in displaying a contemptuous indifference in court towards the importance of fathers (i.e., men) in the lives of their children*
> 8. *Displaying a callous indifference in court to the angst that forcible separation of a father from his children causes the father, implying that men don't love their children, as a form of gender bias*
> 9. *Gender bias and possible obstruction of justice demonstrated 16 October 2008*
> 10. *Gender bias in the acceptance of misandry* [hatred of men] *in court*

In retrospect, I don't think I emphasized the gender bias enough. Oh, well.

I included all the supporting documentary evidence. I also gave them a copy of the Justice Vogelsang decision mentioned earlier. By this point, I had completed my comprehensive *Breakthrough Parenting* course (by Jayne Major, Ph.D.), so I sent a copy of my course report, too. Here are some excerpts:

> *For more than 20 years, this has been a court-referred program, with great appreciation from family court judges who have seen*

results from this skill-building program that vastly exceeded what other programs were able to provide.

If the parent is not able to demonstrate a genuine understanding of his or her current family situation, including changes needed for both short-term and long-term success, we do not certify completion.

Based on my thorough evaluation of Mr. McConaughey's written materials and a comprehensive oral review, my finding is that he has demonstrated an Excellent understanding of this comprehensive parenting program. (The Excellent rating is given to less than 3% of parents.)

Mr. McConaughey has also demonstrated that he understands how to apply what he has learned in his own unique family situation, so that it isn't just theoretical knowledge of the kind that is soon forgotten.

I don't want to make it seem that I was a "super parent" who walked on water or anything like that. I wasn't. Like many parents, I tried to do my best, and generally did so most of the time. It's a bit of a learn-as-you-go process. I believe that I did well in the course for two reasons: 1) I really worked hard at it, as I was motivated to do well and so be able to offer the court proof that I was a good parent; and 2) However imperfect I might have been, I think I was generally on the right track as a father. I learned a fair bit on the course, and its approach to parenting made a lot of sense to me. I highly recommend it to other parents.

Gavelbanger did not put the boys with a father who managed to score in the top three percent on a respected and comprehensive parenting course. No. Instead, she put the boys with a mother who was likely worse than a pedophile. Without trial, against the law, with adamantly disputed facts, and with a CAS application so full of holes that it looked like Swiss cheese. Because she was 'concerned.' In Ontario, Canada, that's justice. In-justice, mind you, but judges can be rather oblivious to the finer points of law, it would seem.

With regards to complaint number 6, after making specific legal arguments, what I wrote included:

> ... Her Honour's order can be held to have constituted or resulted in an offence under article 280(1) of the Criminal Code of Canada... Her Honour's order can likewise be held to have constituted or resulted in an offence under article 281 of the Criminal Code of Canada.

Since judges are above the law and protect other judges, all of the OJC correspondence to me had "PRIVATE & CONFIDENTIAL" written at the beginning. This was to try to intimidate me into not going public with my complaint. Sorry, judges. I've held a TOP SECRET security clearance for most of my adult life. Your pathetic PRIVATE & CONFIDENTIAL thing doesn't impress me at all. This is a public matter, not a private one. Nice try.

Right. Now ask yourself this: Did I or did I not inform the OJC that Gavelbanger had committed two serious and specific criminal offences?

I clearly did.

Suppose we're ordinary men and women who care about genuine justice, which means that we're not judges. We thus respect the Rule of Law, and by now we understand the truth. Gavelbanger is *prima facie* guilty of the criminal offences of abduction as per the *Criminal Code* s.s 280.1 and 281.

So what do you think the OJC said back to me? Some old feminist sourpuss of a judge named Lord Justice P. Penelope Pamplemousse, in her letter to me of 21 May 2010, wrote that I had alleged that:

> The [Gavelbanger's] order constituted a gross abuse of judicial power and in effect resulted in the criminal "abduction" of two children for the purposes of parental alienation, a form of child abuse.

Not "in effect." In reality. Not "abduction." The criminal offences of abduction as articulated in the *Criminal Code*'s sections 280(1) and 281. In accordance with the Rule of Law and the Principles of Fundamental Justice. The OJC had played ostrich, stuck its head in the sand, and pretended that I hadn't stated that Gavelbanger had committed serious crimes. The OJC completely ignored the law. This is what judges do, nowadays. No surprise that the OJC found that there was nothing in the court transcripts—which

Gavelbanger was apparently free to edit—that supported my allegations. The OJC noted that Gavelbanger "appeared concerned" about the level of conflict and how it might affect the children.

Of course she said that. It's called "lying." This apparently is something that the OJC itself is quite familiar with, if not highly adept at.

How about that Ontario Judicial Council? According to them, the Rule of Law no longer matters. It's now the Rule of Estrogen. All that matters is how a woman judge "feels" about the case. To heck with the *Charter* and rights and freedoms. Just so long as she lies about what she is doing, it's okay. I want to be clear here. It isn't me who is being disrespectful to women. It's the Ontario Judicial Council. They effectively said that women can't be expected to do a judge's job, so we have to make excuses for them. We have to pretend that they're as good as male judges, when they're not. Employment equity, don't you know.

If I was a non-feminist woman judge, I would be livid with the OJC's response. It is extremely demeaning to women.

We've seen what happens when we apply feminist 'logic' to come up with the New Duluth Model. Let's try applying the logic of the Ontario Judicial Council and likewise see what happens.

Pretend that I am a fundamentally gender-biased, lying, narcissistic male judge (just like a feminist judge, but in reverse). I want to stick it to some woman in my court. I know that there is a scribe capturing my every word; I have to lie about what I am about to do. So, I say that I am 'concerned' about the woman's "inter-generational wellness." I thus order she undergo an "involuntary, gender-asymmetric, certified-organic cervical wellness examination." Under the 'supervision' of the Fathers' Aid Society, to really make certain of things. Because I am *concerned*, of course. All that matters is how I, the judge, feel. Now it's the Rule of Testosterone.

Besides, it's only going to be a temporary order. Those don't really count, do they?

Man, I sound like one fine judge, don't I? Just ask my judicial council. Only for ordinary and decent men and women, what I've actually ordered is rape. However, applying the 'logic' of the Ontario Judicial Council, it isn't. According to them, if we ignore the Rule of Law and lie through our teeth about what we're doing (and we're a judge), then it's okay to effectively order that serious offences against the *Criminal Code* be committed.

Law is not just what it says; law is what it does. Your words, judges, not mine.

The Ontario Judicial Council should know this: I gave them a fair chance. I honestly reported the truth, the whole truth, and nothing but the truth, so help me God. As it turned out, they chose to conduct themselves in craven fashion.

When I went on the OJC website back in 2009 to research my complaint, I found their procedures for a complaint. Here is what the current version states,* which is close enough to what I had at the time:

> *subs. 51.3(4) Composition*

> *Complaints received by the Judicial Council shall be reviewed by a complaint subcommittee of the Judicial Council which consists of a judge, other than the Chief Justice of the Ontario Court of Justice and a lay member of the OJC (the term "judge" includes a master when a master is the subject of a complaint). Eligible members shall serve on the complaint subcommittees on a rotating basis.*

And

> *subs. 51.4(21) Dismissal of Complaint*

> *A complaint subcommittee shall dismiss the complaint without further investigation if, in its opinion, it falls outside the Judicial Council's jurisdiction or if it is frivolous or an abuse of process.*

The response I received was from the OJC itself. This means that my complaint had been vetted by this sub-committee and had been found to have merit. This in turn means that some Ontario judge felt that my complaint was neither frivolous nor irrational.

So why did the OJC lie to me and try to deceive me? Because it knew I was right. They could not refute my argument that Gavelbanger had committed two offences of criminal abduction. If they could have, they would have. Since they could not, they did not.

* http://www.ontariocourts.ca/ocj/ojc/policies-and-proce-
dures/procedures-document/, accessed 7 July 2013

Their Holinesses then condescended to inform me that I had alleged "abduction" as a way of showing their contempt for me. "How dare you believe in the *Charter* and the Rule of Law?! It's not abduction unless we say it's abduction. We *unelected* judges don't just make the law; we own the law. We ARE the law."

Think about it. What I encountered wasn't an isolated incident. It was the status quo. It was de rigeur. It was widespread and had been going on for years. The OJC must have realized that if they allowed Gavelbanger to be held accountable for her actions, they would have set a devastating precedent. They had to undermine the Rule of Law.

It's what judges do best, nowadays.

The truth is likely that a significant number of Ontario judges, particularly feminist judges, should be in jail for the criminal abduction of children from their loving fathers. The OJC couldn't admit to the truth. It would have been a judicial scandal like no other. It would have shattered public confidence in our judges. Deservedly so, in my opinion. If you're a journalist, don't bother asking the OJC for the truth about Gavelbanger.

The judges will just lie to you, too.

. . . .

I'd love to see any legal authority rationally refute the argument that Gavelbanger committed criminal acts of abduction. Any lawyer, any politician, any professor emeritus of law, or any judge, regardless of stature.

Not deny. Not pretend. Not "play ostrich" and stick their heads in the sand. Not lie through their teeth. Rationally refute the argument, in accordance with the Rule of Law and the Principles of Fundamental Justice.

There is only one way that I can see for someone to attack the argument. It is to allege that Parliament intended that feminist judges could effectively order serious child abuse by employing fraudulent child protection to intentionally and unlawfully deprive me of my sons by taking them away from me against my will. Certainly no judge could make such a finding and not appear blatantly biased. It clearly is in judges' best interests to so find.

I suspect I know what the verdict in the Court of Public Opinion will be.

For those who try to refute the argument, I wish them luck. Despite having attempted for over five years, I cannot. I believe the argument to be irrefutable. Unless someone can succeed where I have failed, know this: In

Ontario, Canada, it is acceptable to be both a judge and a criminal. This is what happens when the Rule of Law is entrusted to the unworthy.

Judge not, lest ye be judged.

Intermission – Part I

The question isn't who is going to let me;
it's who is going to stop me.
— AYN RAND

I began writing this book (during vacation, evenings, and weekends) 18 months ago. I first developed a plan as to its theme, topics, structure, word counts for individual chapters, overall size, etc. In terms of output, the writing didn't really start to happen in earnest until the Introduction had more or less taken shape. This proved to be the catalyst that started the creative process of capturing those thoughts that had been maturing for nearly four years, and others that predated this by up to 20 years.

You might say this book has been a long time in the making.

However, no plan survives first contact with the enemy. The words began to pour forth in a veritable torrent of thoughts and emotions. The structure adapted itself to the creative process. The word counts especially went out the window, so to speak. The book was, from the start, a living thing, and so it necessarily evolved. At roughly the half-way mark, I realize that I must take a brief pause at a natural break in the work.

Yet the work remains a single entity. It is meant to be read as a whole.

Once an earlier chapter had sat long enough that I could look at it with fresh eyes, I'd go back and edit it, when I needed a break from writing. I discovered that I had made frequent errors related to verb tenses. I had too often written in the present tense instead of the past.

In writing about my ordeal, I was reliving it.

The emotional trauma that target parents experience has been likened to that of experiencing the death of a child. It may be worse than that, as there is no closure; there doesn't seem to be a way to grieve. It also has a nightmare aspect. Virtually everyone who is supposed to help you seems to do just the opposite. This happens in slow motion, before your very eyes. Watching your children's personalities being continuously corrupted into something ugly is torment beyond description. It is utter cruelty. It is far too often the norm for fathers in Ontario's fundamentally perverted family "justice" system. Yet, we fathers are expected to remain stoic, lest we be accused of having anger issues.

And so we cry invisible tears.

I suppose it's little wonder that I ultimately needed three or so courses of sleeping pills to get through all of this. I'd fall asleep easily enough. Yet I'd always wake up, typically between 12 a.m. and 4 a.m., dreaming that I was in court. I'd wake up thinking of how I might better explain to the court what was happening. I'd wake up thinking of some new legal argument or tactic. I'd wake up thinking of some new factum (a short explanatory legal paper) or affidavit that might help the case.

It was all a waste. Every single, solitary moment. Every single, solitary dollar. The Rule of Law is the cruel joke foisted upon fathers and children by the Pharisees we know as judges.

Though I did not enjoy my time with the Pathfinders and Ranger-qualified soldiers of the Canadian Army, I remain in debt to them. Were it not for them, I may not have had the fortitude to see this through. So, too, with my father and his lesson to me on the virtue of perseverance when I was in high school. Thanks to men whose duty it was to shape me, I did not quit.

Nor do I cower at the feet of those charlatans who pretend to be worthy of administering justice. They are not the first tyrants to know the resolve of the Canadian military man. In remembrance of those who went before me, I can only hope that I prove worthy in this regard.

Feminism is the enemy; judges are its collaborators.

Perhaps this work will provide me with the catharsis—the emotional cleansing—that I need to completely leave this all behind me. I've done a relatively good job of getting on with my life, but the pain of having your children's lives damaged or destroyed and their personalities warped never really leaves you. It always lingers just a little bit.

I think this has been worse for me than the typical targeted father or mother. I have served my entire life in the defence of Canada, Canadians, and Canadian values and interests. Too late did I learn that those values were the Rule of Lies, injustice, tyranny, oppression, cowardice, slavery, and child abuse. Being a third generation RCAF Navigator on one side and a second generation RCAF officer on the other, I feel betrayed by a nation that my family has faithfully served. I now have little faith in our social institutions and officials.

Especially not the judiciary.

I do, however, continue to believe in and champion: the Rule of Law; genuine rights and freedoms; and the ideals of truth and justice. Judges may be the failed caretakers of these, but they neither own nor defend them.

These are the birthright of all, and are our shared responsibility to protect.

It would have been too easy for me to have become mired in a pit of vitriol and hatred towards those who wronged the kids and me. This is something feminism seeks, just as Mary sought to provoke me to anger. Despite my upbringing, there have been times when I have had to fight the urge to pray to God that He damn the souls of Malyssa B. Kruël and Gertrude Gavelbanger to Hell for all eternity for what these vile women did to the kids and me.

This temptation wasn't an indication of my vindictiveness. I've always been a forgive-and-forget sort of person. What it was indicative of was the extreme emotional suffering that these duplicitous women gleefully subjected me to.

I forgive those who have wronged me. As for wronging my children, this is not for me to forgive. For the record, I do not absolve the Governments of Ontario and of Canada (especially not their judges), and Pasties CAS of their liabilities for the financial damages that I have suffered and persecution that I have endured due to their willful negligence, malice, malfeasance, duplicity, craven and in some instances criminal conduct, contempt for *The*

Charter of Rights and Freedoms, and most especially not for their contempt for the Rule of Law.

Although I choose to forgive, until the day exists when Kruël, Gavelbanger, and others are behind bars for what they did, I cannot honestly say that I live in a just land. Since I cannot honestly say it, I will not. I was brought up to tell the truth.

And, of course, to wear clean underwear.

For the decent people who read this book—the non-narcissists and non-feminists—, thank you for having the courage to see through the distorted mirror of the society in which I live. Were it an honest and just society, no fundamentally decent person such as Dr.s Amy Baker, Marc Feldman, Barbara Jo Fidler, or Richard Warshak (and the others) would ever find themselves mentioned in a book such as this. Sadly, we live in a vulgar and narcissistic age. I have adapted my message as necessary, as I could not remain silent.

Sometimes, to be silent is to be complicit.

Yet I am aware that I am no Margaret Atwood in terms of being a brilliant writer. Writing this book was hardly an effortless exercise on my part. Regardless, my message has a noble purpose, however short that message may fall from perfection.

If I appear intolerant, understand that I come from a very intolerant professional culture. It is rightly intolerant of incompetence, laziness, folly, stupidity, cowardice, deceit, dishonourable conduct, bullying, tyranny, and the like. I make no apology whatsoever for my intolerance of feminists. Nor those moral cowards who appease feminists, nor the foolish or craven men who actively or passively support feminism.

None.

I have tried to balance the full truth of my outrage at the reprehensible conduct of people mentioned in this book with my basic preference for civility. If there were moments where I erred in this regard, I ask for understanding and forgiveness. This hasn't been a fun experience—far from it, in fact.

For social workers, know that I hold you collectively in contempt. In my eyes, social work is the lie that being an unwanted, bossy girlfriend who couldn't get a real degree is both a legitimate academic discipline and a profession. In over four years, I have seen little evidence of legitimacy from any social worker, Professor Kruk's words notwithstanding. While my story is yet to be fully told, there were three women with master's degrees in social work who, in my case experience, either contributed to my children's alienation, or at least acted to reward Mary for it. I believe, based upon experience, that social work is a bogus academic discipline.

I also believe that the Ontario College of Social Work and Social Service Work is worse than a joke. I believe it is an abomination. It deceives the people of Ontario into believing that social work is a profession. In my opinion, social work is not. It deceives the people of Ontario into believing that CAS social workers are accountable. In my experience, they are not. The onus is on social workers to prove me wrong. The burden of proof clearly rests with social workers and the College. Let the Court of Public Opinion judge fairly.

For judges, I admit there remain honourable, noble, and just people amongst their numbers. However, taken as a whole, I maintain that our judges are so deeply biased that justice has long been fundamentally perverted. We divorced fathers and our children have been subjected to systemic persecution and oppression at their hands for decades. Judges routinely and as a matter of covert policy deprive men of the presumption of innocence.

We are, by feminist definition, 'guilty' of being men. We are deprived of equality under the law. We are deprived of our rights. We are deprived of our freedoms. We are deprived of the children whom we love. We are ordered sold into the slavery of onerous and unjust support payments for children we rarely if ever see. Children who are cult-programmed to hate us by the unfit mothers to whom we are economic slaves.

In the Court of Public Opinion, I pronounce our *unelected* judges—even the highest—guilty of fundamental bias. They are henceforth to be presumed guilty of fundamental bias until proven guilty. They are unworthy. They are the lepers of justice of the third millennium. The shoe is now on the other foot; let's see how they like a little of their own medicine. The burden of proof that any judge is fit to dispense justice now rests with that judge. Let's see how they like that, too.

We dads are tired of the Rule of Law being the biggest joke in Canada. So we say to judges: fix the problem. You have proven yourselves unworthy of being entrusted with rights, freedoms, and justice. We have not. It is we dads who care about the Rule of Law and the safety of our children. You do not. It is we dads who care about this society and our families. You do not.

All that our judges really care about is themselves.

We dads have had enough. Judges are not worthy of our respect, and so they have lost it. We now hold judges collectively in contempt, and they've nobody to blame but themselves. It is what they deserve. This will not even begin to change until the day when judges like Gavelbanger are behind bars for their shameful malfeasance and tyranny.

Judges chose to abandon the moral high ground. I chose to occupy it. Nature abhors a vacuum.

There are brave women in our societies who have the courage to speak up against feminism, and its rampant and unrelenting persecution of men. In admiration, I commend their efforts. No matter how humble the blog, the newspaper column, or the speech, I commend them. The compassionate thoughts and sympathies of these exceptional women soothe our tortured male souls in a way that words cannot begin to describe.

Thank you. Thank you for listening. Thank you for caring. Thank you for telling the truth.

For feminists across the land, know this: your time is getting short. You messed with the wrong dad's kids. I wasn't road kill that night when I put traction on my own femur. I wasn't road kill when the Evil Sisterhood thought they'd subject me to a child protection hit-and-run. How does the saying go? What doesn't kill you makes you stronger?

Feminists have made me stronger. For this and this alone, I thank them.

Feminists love to brand men who dare oppose them or offend them as misogynists. This is but a fancy word for "woman-haters." Or, when men object to their manipulative and abusive actions, feminists love to reply that these men are threatened by 'strong' women.

If you're a cunning, manipulative, lying, and abusive feminist, regardless of your stature, you're not a strong woman. You might want to try a certain word beginning with the third letter of the alphabet, instead.

It exists for a reason. I understand this now.

Feminists are used to howling in outrage to get their way. They can howl away like a banshee; see if I care. They can have worldwide feminist marches against me. See if I care. They can even declare a Feminist Holy War against me.

See if I care.

With *Book Two*, feminists will stand naked for all to see. It won't be a pretty sight. Everyone will understand just how uncaring, cunning, manipulative, and dishonest feminists really are. Regardless of whether they're students, social workers, lawyers, judges, politicians, activists, or professors. Just like Echo with Narcissus, everyone will pity them.

And no one will ever believe their lies again.

Feminists will undoubtedly consider this work—what they've seen so far—to be outrageous. Yet another example of narcissistic rage in response to narcissistic injury. I might expect them to try and persecute me for telling the truth. I might expect them to project their shame onto me via all sorts of false accusations. Perhaps I'll be accused of hate speech at a human "rights" tribunal.

It wasn't by accident that I wrote that I might become the most hated man alive.

Once again, so be it. No quarter: none asked; none granted. To misquote John Paul Jones, I have not yet begun to write. I will make good on every promise from the Introduction that has yet to be fulfilled, and then some. I will explain how feminists suffer from penis envy gender narcissism. Whereas covert narcissism is narcissism of the feminine *social* self, penis envy gender narcissism is narcissism of the feminine *sexual* self.

Very simply, feminists are deeply but *unconsciously* ashamed of being women. To the point of hating being women. They envy men. They loathe us for being men. They want to be just like men, especially the narcissistic male stereotype. They pathologically and desperately need *all women to be like men*. Only feminists don't realize this; it is subconscious. Feminists must pathologically perceive— their mirror—any natural order that may exist between men and women as women being 'victims' of men and society.

It is like covert narcissism on extreme social steroids.

When a feminist calls a man a misogynist, it is really narcissistic projection. She is projecting her own unconscious self-hatred and the associated narcissistic shame of being a woman onto the man who is her unfortunate victim. It is so perversely ironic. Her apparent conscious misandry (hatred of men) stems from her own unconscious misogyny (penis envy-based hatred of being a woman).

Like any good narcissist, depending upon the severity, there is no length to which feminists won't go to build and maintain their collectively warped mirror. They need us to reflect this in our beliefs and our words. They need this to be reflected in our social institutions and research results and laws and social policies and judges' decisions. *All of society must be their mirror.* Without this, their perverse need for their false selves of women being inherent "victims" wouldn't be 'true.'

There exists a unified construct of gender narcissism. It explains *everything* about feminists, and it is so, so intuitive and simple to understand. Narcissus will now recognize *her* reflection in the stream. Nemesis spoke so long ago, yet still the doom decreed remains intact. It cannot be averted, for *Book Two* cannot be averted.

Feminism will destroy itself. It is ordained.

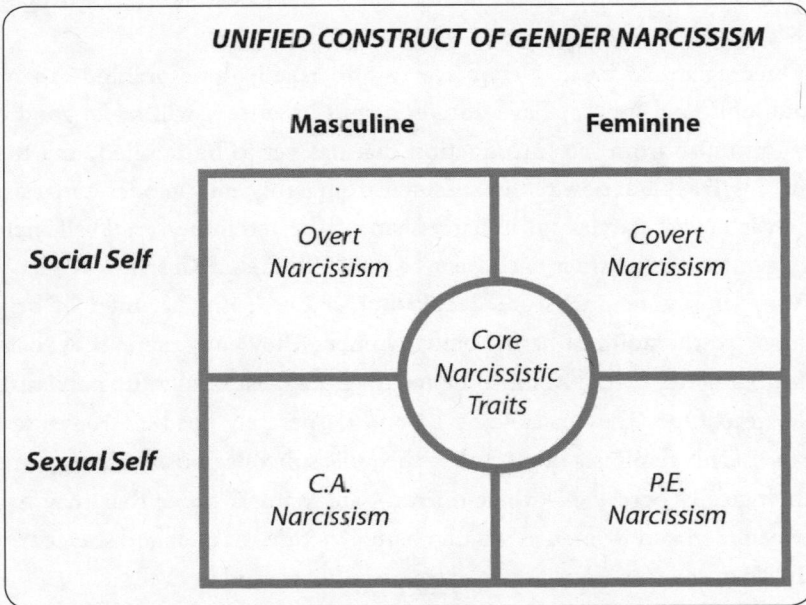

UNIFIED CONSTRUCT OF GENDER NARCISSISM

	Masculine	**Feminine**
Social Self	Overt Narcissism	Covert Narcissism
	Core Narcissistic Traits	
Sexual Self	C.A. Narcissism	P.E. Narcissism

P.S. In *Book Two*, I will try to include a little content specific for the people of various major English-speaking nations. For the people of Canada, this will include thoughts regarding the current Chief Justice of the Supreme Court of Canada. (Although after the bad joke of the Nicole Doucet case, which comes in *Book Two*, perhaps these high judges should start referring to themselves as Court Jesters instead of Court Justices.)

Sometimes being a wood snake is just plain wonderful. As will be unveiled, *Book One* is only a warm up. Feminists have absolutely no idea what's going to descend upon them in *Book Two*. None.

Say goodbye to the Matriarchy.

[NOTE: Just before this book went to print, I discovered what appears to be an online, computer generated report from the Ontario College of Social Workers and Social Service Workers register, dated 12 July 2011.

It shows that Malyssa Kruël's certificate was "... suspended on September 15, 2010." If true, Kruël was suspended six months after the bogus OCSWSSW decision to ignore her reprehensible misconduct in my case.

Not surprisingly, the OCSWSSW never bothered to inform me of this. My opinion of it has not changed.]